Jack Hobbs

Other books by the same author :

Novels

TIMBERMILLS (1938)
THE GOLD GARLAND (1939)
COLD PASTORAL (1946)
THE HOUSE OF THE LIVING (1947)

Criticism

THE SPIRIT ABOVE THE DUST:
A study of Herman Melville (1951)

Cricket

BATSMAN'S PARADISE (1955)

JACK HOBBS

A BIOGRAPHY

RONALD MASON

THE PAVILION LIBRARY

First published in Great Britain 1960

Copyright © Ronald Mason 1960
Introduction copyright © Ronald Mason 1988

First published in the Pavilion Library in 1988 by
PAVILION BOOKS LIMITED
196 Shaftesbury Avenue, London WC2H 8JL
in association with Michael Joseph Limited
27 Wrights Lane, Kensington, London W8 5TZ

Series Editor: Steve Dobell

British Library Cataloguing in Publication Data
Mason, Ronald, *1912-*
Jack Hobbs—(Pavilion library).
1. Hobbs, Jack, *1882–1963*   2. Cricket
players—Great Britain—Biography
I. Title
796.35'8'0924   HV915.H59

ISBN 1-85145-206-0 Hbk
ISBN 1-85145-207-9 Pbk

Printed and bound in Great Britain by
Billing & Sons Limited, Worcester

Cover photograph reproduced by kind permission of
The Photo Source Limited

INTRODUCTION

The last chapter of this biography, which was published late in 1960, may still leave the impression of the happy and relaxed survival of an admired and respected character whose achievements had not only adorned the history of the game but were continuing to enrich his own memories in a retirement which was in no way diminishing his popularity or his reputation. I feel that much as all his admirers might wish that this happy survival might endure indefinitely, it is only right that the story of his life should be duly rounded off by his biographer. He lived on for another three years, dying on 21 December 1963, only a few days after his 81st birthday. Only a few months before, he had lost his wife, partner for nearly sixty years in a deeply happy and companionable marriage, whom he had devotedly nursed through a prolonged last illness. In a sense her death left him with no urgent desire to live longer himself: his own end was peaceful and serene. He went with all honour from the cricketers and cricket-lovers who would never forget what he had meant for them in his prime. A memorial service held in Southwark Cathedral packed that great building to the doors; I was there myself, and from where I sat I could see six England opening batsmen. There was little sense of mourning; rather of a happy blending of love, admiration and honour.

And of course the memory of him, both as a player and a personality, still remains; it is more than half a century since he retired from first-class cricket, and those who remember seeing him play will be sadly decreasing in numbers; nevertheless, his name is one that instantly calls out the happiest and most vivid recollections. Helping to ensure the survival of this vividness is the convivial and illustrious foundation called the Master's Club, a small private group brought into existence during his lifetime to do homage to him and to meet together from time to time to invite many of his colleagues and fellow-players as guests, regularly on his birthday, and frequently on other occasions as well. Founder members included many distinguished players and cricket-lovers of his own and later generations – Alf Gover, Colin Cowdrey, the Bedsers, Doug Insole, Billy Griffith, Raman Subba Row, John Arlott, and many others; and the club still exists, and recruits new members. It is an institution happily and worthily contrived, and it is appropriate that a great player's personality and achievement should be honoured in this way.

Banstead, 1987   Ronald Mason

JACK HOBBS

A Portrait of an Artist as a Great Batsman

by

RONALD MASON

The Oval is not the most beautiful of grounds, nor is it noted for its amenities, but I would go to the Oval and sit on broken bottles for the sake of seeing another hundred by Hobbs
A. A. THOMSON

All stars are angels, but the sun is God
A. C. SWINBURNE

IN HAPPY MEMORY OF
C. M. AND F. C.
MY FATHER AND MY UNCLE
WHO FIRST TOOK ME TO SEE HIM
AND OF
E. R. T. H.
WHO FIRST TOOK ME TO MEET HIM

CONTENTS

Book One
HAYWARD AND HOBBS

Book Two
HOBBS AND RHODES

Book Three
HOBBS AND SANDHAM

Book Four
HOBBS AND SUTCLIFFE

ACKNOWLEDGMENTS

ANYONE undertaking a work of this type is more dependent on the kindness and forbearance of others than is often admitted. I am no exception to this. I have particularly in mind Mr. A. W. T. Langford of *The Cricketer*, who most hospitably received me in his home and went to great trouble to hunt out and lend me various of his archived volumes, and Mr. R. C. Robertson-Glasgow, who at the behest of a perfect stranger unhesitatingly stripped his walls of cherished photographs with unrepayable generosity. Certain of my long-suffering friends I have thanked privately but would like to make it public: Malcolm Barnett, who lent me several essential books of reference, was every bit as cooperative as he would have been if Hobbs had played for Yorkshire; Duggie Dalziel trusted me for months with more than a dozen unassessably precious Wisdens in an indescribable state of decrepitude, and Tom Evans as always was available with both Wisden and wisdom when I lacked for comfort and advice. My Australian pen-friend Colin Johnston, of the New South Wales outback and the Australian Old Collegians touring party of 1960, seized on every hint I dropped and called in aid to my lightest whims the whole resources of his great continent from Ray Robinson to Richie Benaud, a kindness and an honour that I can never hope to return. I owe a great deal to the amused co-operation of one Andrew Sandham, and far more than I can without embarrassment acknowledge to the never-failing readiness of Errol Holmes to exert himself on my importunate behalf. Without him I could not have begun; it is a great grief that his death in August of this year deprived me of the chance of showing him how much I had appreciated his friendliness and done my best to turn it to good use. My wife, who is not as good a cricketer as any of these, has had nevertheless greater opportunities to give help and encouragement than all of them put together. She has been unfailingly generous with both; the book could not have existed without them. As for Sir Jack himself, I have paid him, I hope, some sort of tribute in the pages that follow; but nothing that I can say there or elsewhere can even fractionally render him my real gratitude for his helpfulness and indulgence in face of a barrage of impertinent questions. The honour and the pleasure were all mine. I hope he likes the book.

I feel I should mention here a number of authorities that I have found it useful to consult while writing this book. This is no comprehensive bibliography; a definitive list might fit the definitive *Life,* and can perhaps await it. First in value and importance come the ranged volumes of *Wisden,* orotund and banal by turns and compact of memorable clichés, but indispensable as a quarry for information and a refuge from romanticism. Then there are two books originating from Sir Jack himself, *My Cricket Memories* of 1924 and *My Life Story* of 1935, of somewhat less distinction than his batting but of signal factual value. One of these I received as a present on my twelfth birthday, and consequently know by heart; they both supplement the independent records very usefully. I have found the *Cricketer* (a little underrated nowadays) an abundant and fascinating commentator over the relevant years; Altham and Swanton's standard *History of Cricket* miraculously contrives both compression and vividness and was in constant use. On more particular matters, "Country Vicar" in his agreeable and discursive *Cricket Memories,* and M. A. Noble in his graphic chronicle of 1924-5, *Gilligan's Men,* have shed important sidelights; and especially worthy of mention is Sir Pelham Warner's single-minded, not to say devotional, account of his vicarious triumph of 1911-12 under the title *England and Australia,* a vast *liber amoris* with compelling snapshots which it would have been a delight to reproduce. I must not forget Gordon Ross' compendious *Surrey Story;* I have leaned hard at a memorable moment on R. C. Robertson-Glasgow's enchanting *46 Not Out;* I remember with pleasure a page or two by John Arlott in his *Cricket*; and an essay by Neville Cardus in *Close of Play* deflatingly says with great grace and distinction in a dozen pages nearly everything that I have said in over two hundred.

There remain a handful of small but none the less welcome obligations to discharge. My thanks are due to Central Press Ltd, to the Radio Times Library, and to P.A./Reuters for the photographs; and to Mr. B. O.

Babb and the Surrey County Cricket Club for so readily granting me
access to photographs in their possession and for kindly allowing me to
have them reproduced. Mr. Robertson-Glasgow's great kindness I have
acknowledged already. I have also to thank Messrs. Methuen for giving
me permission to quote from "Country Vicar's" book, *Cricket
Memories;* and Mr. A. A. Thomson for allowing me to enliven an
otherwise bald and unconvincing title-page with a *mot* of his own which
I wish I had thought of myself.

Last of all I would like to pay tribute to the patient self-immolation
of my son Nick, who, by shouldering nearly all the unspeakable drudgery
of the index, converted an expense of spirit and a waste of shame into
a signal act of filial piety.

Banstead, 1960.   RONALD MASON.

Book One

HAYWARD AND HOBBS

CHAPTER I

OVAL-TIME MEANS HOBBS

IMMORTALITY is no easy achievement in any sphere; and at the best of times it is a doubtful thing, dependent upon legend or hearsay, embalmed in tradition, accepted without sufficient question or overlaid by indolence or indifference. Fashion and rumour deny it or destroy it, fancy or prejudice prolong it or re-create it; it is at the mercy of the caprice of a public or a nation, as unstable a sanction as anything could be precariously cursed with. It is bad enough when the work, or the results of the work, which attracted the original acclaim still exist for appreciation by posterity, for even then standards can be overset in a night and the idol shoved without warning on to the rubbish heap. Nevertheless the writer and the painter and the composer live as long as their works are allowed to live. Wren lives in St. Paul's, Shakespeare at the Old Vic, Rembrandt at the National Gallery, Mozart at Sadler's Wells. The actor and the games player, every bit as popular and as accomplished in their life times, have no personal power of survival. They depend on the praises of the audience and the spectator to sustain them after curtain fall or close of play; and these praises are subjective and very often irrelevant and repetitive, until nothing is left of the greatness but a name, repeated and repeated in hollow echoes down the generations; Irving, Irving, Irving; Bernhardt, Bernhardt; W.G. Those who saw them in their greatness strive repeatedly to recapture it. Late comers find nothing but a reflected glory, tantalising, receding.

I wish that the greatness of Jack Hobbs did not depend for its continuing life on me and others like me but could endure for appreciation as his scores endure in *Wisden*. I know that the scores make rich reading enough, and I could think of worse fare for a desert island; but figures are pale simulacra, and the delight that so many thousands felt in his presence for so many years needs perpetuating in worthier terms than these. Words are inadequate in all conscience, but they have a certain power to suggest, as figures cannot, the personality and the character that underlay the overwhelming statistics. It was the character and not the statistics that made Jack Hobbs a representative name far beyond the gates of the Oval, that gave this cricketer a wider dominion in national life than any but the fabulous Grace had commanded before him and none, not Hammond nor Hutton nor Denis Compton even, have enjoyed since. To examine that fame and to look again at the successes and the adversities of his wonderful career as a cricketer is to be conscious more and more of the impalpability of his kind of art. While he played he was the artist complete in his chosen game; once he had retired, his lovely and inspiriting skill was, but for the barren records and the active memories of his admirers, as yesterday's spray on the sea shore. And so much more than the records went into that art and that fame that the task of clothing their barrenness in words that can even remotely hint at the true genius is almost as superhuman as the art itself. Yet it has to be attempted, for memories are short, and Jack Hobbs' admirers do not get any younger. It does not matter very much that Shakespeare is dead, since his plays are as alive and accessible as they were when he wrote them; but it matters a great deal that Hobbs has stopped playing, for no one can now refresh himself with one of his centuries. I wish I could annihilate Time; but I can't.

It was more than fame, it was more than affection, it was more than the widespread rumour of an uncommon skill, that elevated Jack Hobbs at the height of his career into a figure so universally accepted and admired that he awakened responses of recognition far outside the borders of cricket. There have been other instances before and since of a pre-eminent sportsman invading the common consciousness of his time as a kind of representative symbol. In our own day I can think of Gordon Richards and Stanley Matthews; and it may be that Denis Compton could claim the honour too. In Jack Hobbs' time there were fewer accesses to publicity, and the immediacy of impact on the many-headed was achieved with far greater difficulty. Yet he had one great advantage, as a cricketer; that the way to national popularity, to popularity of this immensely authoritative and representative kind, had already been beaten out for him by the massive and overbearing figure of W. G. Grace. This unusual personality, uniting superlative skill with great physical energy, achieved by a combination of nature and art a handsome and imposing presence which fired to universal admiration a Victorian public which delighted in father-figures and worshipped the gods of manly strength and authority. His magnificent beard gives him entrée as an equal to the great gallery of nineteenth-century heroes, Ruskin, Whitman, Tolstoy, Darwin; his phenomenal proficiency in a game which was rudimentary when he came to it and a complex professional art when he left it, combined with his intimidating character and appearance to give him just that symbolic sanction of which I have spoken, to bring him and his game on to the hearthrug of everyone in the country, and to leave his game there when he withdrew from it, accepted for good and all as a part of national manners and behaviour.

While he lasted his dominion was supreme; and there are curious instances of its survival. One of these that stayed in my memory dates back to the hurried preoccupied autumn of 1940, when few had occasion to linger upon cricket. One night between blackout and siren a fighter pilot came to the microphone to relate his experiences of a week or two before, when his Spitfire had been crippled in a dogfight over London and he had been obliged to take to his parachute. As the suburbs swung up below him and the recognisable landmarks took shape, he knew he was above the Oval; and, said he, "I had a momentary vision of a man with a beard." Which suggests a number of things; that the pilot was perhaps not very familiar with cricket, that the game took a very traditional and impersonal symbolic shape in his mind, and that the enormous personality of W. G. Grace still possessed a quarter of a century after his death the magic power to embody the whole of a national habit and pastime to the imagination of a man otherwise occupied. If I had been rotating a few hundred feet above the Oval that fine morning it would not have been W. G. who would have flashed upon my inward eye. I do not blame the pilot for that; he was up to (or more accurately, down from) altogether sterner games. I am grateful to him, and so is the remainder of the civilised world; and in a more specific way I owe him my acknowledgments for the aptness of his involuntary vision. In a momentary flash he illuminated the potent survival of a national myth.

I shall come to it all in good time; but it is hardly premature to remind the middle-aged here and now, and to propose it to their juniors as a fact that they must take for granted, that for the decade that followed upon the First World War Jack Hobbs became as powerful a symbol in his own way as the legendary W. G. had been in his. Jack Hobbs was as alive in the subconscious of the indifferent breeds without the law as the doctor was to be in the preoccupied brain of our parachutist; and to those who knew something of cricket, and to the *aficionados*, he was the game and its god. The Oval without him was an empty shrine, was hardly the Oval at all. On this lovely turf among its conspicuously unlovely surroundings he made his home and informed it with his personality so that history cannot easily separate the man from the place. The Latin poet Ovid coined and perpetuated in exact and beautiful phrase the sensation of awe that the pious worshipper felt in the sacred grove of his worship. *Numen inest*; a spirit is in the place. For a decade and more, and that is a long time in the life of a game, Jack Hobbs was the tutelary deity of the Oval. The great ground was numinous with his personality and his reputation; and at the height of his fame the rest of England was the Oval's province. This potency outlasted his career, outlasted another war, resisted age and oblivion; was naturally modified and attenuated, but survives to this moment. He put his bat away a generation ago, but his name defies time even if his eye and skill could not; he gets birthday letters from anonymous admirers as if he were still able to bat for their pleasure, people send to him from the other side of the world who saw him first, and perhaps last, on his earliest Australian trip more than fifty years ago. W.G.'s formidable character and capacity made this kind of thing possible; in the person of Jack Hobbs the incarnation of a game in an individual received the common touch.

Schoolboys, I suppose, provide the surest nucleus for an enduring popularity; they are attracted instinctively to what is honest and forthright and uninhibited in a character, and when great skill is allied to a personality of their own uncomplicated integrity they take that personality to their hearts. Only a year or two back it was as good as a Bank Holiday excursion to hear how the pitch of the crowd's cheers rose an octave or more higher as Denis Compton came out on to the Marylebone turf; and although perhaps there remained in Compton far more of the schoolboy's irresponsible essence than was compounded in the greatness of Hobbs, the response from these most loyal and sympathetic supporters to the Surrey master in his prime was every bit as eager. They queued for hours in rain and sun to see him, they followed his performances avidly in the papers, they chattered each to each in an excitable and ill-informed manner about his character and exploits, they stood or squatted or sprawled in cramped and inconvenient attitudes in the most damnably uncomfortable seats in the whole topography of cricket, they golloped indigestible picnic lunches and swilled gallons of vile aerated beverages for love of him, they panted after him in scurrying legions for his autograph, they throned him unequivocally in the highest places of honour in their hearts. They spent precious pennies on crude little booklets about him which they left lying about the ground at close of play; they crowded at the bookstall and bought picture postcards, "Jack Hobbs, Percy Fender, and the Surrey team, on a postcard, Two Pence"—(not tuppence, but two pence, like the Good Samaritan's advance to the innkeeper); these postcards they took home and treasured, and swapped, and more often than not Jack Hobbs was worth two of any of the others. When Surrey came out to field they looked first for the slim dark figure moving lightly to cover, and all the day through kept at least one eye on him, reserving the other for the rest of the game; and when he and Sandham came out to bat they strung themselves to a hoarse and agonized tension, establishing with him a passionate and painful identity that made his failures as bitter and his successes as sweet as if they had been their own. When they got home from the Oval and invaded in emulous delight the waste patch or the recreation ground or even the pavement and the lamp post, they would cock up the left toe and twiddle the cracked bat after the fashion of the hero; "I'm Hobbs," they would announce, both those who had just come from seeing him and those who had never seen him in their lives and were never likely to; "I'm Hobbs"—and even the clumsy parody of his own consummate grace was in its own fashion a genuine and a touching tribute. For them, in the egregious words of one of the booklets aforesaid which ventured more than thirty years ago into verse which is quick in my memory to-day,

> "*Summer-time means Oval-time,*
> *And Oval-time means Hobbs.*"

I suppose I remember that verse because it was true for me; and I was only one among thousands who must recall if not the verse then at least the experience—as vividly as I do; who lived this strange hero-worship with an intensity that cannot have vanished without a trace. Those boys who chattered along the benches and strewed sandwich-paper at the Master's feet must constitute now a formidable army of middle-aged men in whom the memory of Jack Hobbs is ineffaceable by Time. I was one of them; in the words of Whitman, I was the man, I suffered, I was there; I took part in this intense and prolonged relationship between a public and its hero, and in recalling it to myself now it comes up in my mind so fresh and unblurred that it can hardly fail to recapture at least a feeble reflection of the original brightness of the experience for my ageing contemporaries who remember it too.

Memory switches one back to a showery, sunny Saturday in the 'twenties, when Middlesex came to the Oval at the butt-end of the season and won the toss before a gay, packed, holiday crowd. Alternately the sun glittered and the clouds lowered, and Dales and Lee began batting circumspectly and confidently as well they might, the opening bowlers being Errol Holmes and Peach, characters of a cheerful and infectious optimism, and the wicket being the Oval wicket of the 'twenties and the bowling the Surrey bowling. A lot happened that day which does not matter here; Middlesex piled up a big score between the thunder and the sunshine, which irked at the time but does so no longer; but the point of the recollection and what it represents in a thirty-five-year-old memory is the remark of a prim bespectacled studious-looking boy of perhaps fifteen some two rows below me on the terrace, as Harry Lee when the game was but ten minutes old, pushed a ball safely into the covers—"Jack Hobbs touches the ball, for the first time."

This gnomic utterance crystallized into a sentence the unusual, almost pedantic ardour with which his admirers collected every infinitesimal action and perquisite of their idol. It would probably

not be true to say that while Hobbs was on view at the Oval the
other twelve occupants of the field might have sat down and played
gin rummy for all the notice the spectators took of them; but in
justification of this extravagance there was admittedly a concentration on him in those days, an involuntary focusing of the limelight,
which for his part he did nothing to encourage. There was another
occasion a year or two before the oracular incident above reported,
Middlesex the opponents then as later, when on a crowded Monday
of eager and humming expectancy a huge spectatorship assembled
at the Oval, partly for Strudwick's benefit but mainly for their
own, acclaimed Hobbs and Sandham with joyful anticipation after
enduring for all Saturday and most of that day's morning the
agony of a vast Middlesex total. The skies were cloudless and the
opportunities for bliss infinite; the honest stock bowlers held no
terrors, the gasometer trembled in the heat-haze, all summer and a
day lay open before the Surrey batsmen on the wicket that has
passed into the classic language of the games history. The crowd
lay back in their shirt-sleeves and took pleasure in their perspira-
tion, deeming it a drop in the ocean of Middlesex's coming discomfiture. Hobbs and Sandham were in no hurry, placing a single
here and a two there; the crowd relaxed, easing into the patient
and relaxed tempo with which these practised openers were clearly
content. All at once Nigel Haig turned one back to the inside edge
of Hobbs' defensive bat; it met bat and pad together and screwed
back towards the stumps; he was down on it hard, but just too late;
the leg bail fell. Hobbs—you could see him do it—let a deflating
puff of exasperation out of him, grinned resignedly at the bowler
and turned from the wicket, stripping his gloves; and a great
dejected sigh of disappointment exploded out of the multitude as
if a giant had ineffectually burst a paper bag. He receded into the
shadows of the pavilion in a murmurous haze of consternation.
That excellent and cultured batsman D. J. Knight took his place
unwelcomed; without anybody on the ground taking a ha'porth of
notice he was caught and bowled for nothing in the next over. The
sun still shone and the match continued as if nothing had happened,
but the frightened hum and buzz persisted along the dense and
disturbed rows of perspiring watchers. A man sitting in front of
me with a knotted handkerchief protecting his head from the
blistering noonday remarked to his companion, "All the interest

seems to have gone out of the game now"; and it is the utterly indefensible fact that so it was. Sandham and Jardine, bringing all their courage and skill to a tricky situation, shored up a tottering innings and gave it a new stability; but I am ashamed to confess that I, and I was not the only one, disloyally left them to it, since the light had gone out of my life that August afternoon. Forgive me; I was only twelve.

What was the secret of this man's compulsive power over the imagination of his public, and of so many more than his public? W.G. had paved the way for such a hero, it is true; but what did the hero have that commended him so closely to such an enormous gallery? You can point to his record; well and good, it was phenomenal, but there were batsmen with figures nearly as impressive and with bats almost as hugely prolific who never unlocked the public imagination as he did. (Think merely of Philip Mead. . . .) Nor was he even a "character" in the sense that he had endearing personal idiosyncrasies like Hendren or Kilner or Godfrey Evans, comical or incongruous manifestations of humour or humanity that conveyed to us comfortingly that these idols were of common clay. He had not W.G.'s intimidating presence, MacLaren's or Fry's patrician dignity, Hirst's or Rhodes' regional cunning and toughness, Ranji's magic or Trumper's incommunicable grace of person and performance, Woolley's indolent ease and power, Bradman's intent and predatory rapacity. He looked, at a distance, rather ordinary. His manner was unassuming and his presence unobtrusive, he affected no gestures or flamboyances, when his side came out to field he was one among the others (and woe attended the rashness of any batsman who mistook this mild diffidence for indifference or torpor). Such part of his personality as his retiring and temperate nature allowed him to share with the public was quietly reliable rather than actively expressive. He was compact of amiable and friendly goodwill without in any way converting this into an item of stock-in-trade. Part of the character known best to his friends was an impish dead-pan humour; this reached remoter spectators in solution only, in a commendable liveliness of deportment and what can only be described as an alert awareness of what was going on. I do not speak of his private virtues and idiosyncrasies to which the public had no call to be admitted; but of those he allowed to leaven his cricket the tally, if you discount his technical and practical genius at the game, seems at a sober audit meagre enough. Yet the public took him to their hearts as they have taken infinitesimally few others.

Do not mistake me; I do not intend to give even the fleeting impression that he was ever ordinary. In his performance at this the subtlest of all outdoor games he attained several altogether exceptional skills. In so doing he awakened uncommon affection and respect in a very wide public and made his name and achievements significant in a far wider sphere than is normally compassed in the limited field of a professional sport. Yet in so doing he remained so commendably inconspicuous in personality that his admirers, so many of them schoolboys, found the natural act of identification with the hero an unusually easy thing. It was impossible for any London schoolboy, however keen, to identify himself in daydream with W.G. or Ranji, but with Hobbs it was different. Jack Hobbs was the friendly, seemingly approachable, living and breathing epitome of the common man's own cricketing dreams and aspirations. His very ordinariness fitted him superbly for the role. His neat slight figure of no more than medium height, his light unhurried movements, his relaxed calm demeanour, his mobile features with the bright wary eyes and the long inquiring nose, dressed up the ordinary man in the ordinary man's own image. Superadd the enormous proficiency, and the image was complete. And the ordinary man, with the ordinary schoolboy enthusiastically in attendance, fell down and worshipped it. This worship was more than a tribute to the wonderful run of scores; it was a salute to a personality whose ready kinship with the worshippers made even his fabulous skill a common possession and a common inspiration.

Even to-day, when the name of Jack Hobbs is introduced into an argument, argument stops. Others abide our question; he is free. The keenest dialecticians and the most arrogant and bigoted praisers of their own county or their own country still fall silent before the bare mention of his genius. Just as when they were schoolboys they proclaimed "I'm Hobbs," now in their maturity their admiration and their loyalty has not changed. "Ah, Hobbs," they say, "now you're talking." "I don't care what you say," said one of these lately to me, who had no intention of saying anything, "there has never been anyone on earth to touch him." He paused a

moment, and the belligerent fire went out of his eyes as he looked
beyond me at some uncapturable but indestructible moment in the
past. "Jack Hobbs," he said, just those two words, but in them a
wealth of expression summing up with complete adequacy all that
I have tried to convey in a dozen pages. It had been bliss to be
alive and a schoolboy, at the height of his great career, and an
especial grace to be a Surrey schoolboy whose hero may have
been the world's but was also peculiarly and intimately your own
and in the worship of whom there need be at no time any sense of
reservation; and in middle age it is a subtler bliss to be able to recall
that dawn and find your feeling unaltered. It is possible that a
little of the ardent loyalty still so widely accorded to the memory
of this great cricketer's playing days is the elemental attraction
that every man feels for his own past; but it is the more admirable
for being linked to such a graceful and accomplished skill. Here in
this book it is my task to trace his progress through the game from
the promise to the honour; and in so doing to find perhaps some
of the essential secret of the personality who for so many years
had the best known name in cricket and enriched its history with
an individual temperament and a technique that no other single
player has approached.

This man was England's greatest professional batsman. He
scored over sixty thousand runs, he made nearly two hundred centuries, he was a model for the young and a continual amazement to
the old; yet preserved throughout an unhurried quietness, a steady
and rooted stability, to which his brilliance was an adornment and
not a danger. Through all the success and all the adulation he
managed without any difficulty to preserve his independence. He
never, as some great men do, dictated terms. He accepted the conditions and made use of them; a boy from the provinces who came
to the metropolis and gave it a new attraction and a new beauty,
yet remained all his life the thoughtful, amused and level-headed
student, experimenting to the end of his career with the com-
plexities of the art he had mastered and transformed.

CHAPTER II

PARKER'S PIECE

THE renown attaching to the birthplace of an illustrious man has often been the making or the breaking of the place. The classic example is Stratford-on-Avon, its beauty and its character overlaid by its own prosperity, the envy and the regret of the civilised world. Jack Hobbs' home town had sufficient of renown already before it engendered him; for he was born and bred in Cambridge, and Cambridge has, even in the hearts of the keenest Surrey supporters, older and more comprehensive associations. The great University has obliterated in the common imagination all significance but its own when the name of the town is pronounced; when we think of Cambridge we think of King's Chapel and the Backs and the life flowing up and down King's Parade, discounting the submerged townsmen and their dwelling places as irrelevant. Cambridge in the wider world means the clear light of science, the home of significant atomic research, learned historians, humanist philosophers and moralists, great romantic poets and ruthless antiromantic critics, invincible oarsmen and triumphant amateur batsmen, a tradition of art and scholarship and sportsmanship from Spenser and Milton and Wordsworth to Trevelyan and Quiller-Couch, Rutherford and Bertrand Russell and Leavis and Percy Chapman and David Sheppard and Peter May, that has only one rival of its kind in Western Civilisation and would not thank me for publicizing its name. The gown has at least partially obliterated the town; and it is therefore a pleasure to record the birth, on 16th December 1882, of perhaps its most distinguished recent extramural citizen. One can only say that were Town and Gown to meet

13

on some Elysian wicket, the Gown, with more than a hundred years of the highest-trained public school material at its disposal and half a dozen or so of the world's finest amateur batsmen to select from, would probably have the edge on the Town; but they would not, I think, be unduly strong in bowling, and the Town could call without hesitation on one of the finest pairs of opening batsmen in the world. Tom Hayward will come very prominently into view a little later on; and it is of the essence of Jack Hobbs' history that Tom Hayward too was a Cambridge man.

Yet even when the distinction is drawn, a reservation must follow. The Town is not really independent of the Gown, or in any way in opposition to it. Cambridge cannot help revolving around the University; there is no reason why they should not give each other reciprocal life. Jack Hobbs' father drew his living from the University and gave his service to it. In his son's earliest years he was on the staff, at Fenner's, bowling at the nets and acting as umpire; some years later he took a groundsman's job at Jesus College. He was of the University but not in it; in truth more essential to the life of its community than any single undergraduate, and more permanent. Jack Hobbs, eldest of twelve (and I take leave to doubt whether either the Cambridge University Cricket Club or the Bursar of Jesus College paid their groundsmen and umpires enough to keep a wife and twelve children in slippered idleness) had admirable advantages at home. His father, and knowing the son one can imagine this, was quiet, reserved, authoritative as the father of such a family must be, but kindly and popular far beyond the home. His mother's life, he says it himself, was all work. She was to survive her husband for many years and to have the reward that one wishes could have been his as well—to see her eldest son generally accepted as the world's greatest living batsman. However much this may have meant to her, mothers not being always accurate judges of the relative importance of this great game, we can be sure that it helped to compensate, if compensations she asked, for the life of selflessness that helped to bring it about. A happy, well-regulated family life, the breadwinner's activity centred upon a game which the boy already loved in his bones, and about him the spires of Cambridge, monastic Jesus and Palladian Downing, Trinity Great Court, Queens' gardens, the Gibbs building and King's incomparable

Chapel—what serener or more fruitful awakening to life for a young observant lad unblessed with the commonly-accepted privileges? The graces of his later maturity may perhaps have owed a little in their origin to the matchless graces of his early surroundings. He was not the kind whose genius had to triumph over childhood tribulations.

His boyhood may be passed over as being, save for his happy advantages, no more and no less interesting than that of thousands of his age. He has recorded it in his memoirs, quiet and unexceptionable, a happy but unrevealing prelude. He liked magic lantern shows and hated rice pudding, he sang in church choirs and kept a pet kitten. He did not excel at map-drawing. At the age of nine he was presented by the headmaster with a threepenny bit as a tribute to his performance at a school concert at which, it pains me to record, he blacked his face and sang a song entitled "I'se a little Alabama Coon" (This is the first suggestion of talent money in his life). He taught himself to swim, he watched the college bumping races, he went out in a boat at Yarmouth and experienced the first of a prodigious and lifelong series of seasicknesses, he attended Sunday school with exemplary regularity, he would appear to have enjoyed reading *East Lynne,* he skated on the frozen Cam, he coveted and acquired a pair of brown rubber shoes, he was reasonably good at football. A full and active and uneventful youth, seen in these impressionistic fragments; and even yet no account has been taken of the ruling passion of his life.

Cricket was in his father's blood and was about him as an essential part of his daily avocations; there can hardly have been a time when it was not present to the boy's consciousness as a central activity of life in which it was natural to be keenly interested, to which it was commonplace enough to be passionately devoted. It must have been the most natural thing in the world to take the baby of eighteen months to see the match between the University and the Australian touring team of 1884. A kind of lay baptism, perhaps, to which the child only contributed the usual yells. Nobody of course knows whether the concentration of the illustrious Murdoch or Spofforth, Bannerman or Boyle, was distracted by the hullabaloos from their not very exacting task of beating a moderate University side by an innings and 81. It did not distract the admirable all-rounder Palmer from taking eleven wickets in the game and scoring 68 not out, nor a future Lord Mayor of London from getting a meritorious fifty; but the tale has been told that one of the Australian fielders, attracted by the innocent disturbance, recommended the proud father to "make a cricketer of that kid, old man." This is a happy story and I apologise for believing it to be a cheerful invention of our old friend Ben Trovato; and it may be that if at some time or other foreknowledge or hindsight had disclosed to that Australian the identity of the infant, his advice might have had more lethal implications. Nine years were to pass before he visited another first-class match; when, in 1893, the Australians were again the visitors, a new generation had risen and Ranji and F. S. Jackson were on view. The Australians were beginning to trim their field-preachers' beards to the less formidable dimensions of bushy moustaches and side whiskers; and Trumble and Turner, Giffen and Lyons were deployed before the keen eyes of the observant enthusiast eating hot pork pie as he watched. Prominent among the Cambridge fieldsmen was A. O. Jones, who fourteen years later captained the first touring side to Australia of which Jack Hobbs was a member.

This, surprisingly, adds up to the sum total of his first-hand acquaintance with first-class cricket right up to the moment when he first stepped on to the Oval. It was natural enough; the only first-class cricket played in his second-class county took place for the most part while he was at school. Furthermore it was not in his nature to rely for his cricket on the essentially second-hand experience of a spectator. He preferred to be playing. He was familiar enough, no doubt, with the general idea of bat and ball from some period that antedated his ability to pronounce their names; and he was at all spare times ready to help his father at odd jobs on the cricket ground, scouting at the nets, fetching, carrying and being the willing dogsbody. He graduated to a species of match cricket at about the same time that his father transferred to Jesus College, where the boy would also play an unofficial version of the game with the college servants, using a tennis ball and a tennis post and defending the latter from the former with a cricket stump. He has high praise for the educative value of this practice, finding in it a wonderful discipline for the eye and the feet. Modestly ascribing to this and not to pure genius the poise and precision of the footwork of his maturity, he gives the weaker brethren a renewal of hope, as who should say, "I arrived this way, by thought and application; there is no reason why you should not do the same." Fascinatingly, he singles out the off-drive as his prime delight at this early period; and as he tells of it, you can call up once again if you are fortunate the sprung-steel timing of the great stroke as he played it in the time of his greatness, trace its free lightness of swing to its origin in the wand-like lightness of the stump he learned to play it with, and divine, as an essential part of the genius that he imprinted on cricket, the intent swiftness of the boy's instincts and movements innate and enduring in the experienced finish of the grown man's art. He was blessed all his career with a spare youthful frame; and the arrowy intuition of the boy in Jesus College Close never left him.

The first cricket team he ever played for was St. Matthew's Church Choir XI, but his first innings in a proper match took place when he was twelve on Jesus College Close, when he assisted Jesus College choirboys who were one short. He got one or two runs, he says, and from the happy relieved way in which he says it, one surmises that it might have been three or four. A number of these games were played in the evenings, and after he had been playing for some little while and scoring apparently with some consistency for one of his age, twenty being something of a feat it seems, he suddenly occasioned unexpected and lasting delight, particularly to his father, by scoring 90 and getting it into the local paper. According to his account, he was given out l.b.w. but the decision was afterwards found to be an error and he appeared in the paper as 90 not out. I do not find this explicable by any rational standards, and I can make no useful comment either on the umpire or on the person or persons unknown who caused the belated reversal of the decision, except to remark that this seems to have been the one occasion on which a protest to the umpire by the batsman could hardly have been met with cogency by the stock adjuration to look in the evening paper.

Life went on, more and more leisure time was devoted to cricket. Yet he never let go of a remarkably adult sense of responsibility; for a year before leaving school he earned half a crown a week in a situation which he describes as Jack of all jobs at a private house, getting up early and busying himself about the chores before school. After leaving school altogether he worked at Jesus College, as a subordinate to his father, oiling bats and cleaning up the pavilion, a general factotum whose seven-and-six a week was augmented by tips when he fielded at the nets. Undergraduate cricketers at Jesus, coming for a knock, would see Jack Hobbs in off moments and in odd places practising strokes with a stump. In his off-times he was a member of a boys' club which he had helped to form. It was called the Ivy Club, and it played matches on Parker's Piece.

Parker's Piece, in the fullness of the years, has become in the literal sense of the words a *locus classicus*. It represents the chief contribution of the Town to the tally of hallowed sanctities that in a town like Cambridge are normally the principal perquisites of the Gown. A large squarish open space of green eastward of Downing grounds and to the south of Emmanuel down St. Andrews Street, it derives of course from a time-honoured College gift—was in fact demised to a respected college servant of Trinity named Parker —and slumbered in local honour but national indifference until the end of the nineteenth century. Up till the 'forties the University cricket team used it; but then they migrated to Fenner's, and the stones of a damnably ugly prison, that used to overlook Parker's Piece and was now turned over to the demolition squads, were used to build a wall round this most honoured of Cambridge enclosures. Parker's Piece was delivered happily and permanently to the people of Cambridge, a municipal open space dotted with football and cricket pitches. With its green and tree-lined levels, its fringe of comfortable nineteenth-century gentleman's residences, its crisscrossing paths and vistas of simultaneous games, it resembles a more easily circumnavigable London park, with a provincial friendliness and intimacy added. It is Jack Hobbs who has given this genial expanse of turf its place in history; but even before his time it had its vital connections with the great. Ranjitsinjhi would frequently practise there, and play there in matches too; and fact and legend between them have perpetuated the story of the notable afternoon on which after scoring a quick century in his own game he strolled round the ground and was roped in somewhere in a remote corner to bat in another match in place of a last-minute defaulter. He is there reported to have scored another quick century in time to hurry back to take part in his own match as if nothing out of the ordinary had occurred; and I have seen in print the impossible piled on the improbable by the addition the same afternoon of another hundred in the second innings of the first game. The essentially prosaic Englishness of Parker's Piece, impinged on by this miraculous Oriental, was no doubt fertile ground for this kind of superstition, and there could be no more promising subject than Ranji, who of all people on earth could make the unlikely feat of occupying two places at once look simple; but let the legend stand as a record of the first arrival on Parker's Piece of a genius from without. It was very soon to be reinforced by the steady maturity of a different kind of genius, native to the place, engendered and fostered from within.

It was fostered, of course, by those twin concomitants of genius, enthusiasm and application; and the boy used frequently to get up at six in the morning to practise on Parker's Piece before breakfast. By the time he was seventeen he was playing or practising morn-ing, noon and night, and the end only came when it was too dark to see. The energy and concentration of a boy in pursuit of his keenest enthusiasm is the most single-minded and ruthless spec-tacle in nature; and in his case natural ability and aptitude were most happily assisted by the third advisable if not absolutely essential ingredient in the recipe for conspicuous success—good fortune. There can be little doubt that whatever his luck had been, the young John Berry Hobbs would have found success sooner rather than later, there being every quality in his temperament to ensure stability for his own particular capacities; but it was fortune, or luck, or blind or benevolent Providence that determined that his boyhood enthusiasms should be cherished on Parker's Piece during the wise groundsmanship of Dan Hayward, whose son at the time we have now reached was the idol of Cambridge town, standing at the threshold of one of the most conspicuously successful careers that have ever been enjoyed by a first-class professional batsman. It might have been thought, as the nineties drew to their close, that to send one local boy to play with immense honour for Surrey and England was as much as the county town of a minor county could expect to hope for in any given century. It is an altogether happy accumulation of glory that has been visited on Cambridge in the fact that the unpredictable emulation and eclipse of Tom Hayward's own wonderful performances by his protégé and fellow-townsman in the ensuing quarter of a century should have been due in large part to his own active and energetic friendship and encouragement. Tom Hayward was as much the hero of Jack Hobbs' boyhood as Jack Hobbs was later to be for the boyhoods of multitudes of anonymous worshippers; and it was ultimately through Tom Hayward that Jack Hobbs' genius was eased gently into the course it took in the end. Hayward directed rather than inspired or educated the incipient talent. Without him its quality would perhaps have altered little, but it might easily have found itself flourishing elsewhere. Before Surrey men drink off their copious toasts in honour of Hobbs, they should devote at least one modest glass to Tom Hayward, but for whom they might not have been able to enjoy that privilege and pleasure.

Yet it has to be emphasised that Tom Hayward never coached the young Hobbs. Indeed it may perhaps be wickedly suggested that if his coaching methods could be judged from his performance in the Oxford nets after his first-class career was over, when he had no constructive observations to offer other than " 'It it, sir," this was just as well. Luckily the young Hobbs was one of those naturals off whom any sort of set coaching, good or bad, slid easily and gracefully and left little trace. I have no doubt that there were plenty of occasions in his early life when older men watched him as he practised and proffered advice, in face of which he was, I imagine, polite and non-committal; and he has himself related that his father bowled to him on Jesus College Close and told him to stand up to the ball and not to draw away. But apart from these incidentals he is emphatic in repeating that he never in the accepted sense of the term had an hour's coaching in his life. He was quite content to teach himself, and who can be other than satisfied at the result?

By 1901, when he was eighteen, he seems to have outgrown the Ivy Club, which was perhaps less tenacious than its name, and was equally assisting two clubs at once. One of these was the Ainsworth, which had grown out of a Bible Class renowned for its ferocious renderings of Moody and Sankey hymns, and the other was the Cambridge Liberals, which (through modesty or shame or diffidence or pride he is at pains to explain) he joined originally for the football and not for the politics. There naturally ensued, on the occasion of the annual match between these clubs, a foreseeable dispute over which one was to have his services. It is pleasant to record that whatever religious scruples the Bible class may have harboured over allowing their decisions to be dictated by blind chance, the issue was settled in their favour by a spin of the coin and any potentialities for devilish political machinations on the part of their opponents were nipped in the bud. What is more, fortune's favour was not only extended to the devout, but to her own puppet whose destiny she was directing; for in this very match he went in at number four and scored 102. This was his first century, and there has never been another like it in his life. In his whole career, the statisticians tell us, dredging up their data from God knows where, he made 244 of these scores. I suppose, and hope, they have duly included this one, which in a peculiar and subtle way gave him greater pleasure than any of the others.

He did well for Ainsworth that year, making incidentally a big score against the Ivy Club, and his reputation was beginning to extend beyond the edge of Parker's Piece. Towards the end of that season there came another of these happy tricks of fortune which determined that there should be a man short at a crucial moment. This time it involved the annual charity match on Parker's Piece when Tom Hayward brought a team of county players down to meet the pick of Cambridge. Young Hobbs had naturally watched this match year in and year out for as long as he could remember it happening—just as, thirty years later, my contemporaries and I at school in Wimbledon piled annually into the constricted little enclosure at Merton to see J. B. Hobbs' XI play a Wimbledon and District XVIII. This year of 1901, for some reason or other, a man was absent. Jack Hobbs (could it have been connected with the fact that his father was umpiring?) was invited to fill his place. He duly batted, he faced the bowling of his idol Tom Hayward, and had his father the umpire's word for it that he played it quite well. He was tolerably satisfied with his 36 not out.

An even greater distinction awaited him in the last weeks of that season, and this cannot have been contrived by anything but a wise and encouraging planner. He was invited to play for Cambridge-shire in a couple of matches as an amateur—he was still not yet nineteen, remember, and had no very astonishing club figures to boast of, so the invitation can be very justly labelled as imaginative. He duly played, in a state of commendable nervousness. He did nothing to set the Cam on fire, but in one innings, going in number nine he stayed to make 30 while a batsman named A. J. Rich made 92, and helped Cambridgeshire to a substantial victory. He strained his thigh in the second game and was too scared to mention it; and if he troubled the scorers at all it was only very temporarily. In this characteristically unobtrusive way he made his first appearance in *Wisden*, figuring last but one in the Cambridgeshire batting averages in the unfamiliar guise of "Mr. J. Hobbs, junr.", offering substantial encouragement to all other aspiring beginners by clocking up an average of 8.75.

By this time it seems to have been a clearly understood thing that he was to try the career of a professional cricketer. His father, in his humble and valuable fashion, was one already; the boy was coming up the hard way, being offered few starry illusions and entertaining none, but the ambition and the application were developing together, and the experience and the local contacts embodied steady and useful prospects in the trade. Early in the next season he applied for and obtained a post as assistant professional at Bedford Grammar School. Until he left to take this job, which was specifically for the summer term only, there is little indication that he had ever left Cambridge for more than the odd holiday. With the vision of the calm, self-possessed, cosmopolitan cricketer of his heyday in our minds, it comes as a sudden shock to us to realize that until he travelled up that summer with the school elevens to umpire the second team game against St. Paul's School (where it is more than likely that a nine-year-old Percy Fender cast an unseeing glance at him*), he had never been to London in his life. His chief recollection is of topping up the day by visiting the Tivoli and laughing so ecstatically at the performance that everyone else in the audience laughed at him. The teams travelled back the same evening, the young Hobbs still dazed by the impact of the metropolis, having passed within a mile or two of Lord's and the Oval without being able to visit either.

At Bedford that summer he tasted the drudgery of the coaching professional's routine. He worked at wicket preparation and cognate matters in the mornings, and bowled at the nets for two hours every afternoon. He did not take to it, finding it dreary and

---

*Alas; this is what William Blake would have rightly called a Memorable Fancy, and must remain so. Percy Fender did not go to St. Paul's for some years after this. A pity.

monotonous; but he still found that he learned as much from these practices as his charges did. The boys of that year at Bedford Grammar School, now over seventy years of age, may find it sweetens their declining years to reflect that they may have had individually a larger part in coaching Jack Hobbs than even Tom Hayward had.

Soon after the end of term he played his first match as a professional. The little country town of Royston, a few miles south of Cambridge, was playing Hertfordshire Club and Ground, and co-opted his services for ten shillings and expenses. He gave them good value, for he made his first hundred in good club cricket, and found himself not only the talk of Royston, but of Cambridge too. No one, of course, was more delighted than his father at the boy's first substantial success. He was on a sick bed at the time and his son says wistfully that he was in raptures. It was Jack Hobbs' first tangible return for the hours of ambition and devotion that had gone to his wise and circumspect training; and it was the last he ever had power to render, for his father was dead within the week, leaving behind the memory of a careful and contriving solicitude, and a lasting regret in his son's mind that he never shared in its limits. He is a remote, shadowy figure, the elder Hobbs; in a group photograph reproduced in one of his son's autobiographical volumes, he is shown in that curious, sidelong, disinterested attitude common in nineteenth-century team pictures, where eleven or more fierce and unshaven individuals stand or sit about in postures of unco-operative independence. In this group the elder Hobbs presents a three-quarter face at the camera, regarding with mild benevolence the countryside behind the photographer's right shoulder, and exhibiting for recognition the famous Hobbs nose. Worthy and anonymous, he was characteristic in his death, conducting his son to the verge of his transcendent career and unassumingly retiring. There is no need to look further than the father for the source of the gentleness and modesty that are so much of the essence of the son's nature.

Tom Hayward with ready generosity arranged a charity match for the widow and large family, and this brought in a quite considerable and much needed sum of money. Jack Hobbs for a time took over his father's duties at Jesus College; but the death of his father, as well as his own development, seems to have brought

the question of his future career into urgent question at this very
moment. It was at this stage that Mr. F. C. Hutt plays a transitory
but vital part in the story.

Mr. Hutt is visible in the same group photograph as displays the
elder Hobbs, standing in the back row and discernible as a beard
and a straw hat. He was the regular scorer for the Jesus eleven,
and a man of patience and goodwill. More important, he had the
ear of Tom Hayward, and on his recommendation the young Hobbs
was submitted one day to a twenty minute net on Parker's Piece,
being bowled at by Hayward himself and Billy Reeves of Essex
(who later became, by reason of a witty and resourceful disposition,
the central figure of pretty nearly every apocryphal umpiring
story ever repeated). At the end of this test Tom Hayward mur-
mured something about "getting you a trial at the Oval next April."
This encouraging remark, which was the best outcome that could
possibly have been expected from the encounter, had the
ambiguous effect of transporting the aspiring youth at one and the
same time to the seventh heaven of delight and the deepest hell of
imagined frustration.

He had dreamed of playing for Surrey for as long as he could
remember idolising Tom Hayward. Cambridgeshire being out of
the first-class question, Surrey and its Cambridge associations
were naturally next on the list. Hayward's recommendation was
sure to get him at least a tentative entrance; or was it? And if it
did, would he be equal to the trial when it came? He spent the
winter in what must have been a pitiful dither; his anticipations
varied from brilliant success to a sickening failure, with a deathly
intermediate stage which envisaged a complete blank, not success
or failure but just no trial. It must be recorded that he took it out
on Mr. Hutt. That admirable friend was patience personified and
extended; he told the boy not to worry, everything would be all
right. But just to have two strings to his bow, he suggested, it
might be a sensible idea to approach another county beside Surrey,
to lessen the chances of disappointment. On the boy's behalf he
accordingly applied to Essex. Essex, without so much as a by your
leave, turned him down flat.

All right, they were not to know. Nevertheless there can be no
doubt that somewhere in the flattest and dreariest swamps of that
county is the unmarked and dishonoured grave of the official who

rejected Hobbs without a trial. His homeless ghost has for company that of the legendary secretary of that other county among
whose unopened letters at his overdue resignation was found, many
months too late, an offer of the unappreciated services of
W. R. Hammond. Together they contemplate the might-have-
been, without avail. Jack Hobbs and the good Mr. Hutt faced the
disappointment as best they could and waited for the spring. He
was still on edge, and the older man was unfailing in encouragement. Hobbs dared not approach Tom Hayward again, as he was
shy of him still. (This shyness persisted; three or four years later,
when Hobbs was a well-established member of the Surrey eleven
and he and Hayward had several times put on over 100 for the
first wicket together, the young man was still too diffident,
though all his inclination was in favour, to invite the other to his
wedding.)

Tom Hayward did not forget. After the prolonged anguish of the
winter there came in early April a summons from the Oval. The
trial had been granted, Hayward gave him precise instructions
about where he was to go and whom he was to ask for, he collected
his bat and pads and boots in a green carpet bag, and waited for
the day. It was 23rd April, and whether it is a coincidence that it
was St. George's Day and Shakespeare's birthday I neither know
nor care, but on that day of 1903 Jack Hobbs got up at dawn,
journeyed for only the second time in his life to London, and went
in at the gate of Kennington Oval for the first time.

He stood there waiting with his new boots and his green bag,
taking anxious stock of his companions. Some of them were nervous, some confident. If we make an effort of the imagination we
can resurrect, from far beneath the familiar friendly features of the
man who became so famous, the dark alert shy youth of twenty
who was the only one of that day's batch to make good; the long
nose, the prominent reflective eyes, the pouting lower lip, the
reticence. Thinking of him at this moment as beginning to build
on a sure foundation as impressive a single structure as any man
in the game's history has achieved, it is appropriate to remember
the application and the devotion and the solicitude and the tradition
that had made that foundation so firm. Not only his own
intelligence and talent and perseverance, though the rest would
have gone for nothing without these; but his mother, who worked

all day, and his father who had died short of his ambition, and the Ivy Club and the Cambridge Liberals and Mr. Hutt and Bedford Grammar School and Tom Hayward; and at the centre of all the historic turf of Parker's Piece, that compost of anonymous and enthusiastic cricketers, that had bred out of its rich fertility such a sturdy and classic bloom.

CHAPTER III

KENNINGTON OVAL

THEY bowled at him for twenty minutes in the nets that morning; and he performed well enough to be invited to play in a trial game on the same day. J. N. Crawford and N. A. Knox, captaining the two assemblages of nervy tyros, would have been interested that day to be informed that two of those unfledged lads would between them make three hundred and fifty centuries in first-class cricket, but they would no doubt have told you where to take the tale; especially as one was played for his bowling alone. As it was, Philip Mead bowled Jack Hobbs for 37. Retained in town overnight to play in another trial on the next day, Hobbs put up for the night at Islington and refreshed himself with a visit to Sadler's Wells, which did not provide then the kind of fare it provides now or I am prepared to guess that he would have opted for the Tivoli instead. Next day Mead bowled him again, for 13. They were to be colleagues and opponents for thirty years before and after Mead departed for Hampshire; but the feat would not be repeated very often.

That day at lunch time, C. W. Alcock, the Surrey secretary, called Hobbs into his office and offered him an engagement to qualify for Surrey. It meant that he would have to live in the county for two years and that during that time he would be given a salary as a member of the ground staff. It does not look very princely by the colour of to-day's money; but he was to get thirty shillings a week during the summer, with a pound a week winter retainer and expenses for Colts matches. For his part, he felt it gave him the key of the Bank of England; and he has emphasised later that

27

although he realises it was short commons enough and knows very
well that modern rates of pay have left this far behind, yet he
found he had enough to live on and to send a little home as well.
He dashed straight back to Cambridge to tell Tom Hayward the
news. Tom Hayward said all the appropriate things and, without
the boy knowing it, a few more beside; for he took an early opportunity to drop a hint to the Surrey secretary about Hobbs' home
circumstances, which got him an unobtrusive and highly appreciated £10 bonus.

One foot on the ladder at last, Jack Hobbs made excited
arrangements to leave Cambridge. Established in lodgings near
the Oval, which he shared with a stocky genial cockney called
Joe Bunyan, also on the ground staff, he prepared for his first
professional playing season. He was now for better or worse part
of one of the oldest and most illustrious county clubs in the
country. Being a lad steeped in cricket and its attendant tradition,
he did not fail to be impressed by this; the Oval turf excited him to
walk on, being already alive with associations to anyone of kindred
mind. Being at the same time a level-headed and not unduly
imaginative fellow with a cut-and-dried job to do, he never let his
historical sense overawe him. He kept his humility, but he kept
his independence too.

Active life for the young lads on the ground staff was roughly
divided into Colts and Club and Ground matches. The Colts are
what they say they are, trainees as one might call them, anxious
and ambitious and inexperienced. The Club and Ground vary considerably from match to match, selecting their players partly from
the younger professionals and the Colts themselves and partly from
amateurs of good club or even of county standard. They meet
high grade clubs and schools all over the county, and to these
opponents the match carries an unusual glamour and sanction.
The county representatives themselves, Colts or not, run one feels
a curious gamut of responses and attitudes to these games. With
part of themselves, being often technically a good deal more
accomplished than their opponents, they no doubt do not feel
extended; with another part, and this applies in particular to the
emulous Colt striving to create a good impression, they must be
keyed to an unnaturally competitive intensity, and every match
must seem like a kind of Test match. Either way, it seems likely,

every match must be something of an ordeal for the aspiring.

There is no point in detailing the young Hobbs' scores and achievements for these junior county teams in this season of 1903. He played in all about twenty games and collected nearly five hundred runs, with a sprinkling of not outs to help his average; he bowled on the average four or five overs per match, and, on the average, each match brought him one for 14. He began with a duck but he did not let that perturb him; he did not once reach the century (he never got 100 for the Club and Ground until after he had toured Australia twice), but he wasn't far off it; and he most happily and appropriately put up 100 for the first wicket in a Club and Ground game with the great Bobby Abel as his partner. He disclaims any memory of nervous tension on his own account during these, his qualifying days, though he would still shake like a leaf when he watched Tom Hayward go in to bat (a sensation, *mutatis mutandis,* which we, his own admirers, were to understand and share two decades later when he himself took guard). His results broke no records, but he was confident. Vaulting ambition never seems to have been his; a key to the quiet cumulation, rather than immediate explosion, of his ultimate achievements. He settled down, he nosed about London, he listened to the band in Hyde Park, he visited Madame Tussaud's, he was a constant attender at the music halls. He seems to have been the ideal public; everything, he says, made him laugh. He enjoyed a little billiards and occasionally went wild and played whist. There was a special thrill one evening when someone took him to dine in Soho, eight courses for half-a-crown. London belonged, in a modest and unexacting manner, to him.

His twenty-first birthday came and went; he entered confidently into 1904, with a full year yet to work out before he could play for his adopted county. With the great procession of his career's achievements in our minds, we are often forgetful of what was, in the cricketer's context, a rather tardy beginning. If we look at comparable figures in the recent history of the game, Hutton by the time he was 21 had made over 3,000 runs in first-class cricket, and Denis Compton 5,000. It is to his credit that nowhere in his reminiscences of what might have been a frustrating time is there any hint of impatience. He appears to have been content to wait, taking life on the terms it offered him, not on those he laid down.

He began, and continued, his second year's service for the Club
and Ground only. He felt more at ease; the Oval was home. He
fledged himself with a number of longer scores—96, 90, 73. The
hundred still eluded him.

At this point in his career the Cambridgeshire authorities, alive
to the realisation that the nervous and reticent Mr. J. Hobbs
junior of 1901 had put on weight and confidence and could use his
name in his own right, asked him to play for them in half a dozen
matches or so in July and August. Here in his first extended stint
of two-day cricket, where the batsman's skills are less circum-
scribed by time and the even rhythms of the game are given fuller
scope, he cut loose for the first time and exhibited first-class capacities. It is not to be supposed that the opposition was of more
than average quality, and in his favour was the inestimable
advantage that his home county enjoyed in playing their matches
on such a perfect wicket as Fenner's. Nevertheless, these games
were the making of the young batsman, who achieved what by
any standards was a memorable month's work by making 696 runs
in thirteen innings, with a single not out to perk his average up to
58. He pleased himself very much by getting 50 in each innings in a
match against Oxfordshire, on which occasion he was if anything
even more pleased to be congratulated by an old friend, J. F. Marsh,
who had been at Jesus College in the days of the elder Hobbs'
groundmanship and who had lately distinguished himself by
making 172 not out in the University match, a record that was
not to be overset until Ratcliffe and the Nawab of Pataudi
beat it twice in two days in 1931. But this success was only a prelude. In the next game, against Norfolk, when he had been tipped
off that the authorities at the Oval had their spies out among
the spectators, he ran to 92 in two and a half hours; and a week
or two later played an innings of 195 against Herts that got him
a paragraph in the London papers. In ten days' time he had
rammed his point home by subjecting Hertfordshire to yet another
hundred on their home ground at Watford; completing as happy
and practical a four weeks' tour of duty as any aspiring lad
could wish to achieve. The records credit him in addition with
fifteen wickets, and it is clear that he bowled more than anyone
but the two stock bowlers, who between them took 91 of the 125
wickets that fell. *Wisden* gives him a passing but honourable

mention. "A new player in Hobbs," runs the Cambridgeshire commentary, "rendered fine services as a batsman and came out with a remarkable average." The old yellow-backed oracle had opened one eye and spoken, if only laconically.

There is a pleasant individual reminiscence of one of these games on record. Regular readers of that assiduous periodical *The Cricketer* will perhaps recollect, if they have been regular readers all their lives and if their lives have been long enough, an engaging series of articles embodying the memoirs of an unassuming enthusiast calling himself "Country Vicar." His real name was Hodgson, the Rev. R. L. Hodgson, and in the days of his youth he played occasionally for a county he must needs call Loamshire, but which was in fact Suffolk. He was, at the time of which he writes, the honorary secretary of that county. On the first occasion on which he played at Fenner's against Cambridgeshire—he thought it was in 1903, but it is clear from all attendant circumstances that it was a year later—he had a brief encounter that he describes in this way: —

"Almost the first person I met on reaching Fenner's was Tom Hayward. He was an old acquaintance, and we talked of old times. He explained why he was not at the Oval or elsewhere. Then he said, 'There's a young fellow playing for Cambridgeshire I want you to notice.'

" 'Is he good?' I asked.

" 'He's very good, and he's going to be great.' Tom affirmed.

" 'Batsman, bowler, or all-rounder?' I queried.

" 'He's a bit of a bowler, but it's his batting that's worth seeing! Just watch him!'

"I said I would. 'And his name?'

" 'Hobbs,' said Tom. 'Jack Hobbs. He's qualifying for Surrey.'

"Cambridgeshire won the toss. I think J. B. Hobbs came in second or third wicket down. He was a quiet, modest-looking young man. He played very correctly and very carefully; every ball seemed to be met with the middle of his bat.

"Just before lunch I had an over at him.

"I tried to bowl leg-breaks in those days. Sometimes the ball turned a little; more often it continued its course, undisturbed by my attempted finger-spin. But for five balls, young Hobbs treated me as though I were a great bowler. He played each delivery gently back to me.

"I determined that the last ball of the over should be fast. With no change of action, I would bowl one which would really rip off the pitch and hurry along, beating the batsman by its change of pace.

"Were I writing a romance, and not a narrative of simple fact, I should say that that ball was the best I ever delivered—that it spreadeagled all three stumps—and that I clean bowled Hobbs without his scoring a run off me; 1 over, 1 maiden, 0 runs, 1 wicket would have formed quite a pleasing analysis.

"Alas, like George Washington, I cannot tell a lie. My fast ball was a most outrageous long-hop, about a foot outside the off stump.

"Hobbs cut it prettily past point, but the stroke failed to reach the boundary. They ran 3 only. Third man was very fleet of foot and a fine thrower.

"Then the luncheon bell rang and I bowled no more. Somebody else got the young player out when he had scored about 45. But, at least, I can truthfully say that I once bowled six balls at J. B. Hobbs and he scored no more than 3 runs off them! If I live long enough for my memory to become sufficiently faulty I may even imagine, some day, that I bowled him out."

"Country Vicar" lived long and wrote much; of his salt is the cricketing earth savoured. The little memory comes up after nearly sixty years fresh as the new May flowers. Yet the averages for Suffolk in the appropriate *Wisden* do not credit him with a single over, though they allot him four innings. And he was secretary himself, and must have been in a manner responsible for them. I do not doubt him for a moment; to dream that he bowled at Hobbs without triumphantly dismissing him would have been an imaginative refinement which his genial romanticism would not have permitted him. We must put down the discrepancy to *Wisden,* whom it is always a malicious delight to catch out.

Jack Hobbs, coming out of the Cambridgeshire season with his highly creditable average, attended at the Oval for the closing days of his engagement. This signed him off at the end of August, but he watched the last first-class game or two and on the very last day was called upon as a substitute fielder. He had performed this duty earlier in the season when Hampshire ran short of substitutes

and distinguished himself by taking a blinder in the long field which
disposed of a surprised Surrey captain. In this last Leicester game
he patrolled the long field once more, and accepted three more
catches off "Razor" Smith which helped to precipitate a steam-
roller victory. For this he received honour and glory and five
pounds.

At the very end of the season he batted for the first time at
Lord's; not in a first-class or even minor county match, but in one
of those strange autumnal fixtures with which the Cross Arrows
seek during September to postpone the inevitable night. It is
becoming a monotony for the chronicler, but it has once more to
be noted that he was asked to play because a side was a man short.
The side was George Robey's XI and the obliging defaulter was
Tom Richardson; among those lined up with the comedian were
Ernie Hayes and the fabulous Jessop, while the opposition
included a disproportionate number of Hearnes and a young all-
rounder whom Jack Hobbs was to respect warmly all his life,
Johnny Douglas. The Cross Arrows play their games nowadays
on the practice ground, which gives them rather the air of being
in Lord's but not at it; but in those remote days they trod the
authentic turf and no mistake, and the last-minute substitute
helped himself to seven fours in making 55. Then, with the savour
of first-class cricketers around him, he bedded down for the winter.
He entertained few wild dreams; he had found himself happy and
confident with Surrey, had stretched himself to his great content
in the few second-class games he had had the chance to play in.
But there was nothing out of the common in his performances. It
was not his way to begin by blowing the top off the gasometer, and
he never expected it or in fact desired it. He looked towards 1905
in the hope that he would next get a place in the Second Eleven of
his county. As it happened, he never played for Surrey Second
Eleven in the whole of his life.

Here on the threshold of his county career, we may be said, I
hope, to have got to know something of the man. It is time to look
for a moment at the county he was about to represent; for by the
accident of history he came to this county at a moment of its fortunes at which he was best fitted to supply its needs, or some of
them. It would be a mistake to think that the events of Jack Hobbs'
life fit with wonderful appropriateness into a story book pattern;

its many wonderful climaxes sometimes appear in what a romantic would take to be the wrong order; but there can be no doubt of the aptness of his arrival, when a once great and illustrious county had suffered leanness and humiliation for which a decade of success had done nothing to prepare it.

The 'nineties had belonged to Surrey almost as exclusively as they had seemed to belong to the aesthetes and the decadents; between 1887 and 1899 they had headed the championship nine times, and during their great decade they never fell lower than fifth. Immense talent and resources capably guided and led; these are the assets essential for champions who retain their leadership as well as snatch it. The honours of the 'nineties should properly go to the great captains, John Shuter and Kingsmill Key, who gave character and authority to the rich regimes they controlled; but the teams they built up and so successfully directed contained names and reputations enough to scare the heart out of all but the toughest captains, let alone opponents. Five or six names should suffice to convey the essential quality of this classic side; for it began with Abel and Brockwell, it carried on through promising newcomers like Fred Holland to tried and honoured echoes of past greatness like Walter Read, and in its happiest days it boasted in George Lohmann the most brilliant all-rounder of that generation. The miracle did not end there, as knowledgeable observers of championship contestants will know very well. The real keys to success are in the penetration of the attack; and it will be sufficient to bring the list to an end with the pair of names which in all the rich cricket of the 'nineties spelt devastation more certainly than any other—the supreme fast bowlers Richardson and Lockwood. With this superb combination Surrey held the head of the championship and thereabouts with something of the arrogant ease which it did not show again for over fifty years. Changes were alive in the organism, it is true; Brockwell began to yield his particular pre-eminence to Hayward (an evolution of portentous moment). Lohmann's health broke down, a curious character named Digby Jephson, who bowled lobs, fluctuated moodily between success and despondency, the standard wicket-keeper Harry Wood was succeeded after a short interval by a newcomer named Strudwick, the shattering violence of Richardson and Lockwood was slowly abated by time and temperament, and Key resigned the captaincy at last. It was not the fault of Jephson, who took the side over and led it for three seasons, that it came to pieces in his hands. New and energetic material in the forcing batsman Ernie Hayes and the fast medium seam bowler Walter Lees was introduced and flourished; but the organic power of the united group faltered with the natural defection of some of the individuals. Although at the beginning of the century Abel and Hayward were as solidly established as opening partners as Brown and Tunnicliffe themselves, they could not on their own keep the county from its inevitable landslide. Richardson dropped out; Lockwood, seeming for a while to defy earlier hints of decline, was defeated at last. Lohmann died in South Africa. The side faltered and lost grip; dropped to seventh in the table in one year, pulled up a little the next, alternated brilliance and unreliability, and forfeited in the end the erratic confidence of their captain, who despairingly resigned.

In 1903, when Jack Hobbs played for the first time for the Colts and the Club and Ground, the proud Surrey eleven was undergoing penitential experiences. Not for the last time, they suffered from captain trouble, falling back in distress on an unknown without any experience of first-class cricket, a predicament which only Yorkshire has ever been able to survive with honour. Hayes made a great advance and Strudwick in his first full season created sufficient of an impression to get himself chosen for Australia; but Abel's eyesight began seriously to trouble him and his decline took the heart out of the batting as the passing of Richardson and Lockwood had blunted the point of the bowling. The county finished eleventh, the lowest they had ever been in the table.

1904 was in the upshot no improvement; they went neither up nor down, and they had one victory fewer. In fact it is a toss up whether they had more victories than captains; at least five harassed amateurs tried their hands, and at this late time it is difficult and unprofitable to determine whether there were not in fact more. Abel played again, but finally had to yield to the encroaching dark; the great fast bowlers made positively their last appearances. Only the admirable Hayward blossomed like the rose, scoring over 2,700 runs and becoming the first Surrey player to score 100 in each innings of a match. Hayes assisted with spasmodic brilliance, and fresh from the cradle came the Repton schoolboy prodigy J. N. Crawford, who had still a year to do in the sixth

form. Destined for a strange flaring career like an entrancing but
intermittent firework display, he brought an unnatural maturity
with him that promised exceptional things. He seems to have possessed everything but stability.

For stability it is a refreshment to turn once more to Hayward.
Once more only, because from this moment onwards it will not be
easy to think of Hayward in terms of the rightful pre-eminence he
enjoyed in these early years of the century. His name cannot avoid
being coupled for the last ten years of his career with that of the
young partner whom he fostered and for the time being overshadowed in performance, but who in retrospect so outshines him
as to dim the value of the older man's quality. Setting him in the
cold light of history it is difficult to rate Hayward too highly.
Before Hobbs came, only the great Shrewsbury could rank with
him in talent and accomplishment among professional batsmen.
We have already seen, in the early stages of young Hobbs' career,
glimpses of the considerate and generous graces that underlay Tom
Hayward's solid and patient character. Like all great players he
reflected his inner graces in his play, a commanding and upright
affair of watchfulness and strength, culminating in an off-drive of
great power and splendour. Tall and finely built, he qualified his
natural good looks, like so many of his eminent contemporaries,
with a bushy cascade of moustache that along with broad shoulders
and a deeply-tanned benevolence of feature, gave him the air of a
reliable regimental sergeant-major. And indeed it was a cognate
position that he occupied in the Surrey eleven of the years before
the 1914 war; senior professional and chief N.C.O., aware and
careful of his authority and responsibility, he was as sturdily reliable off the field as on it. It is difficult to think of him during these
years, with his portly grocer's demeanour and avuncular church-
wardenly rectitude, as being in his middle thirties only and the
best player of fast bowling in England. Now in 1904 he was still
two years away from the greatest season of his life, when in hoisting an aggregate of 3,518 runs he established a record that even
his famous protégé never came within telescopic view of, and which
took the bone-hard wickets and rusty post-war bowling of 1947 to
lower as accessories to the gay insatiable prodigality of Compton
and Edrich. It is not being quite accurate, or quite fair to
the individual genius of the two players to say that on the shoulders

of Hayward's character and talents Jack Hobbs forced his way to the forefront of professional cricket in quicker time than he otherwise might; but he himself has never failed in acknowledgment of his debt, and it is mainly from his own memories that we become aware of the enormous love and respect that went into both the public and the private relationship. Only he can know precisely what an inestimable advantage he enjoyed, in coming to the Oval at the time when he did, in having the illustrious Tom Hayward to see him through. Of the other end of the relationship we naturally know less, as Hayward himself was apparently suspicious of speech as a mode of communicating thought; but there can hardly have been far absent from his long and tranquil retirement a strong sense of very pardonable pride. He lived until 1939, right through to the end of Hobbs' career and well beyond it; it was an admirable thing that he was given the chance to enjoy to completion the entire harvest that he had helped to sow.

Hayward had during the past season been deprived by the ravages of time and health of his long-established opening partner. Abel and Brockwell had begun the 'nineties with consistency and success; Abel and Hayward had continued without faltering, a very good batsman being supplanted by a great one. With Abel's defection the succession temporarily faltered. Fred Holland, Baker, the gifted Oxford Blue J. E. Raphael had all at one time or another filled the gap with more or less success. Raphael had held it longest, but being still at the University was available only for the second half of the season; and as a regular opening pair of batsmen is as essential a factor in a county team of quality as a regular opening pair of bowlers, there was a wide open vacancy for anyone with application and the flair. Jack Hobbs may have been aware of this objectively, as an academic matter of tactics; he does not seem to have felt himself as in any way personally concerned. This seems natural enough when we consider that in the Cambridgeshire matches he was not opening the innings and even in the Club and Ground games there would seem to have been no regular understanding about it. In any case, as I have already made clear, he did not expect to find an immediate place in his county's first eleven. That he attained it right away may be due partly to his obvious quality, but even more perhaps to the fortuitous vacancy occasioned by Abel's premature departure. Once again a side were a

man short; not at the last minute, this time, of course, but short all
the same.

He got the shock of his life when he turned up at the Oval in
April 1905 and found his name posted as a probable for the first
match of the season. He says he can still remember his excitement,
and no wonder. First-class cricket seems to have started a week or
two earlier then than it does now, and Surrey's first match began
as a matter of time-honoured ritual on Easter Monday, a practice
that with all its attendant drawbacks many of us would be happy to
see reinstated. It was not a championship match; they came later.
As in previous years, Surrey were to open their season by opposing
a team called the Gentlemen of England, a comprehensive rather
than a representative title; and the captain of the visiting side was
to be, as always, W. G. Grace. On Easter Monday, 24th April
1905, two years and a day after he had arrived with his green
carpet bag, Jack Hobbs played for Surrey for the first time.

CHAPTER IV

HAYWARD AND HOBBS

WE have the very good authority of Mr. H. S. Altham, the historiographer of cricket, for the fact that Easter Monday of 1905 was a bitterly cold day. He was there as a spectator, a schoolboy of sixteen, and remembers it well. In the pavilion Surrey assembled; Lord Dalmeny was at this point of time their duly elected captain, but he was not available for this match, and Tom Hayward led the side with three amateurs under him, an admirable choice. And right at the outset of the match he brought off two manoeuvres of commendable skill and judgment; he won the toss and elected to bat, and he took the young Hobbs in with him as his partner. Hobbs was too much overwhelmed with surprise and pleasure to be nervous; it was clearly an unexpected advance on the wildest of his anticipations, and he took it gratefully as a wonderful compliment. And so it fell out that the shivering spectators on that bitter Bank Holiday, after applauding W.G. and Walter Brearley, C. L. Townsend and V. F. S. Crawford and a number of other keen and estimable cricketers to their places in the field, were privileged to see the opening not only of a great career but of one of the most signally successful batting collaborations in the history of cricket.

It may properly be said to have begun on the way to the wicket, when Hayward reminded his partner to go all out for the first single, a precept which appears to have struck deep into the imagination and practice of the younger man from that time on. Arrived at the wicket, they prepared to face George Beldam of Middlesex, a renowned action-photographer and a prodigious swinger of the new ball, and Walter Brearley, a formidable and resourceful fast bowler of Test quality. W.G. loomed watchfully at point, presiding unknowing at the genesis of his most worthy successor. Tom Hayward, true to his intention, took a quick single in the first over; and only a ball or two later the Oval score-board clicked into position the first of 61,237 runs. It is tantalising, but only natural, that he cannot remember the shot which brought him his first run. If he started as he meant to go on, we may conjecture that he laid it dead within ten feet of the bat, and that he and Hayward walked it. There is not much more to say about the first innings, for Surrey tumbled ignominiously for 86; Hobbs touched an out-swinger to slip when he had made 18, and had the pleasure of tying with Ernie Hayes for top score. Brearley and Beldam polished off the whole collection before the taste of lunch was out of their mouths; but when the Gentlemen followed in they were barely more successful themselves, the fiery and erratic Knox playing skittles with the early batsmen, including W.G., and confounding everyone but the wary Townsend with his pace. They were all out for 115 and left Surrey an hour's batting; and it seemed as though practice and experience had already taken charge, for the ball was no longer master, the runs came steadily and freely, and when stumps were drawn Hobbs was 44 not out. He says he felt remarkably pleased with himself, was effusively congratulated by an old Cambridge friend who had come to town specially to see him "and was so delighted he could have eaten me," and after buying an evening paper to read all about himself, went off in the most relaxed and modest manner to spend the evening where we would have expected him to spend it; at the Tivoli.

Next day he went on where he left off, playing with an impressive freedom that was noted with approval in the pavilion; and refused to be scared by the foxy old W.G., who wheeled up an over or two at him and at least once put him off a contemplated short single by asking him to save him trouble by hitting the ball back to him. He got to 88 before impetuosity overtook him and he hooked at Brearley once too often, giving a catch to square-leg. That most amiable of bowlers remarked to him as he passed, "I should drop that stroke if I were you." "I didn't drop it," says Hobbs, "but I learned how to do it properly." The game itself took a spoiling from some heavy rain, but Hobbs came out of it with new pleasure and confidence, awaiting with what may have been in his particular circumstances an ironic interest his first county match, against Essex.

This began on Thursday, 4th May. Surrey stiffened their side with Fred Holland and Baker; the new captain, Lord Dalmeny, took up his duties, and Surrey won the toss. The shape of the game was vaguely reminiscent of the last one, for once again a fast bowler and a resourceful medium pace swinger, in the respective persons this time of Claud Buckenham and Billy Reeves, toppled the side's balance early and had them out for 138. Hobbs did well enough, getting 28, the second highest score, and his was the one wicket that the two triumphant slayers had to farm out to another bowler. Surrey then recouped on the bowling roundabouts what they had lost on the batting swings, Walter Lees being chief spearhead in a thrust that drove Essex to the wall for 123. In the second innings the previous week's history repeated itself and more also; Surrey made a fine recovery, they ran to 383 in under 4½ hours, and for three of those hours Hobbs led the scoring from one end at the cracking rate of fifty an hour, and was eventually caught by his old friend Billy Reeves for 155. He made it against active and belligerent bowlers with their tails up, and he made it with a borrowed bat; and he walked on air while Lees bowled Essex to their certain destruction, and he finished the match schoolboy-fashion by taking one of his familiar style catches in the long field. The crowd ran after him to the very gates of the pavilion; and Lord Dalmeny made the handsomest recognition possible to the young professional's skill and value by awarding him his county cap on the spot. There can be very few instances on or off the record of a cap awarded after only two games for a county.

Local immortality was established after this innings. For some years there had flourished on London grounds, but particularly at the Oval, a strange character by the name of Albert Craig. This enterprising original, a Yorkshireman by birth, had tired of a clerkship in the Post Office and descended early upon London to live in the most innocuous and praiseworthy manner on his wits. His habit was to attend county matches and improvise rhymed commentaries on them, printing them off in broadsheet form and hawking them in person among the crowds to the accompaniment of light-hearted and impromptu badinage. The verses were for the most part of a paralysing badness, for his literary style tempered a

cursive facility of cliché with a dire metrical uncertainty; but a
resilient and engaging personality overcame technical ineptitude,
and perseverance and familiarity won Craig the heart of the
generous and good-humoured Surrey crowd. Craig the Surrey
poet became as permanent an institution at the Oval as the gasometer itself; one of the last of the great public jesters, he played
jongleur for a generation to the gods of the London cricket grounds.
His returns were mainly in coppers, but there are still many who
remember his pockets weighed down with the takings as he progressed jauntily around the ring. He had no authority but popularity, no recommendation but gaiety, no talent but wit. He knew
all the cricketers and the cricketers all knew him; and when he
died in 1909, Bobby Abel and Tom Richardson went to his funeral,
and his portrait hangs to this day in the Oval pavilion. When
Hobbs made his championship debut, Craig was in his last years,
and his style was in what might be termed its late degenerate period;
but he wore his laurels with a conscientious application to duty,
and the young batsman got his celebration.

> *Joy reigned in the Pavilion,*
> *And gladness 'mongst his clan*
> *While thousands breathed good wishes round the ring;*
> *Admirers dubbed the youngster*
> *As Surrey's coming man;*
> *In Jack Hobbs' play they saw the genuine ring.*
> *'Twas well worth going to see*
> *Illustrious Hayward's smile,*
> *While Razor Smith and Walter Lees*
> *Cheered with the rank and file.*

Acclaimed by Craig on his first county appearance, knighted by
his sovereign nearly half a century later; what greater glory could
a man desire? In his new chocolate cap he prepared happily for the
long stretch of the season; and somewhere in Essex the man who
harboured in his breast the cankering secret of his silent rejection
faced the ironic future with what courage he could muster, preserved as yet from the ensuing turn of the screw that was to come
in the return match at Leyton three weeks later, when Hobbs was
to help Hayes add 216 in just over two hours and with his only
other hundred of the season guide Surrey to a five-wicket victory.

Before that came about, however, he had faced his toughest assignment yet. Pleased with his early successes, and in no way abating his confidence by a first innings failure against Hampshire which he atoned for satisfactorily with 43 in the second, he was mildly disturbed by a comment in the Press that the match against the Australians, starting at the Oval on 11th May, would be "his real trial." As he went into that game with an average of 56, the jolt may have been a genuinely unexpected one; and the sight of Victor Trumper, Clem Hill, Warwick Armstrong and Joe Darling among the team taking the field may have justified the truth of the comment if not its veiled implication. His luck was with him to reinforce the defiant skill the newspaper comment had called out; and he withstood Cotter, Laver, McLeod, Noble and Armstrong to the very verge of his hundred (giving he thinks at least four chances on the way) until at 94 he was magnificently thrown out by Clem Hill from the boundary, aiming at the one stump and hitting it. Hobbs, who has never allowed false gestures of insincere diffidence to obscure his sense of right and justice, stoutly maintains that he was well in; but in or out he had won for ever the tardy confidence of the Press and the settled admiration of the hard-headed traditional enemy. Surrey were out for 225 and the tourists led them by 67. Going in again, Hobbs failed, but Hayward batted through the innings for a wonderful century with sufficient support to put it just outside Australian powers to overtake Surrey at the end. Surrey provided the Australians that year, in a season when they were only defeated three times, twice by England and once by Essex, with two of their closest contests. Late in July Surrey were all over them for two days, Hayward and Hobbs hoisting the century together for the first time, but with the game in their pockets they dithered in the last innings before the hypnotic Armstrong and lost by a mere 22. In these two games alone is a potent indication of the vertebrate power that was once more native to Surrey cricket.

The season of 1905 is for the county a heartening tale of recoupment and refreshment. They won half their championship matches, they lost only six; they climbed up the table from eleventh to fourth; they put into the field, after an abeyance of two or even three seasons, an organism and not a collection. All the signs of that season are that once again they had found their way, if not to the secret of consistent success, at least to the clue to that secret, which in the golden decade of their victories had been, we remember, talent capably led. After much halting and retractation, they had hit upon a leader whose powers of control and organisation were the key to a success for which he has perhaps never had the credit he deserves.

Lord Dalmeny, son of the very illustrious Lord Rosebery, and now at this moment of writing an illustrious Lord Rosebery himself, had too various a talent and too urgent a sense of public responsibility to feel able to devote a whole career's time to first-class cricket. Because he began in county matches with no great school or University record to recommend him and because his early performances were modest, he is too often accepted by history as just another figurehead amateur imported from the leisured classes to control the uncontrollable professionals and seal the county representation with respectability. The fact that he was one of the half dozen or so captains shuffled through by a desperate county in its leanest year should not tell against him; and when he engaged in 1905 to lead the side until Raphael could join it as captain after the University match, he showed an entirely commendable modesty and sense of fitness. It is a measure of his success that when mid-season came the Surrey authorities were unanimous in urging him to carry on and Raphael for one was proud to play under him. A powerful and upstanding player, he brought his batsmanship to something equivalent to the maturing of his character. Winning the generous commendation of *Wisden* for the intelligence of his leadership and the wisdom of his handling of both amateurs and professionals in his team, he gained the even more spontaneous tributes of the spectators by a series of electrifying displays of violent hitting. It is probable that for his captaincy he sensibly leaned much upon Hayward, and that for his batsmanship he trusted to his eye and his might. He scored over a thousand runs and began a most popular and successful run of seasons as captain of the new Surrey; and his run getting success earned for him in *Wisden,* in the section on Surrey batsmen, a sentence which then meant less than it does now but which he could be forgiven for causing to be engraved over the doorway of his ancestral home—"Hobbs and Lord Dalmeny demand more extended notice."

His maturing leadership added incalculable power to the existing talents of the leading players. In particular, in a season of hard wickets, two of his bowlers did wonders. Walter Lees was a stock bowler in a thousand, and the reward for his tireless loyalty was 169 wickets in championship matches alone; and no one appreciated more, or responded better to, wise handling than the inexperienced and terrifying fast bowler N. A. Knox, whose pace matched anyone whom we have seen or heard of since, but whose vulnerability to strain and sprain confined his real effectiveness to two or three seasons. In this year of grace Lees and Knox, with the help of the energetic Hayes and the sardonic and guileful Razor Smith, cleaned up all but about fifty of the championship wickets that Surrey took. Their thrust and aggression was backed by admirable fielding; and when it came to batting Hayward and Hayes were dependable and prolific, Baker and Holland were free and attractive, and, as already recorded, in the cold light of *Wisden's* balanced objectivity, Hobbs and Lord Dalmeny demanded more extended notice.

It cannot be too wearisomely insisted on; the hero accomplished no miracles. He did not blind all beholders with the thunder and lightning of his blazing genius, it was not through him alone that Surrey's resurgence of power returned; he merely, in the most unassuming manner possible, demanded more extended notice. He was not, in any sensational sense of the word, a phenomenon. I find this altogether admirable. As it happened he fell away after the gratifying start. Even if you include all the innings I have mentioned, he exceeded 50 only six times that season. In the game after the second Australian match recorded above, he and Hayward cut loose in the concluding stages and achieved a ten-wicket victory over Middlesex with a remarkable unfinished opening partnership of 168, made in just over two hours. Hobbs was 75 not out at the finish, and the innings showed his contained aggressiveness at its best. But apart from that display, and the 58 against the Australians a day or two earlier, his highest score after the first of June was 38. He may be forgiven for having felt from time to time the nudge of despondency. In particular it is not out of place to record that his four completed innings against Yorkshire aggregated seven runs; Hirst got him out once and Rhodes twice. He registered a string of four failures against Kent, and Blythe had him all four times. He says himself that to plunge straight into a full season of three-day

games is an unbelievably tiring experience, and the downward
graph of his scores in this first season is a clear indication of an
endurance tested to the limit. They rested (or even dropped) him
in one or two late matches, and there were four occasions in August
on which he went in lower down in the order. To complete the tale,
which has degenerated perhaps unfairly (and assuredly only temporarily) into a tale of woe, the grimness of irony decreed that on
his first visit to Cambridge as a first-class cricketer, he opened the
innings against his home University and was promptly caught at
the wicket for 0. Illustrious Hayward did not play in that match;
otherwise no doubt 'twould have been well worth going to see his
smile.

Nevertheless there was clearly so much quality there that nobody
with any sense was going to worry about quantity; and he himself
has said that as the Surrey Committee were satisfied, so was he.
All told he had made 1,317 runs in 51 completed innings, and
although an average of 25 was nothing extraordinary, there was
no doubt in the mind of *Wisden* that here was the best professional
batsman that Surrey had brought forward in recent seasons. "Easy
and finished in style," runs the comment, "he is particularly strong
on the on-side, scoring in front of short leg with great skill and
certainty." Later it was remarked that he "developed a tendency
to play too much with his legs" (against which it may be noted
that he was l.b.w. only twice during the season, and the first of
those occasions was in early May). *Wisden* saved up its schoolmasterly admonition until last. "He is a cricketer from whom a
great deal may be expected, but he should endeavour to brighten
up his fielding. Though a safe catch he is not at present very quick
on his feet."

When the last match ended he could hardly move his feet at all,
much less be quick on them; and he went down to Cambridge for
a holiday and made up for his slowness in the field by being very
quick through the air over the handlebars of his bicycle half way
down a steep hill. The enforced rest which followed eased his
muscles back into order; never again in his career was a season's
cricket to tax him too far. In later years he had less strength to
spare, but he knew how to husband it.

As the spring of 1906 opened out around him he was prey for a
few weeks to an unaccustomed onset of nerves. Establishing him-

self in a county side had been one thing; but the coming season
would be the ravaging test of his ability to retain his place and
improve on his quality. There have been many occasions of a
successful first season followed by ruinous disappointment as the
bowlers whom fresh and reckless talent plundered at the first
attempt returned with knowledgeable guiles to defeat ambition
once for all. Doubts of this kind crowded in as the season began;
he seems to have shared them with some of his fellow-professionals,
for he says that their cheerful encouragement bucked him up a lot.
He no doubt improved in spirits after the first few matches, as he
began by taking an undefeated 85 off the Gentlemen of England,
whose attack was less powerful than it had been the year before,
and followed this up with 79 and 69 against Hampshire. This was
the first match in which he ever scored two fifties; Mead, now
migrated, got his wicket again.

He clearly need not have worried. It was a dry hard summer,
and his skill flowered under the sun. In the first weeks of the season
not only the Gentlemen and Hampshire had a taste of his powers,
but Leicester were subjected twice to innings of over 70, Worcester
fielded out to his first century of the season and all the Aeschylean
ironies descended once more upon Essex, who were thrashed in
the Oval game to the tune of 80 and 31 and at Leyton provided him
with yet another 100. The combination of Hayward and Hobbs
was gathering experience and proficiency; the younger very properly dwarfed in this season by the older, and learning from him
in every match. On the crest of Hayward's magnificent wave Hobbs
rode into the security and prosperity that were to be his own province for the rest of his career.

It was fitting enough that he should do so, for this was Hayward's
greatest year, when he broke the aggregate record and stood established beyond any challenge save Johnny Tyldesley's as the greatest
professional batsman of what we like to think of as the Golden Age
of English cricket. It may be an illusory view *sub specie
aeternitatis*; but the first decade of the twentieth century cannot
fail to lie broadly under the eye of the historian as the age when the
main tradition of this maturing game entered upon its high summer.
An age untroubled by serious controversy or complexity, it saw
orthodoxy gloriously enthroned. Batsmanship, a brilliant but not
always stable art on the lifting uncertain wickets of the nineteenth

century, had been massively manhandled into a consistent and
formidable science by the immense skill and personality of
W. G. Grace; and on his unshakeable foundations had been erected
the firm classical lines of memorable style and beauty by MacLaren
and Palairet, Spooner and R. E. Foster, Jackson and Fry and
Ranjitsinhji—amateurs of free and independent bearing whose
freedom and independence never scouted the true principles of
orthodoxy, unless a scientific intelligence like Fry's thought out a
better way, or a preternatural intuition like Ranji's by-passed the
normal, or a deliberate cool-headed apostasy like Jessop's trans-
cended it. For the most part these great and graceful players set
the tone which dominated the decade; the free upright stance, the
rhythmic swing and punch, the timed flow of the front-footed
drives, the late cuts and leg-glides that were the second line of
resource when the bowlers countered the power of the forward
technique by pitching them shorter. Among the professionals at
this period only Tyldesley and Hayward shared this aggressive
and orthodox pre-eminence. Tyldesley's Northern training and
circumstance moulded him, with the aid of a quicksilver adaptability that his compatriots MacLaren and Spooner lacked, into
the greatest bad-wicket batsman playing bar Victor Trumper;
while Hayward for his part concentrated into a watchful method
and formidable powers of attack all the virtues of the orthodox
classical style which the leading amateurs had individually and
collectively founded. Here in 1906 we can watch for a moment the
last enchantments of that golden age: epitomised in the Gents. v.
Players match at Lord's, a classic of the series, a game of lowish
scores and flying stumps, when Fielder took all ten wickets in the
first innings and Lees and Fielder all ten between them in the
second, and Brearley and Knox twice went through the flower of
the professionals like twin flames out of hell's mouth and only Hayward, bloody but unbowed, and his Surrey co-evals Hayes and Lees
could present anything like a defence to the onslaught. On the
positive side of batsmanship moved the supremely graceful
Spooner with a classic hundred, and Jessop bludgeoned 73 in less
than an hour; but the day, and the year, and the decade, belonged
to the patient and courageous Hayward at the height of his prolific
strength. 1906 was Hayward's year and not Hobbs'; but for the
most part, while the fabulous scores were being amassed, the

younger man was at the other end or thereabouts, reflective and receptive. For a player of Jack Hobbs' remarkable powers of assimilation, Hayward's year was almost as solidly and productively educative as if the success had been his own. When Hayward in successive matches collected two separate centuries from Notts and two separate centuries from Leicester, his partner's performances, except for the first innings of the Leicester game when they put on 178 together, were modest enough; but we may be sure that the lessons of these grandiloquent innings were docketed neatly away, whether from twenty yards' distance or from the pavilion. The culmination of Hayward's classical completion was absorbed into his partner by a kind of chemical action. By the end of that season Hayward had virtually perfected two batsmen and not one.

In late July and August Hayward began to slow up. On several occasions Hobbs seized the initiative. Once against Worcester, when Surrey were set to make 286 and Burrows swept away Hayward, Hayes and Crawford for negligible scores, Hobbs took charge at a moment of some crisis and led his county at a spanking pace to a six-wicket victory, accompanied most efficiently by an Oxford Blue named Gordon in his second county match. Hobbs made 162 not out and Gordon 69 not out and their unbroken partnership totalled 176 in just over two hours. In the last home match of the season he tried the same trick in kindred circumstances against Middlesex; he took only a hundred minutes over his own hundred, but there was not enough solid support, and when he was out Baker and Rushby had to hold on with all they had got to avoid defeat. Ending this season with a flourish, he proved that his stamina, as well as his skill, was being reinforced by experience. His 1,913 runs for the season gave him an average of 40. *Wisden* said roundly that good as he was it was not in the least degree likely that he had yet reached his highest point; it noted a gain in all-round hitting ability with a continued penchant for on-side play; it observed with satisfaction that his fielding at third man and in the deep had improved out of knowledge. It mentioned him without disparagement in this context in the same breath as Denton and Johnny Tyldesley.

Surrey came in on the high waves, only Kent and Yorkshire beating them to the top. For this they naturally returned prime thanks to Hayward, but Knox and Lees must without any reasonable reservation be bracketed with him in honour, and so must the phenomenal Crawford, who made 1,000 runs and took 100 wickets at the age of 19. The invaluable Hayes came roughly equal to Hobbs in runs and average. Dalmeny's personal record was slighter than it had been the year before, but there is no doubt of the positive and dynamic quality of his captaincy. "The Oval," says *Wisden,* "was in every way its old self."

Hobbs did not, apparently, find his 53 first-class innings too exhausting that season; for he played at odd times in a few club matches, and on one occasion made two centuries in one day for the South Kensington Club. He had also been active in other directions, and at the end of the season was married at Cambridge to a girl he had been courting since he was seventeen. Here began the happiest and the longest partnership of his life, a stimulus to all his many successes and a ready solace to his widely-separated failures. It is the career that concerns me here and not its essential and harmonious background, which is not our business; only Jack Hobbs himself can know what part serene stability can play and has played in the perfection of an art.

CHAPTER V

REPRESENTATIVE CRICKET

THE horizons were expanding; experience was completing the young player's natural competence, and the varieties of climate and condition which two English seasons impose upon the routine of a cricketer's life were teaching him adaptability as quickly as he could assume it. 1907 was to extend him in many new ways. The season, by contrast to the baked bright summer of the year before, was all drench and drizzle, sweaters and sawdust; a writer in *Wisden* called it the wettest within living memory; the word "quagmire", excellent in itself, is over-familiarly used in the official descriptions of the matches and loses force; in this central year of the golden age of batsmanship C. B. Fry heads the batting averages with a figure of 46. (Hayward's the year before had been 66 and even then he wasn't at the top.) The bowlers, correspondingly, revel and riot among the wickets, Hirst, Rhodes, Blythe and the rest; George Dennett, excellent county bowler, collected over 200. Not a season for batting records, even if records were in themselves of great importance, which they are not. It is more the concern of Jack Hobbs' biographer to chronicle the expansion of a personality and an artist than to juggle and amaze with the juxtaposition of figures which have already been adequately marshalled by the statistician; and it is perhaps sufficient to note, broadly, that in what Tennyson might very well have called a death-dumb, autumn-dripping gloom of a so-called summer this newly-fledged county batsman made over 2,000 runs. Hayward bettered him slightly, both in aggregate and average; he himself performed the same kind office, by the breadth of three runs and a decimal point, for

Johnny Tyldesley. He clearly had the measure, in his own established and sub-international context, of whatever weather and bowling his own native land could front him with; and this in spite of an uncertain beginning to the season, a bitty and uneven row of small scores in May being enlivened by a few scattered successes only, when he and Hayward minced Hampshire's mediocre attack and he and Hayes made brave and brilliant onslaughts on Northants and Derby. These successes were fitful skirmishes to keep up his spirits while deep inside himself he reorganised his technique to combat the changed condition, varying the bold forward play he had learned and perfected with Hayward with new back-foot tactics that exploited defence and deflection, measured the probabilities of spin, cultivated the dead bat or the unexpectedly live one, and above all trained the feet in their economical placing and poise.

It was not only the weather that season that threatened new dangers. The year was memorable in cricket history for the visit of the South African touring team. It was by no means the first, though certain of its predecessors had barely touched the fringe of first-class status. The first really capable South African team to visit England was the 1904 party under Frank Mitchell, which lost only three out of 26 matches and threw up certain signs and portents for the immediate future that had not to wait very long to be realised. Their batting, though sound, was nothing out of the ordinary; but they boasted an unspeakably fast bowler named Kotze and a strange Mephistophelian spin bowler named Schwarz who had had a little experience of English cricket and had been present at the birth of B. J. T. Bosanquet's disconcerting "googly". When the team went back to South Africa Schwarz went back with them to think out the implications of his experiments; and when in 1905 a fairly strong and hopeful M.C.C. side landed in South Africa under Plum Warner's captaincy they found waiting for them not one googly bowler, but three or four. As it happened only two of them were thrown seriously into the firing line against the M.C.C. tourists—Schwarz himself and an even greater all-rounder and artist, Aubrey Faulkner—but they were in all conscience enough and to spare. The tourists, after one really magnificent Test in which South Africa triumphed breathtakingly by one wicket, were comprehensively annihilated; the double advantage of the fast matting wicket and a very disconcerting and unfamiliar technique unseated the reasoned defences of our most capable and resourceful batsmen. Schwarz was a special case, being it would seem congenitally incapable of bowling anything beside the googly; but the fact that this considerably detracted from his surprise-value was almost completely nullified by the extraordinary pace and variation of his spin. On mat he would seem to have been a uniquely dangerous force; at any rate the English batsmen, schooled in resolute and flowing forward drives, found him disturbingly penetrative. Faulkner, varying his attack with great subtlety, was potentially even more destructive. Vogler and Gordon White, the other links in an apparently endless chain, were kept at this stage discreetly in reserve.

All four were among those present when P. W. Sherwell's team set out on its journey round the counties in this wet May. By the season's end there was no one in any doubt that this lively combination was a serious challenge not only to English cricket but to many of the most carefully-taught principles of batsmanship. It is true that their record was not the all-destructive one that their home success against Warner's tourists might have suggested; they did not win a Test, and they were beaten by Surrey and Notts as well as by England and the M.C.C.; but the one Test they lost was a desperately close affair, Blythe striving past the limits of his endurance to take 15 wickets and win the game virtually single-handed, and for the major part of the tour even the most experienced of England's batsmen found the South African attack difficult to counter. Only in the Lord's Test, which before being ruined by rain was conducted on a hard batsman's wicket, were these bogies really contained, partly by the patience of Braund but primarily by Jessop, who made 93 in an hour and a quarter, largely off Vogler. (The luckless Kotze, whom the softer wickets did not suit, but who was in C. B. Fry's later estimation every bit as fast as Tyson, had at one time four men in the deep field to Jessop in this innings, but it availed him nothing.) That match apart, the bowling strength of South Africa was the talk of the town that season; Schwarz and Vogler, with 256 wickets between them in first-class matches, were most ably seconded by White and Faulkner, with a combined bag of 120; and all the other South African bowlers' wickets totted up to 87. The striking power of the googly has never been more formidably demonstrated, and

one supposes that had all these games been played on matting and
not on the uncertain sponges of the 1907 water-meadows, the toll
of these menacing newcomers would have been even greater.

Wisden was fully alive to the peril. Schwarz and Vogler were
accorded the honour of places among the Five Cricketers of the
Year, and R. E. Foster, England's current captain, devoted an
article of considerable length to the new technique. It is highly
appreciative in tone and he hands out compliments all round with
all the charm and directness of one of his own cover-drives, but it
is impossible to escape the haunting ground-bass of foreboding.
"This new kind of bowling," he said, "is a very great invention,
and it is possible it may completely alter cricket . . . such bowling
never allows a batsman to get really set . . . the ball he is accustomed
to drive between cover and extra-cover fearlessly now bothers him
and prevents him doing so . . . as this bowling improves the difficulty will become increased, till those beautiful drives we are wont
to expect from our great batsmen will become a thing of the past
. . . if Hayward's off-driving and Tyldesley's cutting are to be
seen no more and such strokes to be a lost art to future generations
cricket must lose a great deal of its attractiveness."

This is without any doubt a cry from the heart of the golden age
from one of its most golden exponents; it calls strongly to mind the
tone in which the word of the Lord came once again to Jeremiah
his prophet in the days of Jehoiakim, as well as the succinct and
more contemporary realism with which Hilaire Belloc reported
that the ice was breaking up on every side. There was little
exaggeration in Foster's words, for their truth was apparent to all
who saw the South Africans that summer. They took back with
them to South Africa the comfortable knowledge that they had
shaken the tradition of English cricket to the marrow of its bones.

Jack Hobbs was barely involved in this. He encountered the
South Africans twice only that summer. The first time was for
Surrey in July, on one of the rare occasions when the visitors were
bettered. He himself performed with sufficient but not conspicuous
distinction, making 18 and 41; in the second innings he helped
Hayward to raise the hundred before being stumped off Vogler.
It was a hard wicket game and Vogler was the only danger. Hayward and Crawford made big scores and the South African batting
broke before Knox; the real revolutionary might embodied in the

South Africans could only be communicated in this match as it were at second hand. The second occasion was in a festival game at Scarborough at the fag-end of the season, when everybody got runs on a bone-hard wicket against tired bowlers. He got a quick 78, before lunch; an enjoyment rather than a business.

Nevertheless he was being watched. He brought his lean uncertainties to an end in early June. Possibly he stimulated himself by a visit to Cambridge, where he made 37 (nothing to write home, or even visit home about) but took 5 wickets for 22, no doubt a source of innocent merriment on and around Parker's Piece. He followed with successive innings of 66 and 55, enjoyed two hearty failures against Yorkshire and Lancashire, and then moved into a week which is still historic, when he helped Hayward to put up over 100 for the first wicket in both innings of two consecutive matches. Against Cambridge University, this time at the Oval, they scored 106 and 125 together; and in the next game, against Middlesex at Lord's, they hoisted 147 and 105. Hobbs made 72 and 56, 70 and 65 not out; Hayward 54 and 66 not out, 119 and 50. It was one of those triumphs of efficiency and solidarity which only the great opening pairs achieve. When, two matches later, Hobbs made his first century of the season on the last playing day of June, a glorious display of aggressive batting against Warwickshire that left him not out for 150, there came to him at last, for the first time, an invitation to play in a representative match.

Two representative matches, in fact—the Gentlemen and Players fixtures at Lord's and the Oval. Now, in the 'sixties, our perspectives have altered, with the acute publicisation accorded to the Test cricket that is with us every mortal moment, and it is perhaps not easy to recapture the sense of occasion and importance which surrounded these two fixtures half a century ago. In particular the Lord's game ranked as the focal point of the season; to appear in it was almost as signal an honour as to be selected for England; and the Oval game, though of lesser status, carried the unmistakable representative *cachet*. For a variety of deplorable reasons this attractive fixture lost caste and finally lapsed, after carrying about it for several seasons the curious imprint of a crazy mixed-up beer-match between Surrey and Hampshire. Even the Lord's game looks at times like somebody's afterthought and not a grapple between the toughest cricketers in the country; but in

1907 these two matches had an illustrious savour, and to the young player invited to take part they must have had the air of the ante-rooms to the international holy of holies itself.

It is one of the ties which bind Jack Hobbs firmly to the common cricket-lover that his beginnings never bear the infuriating stamp of omnipotence or infallibility that, try as we will, act as an involuntary estrangement between us and other heroic paladins. It is a very great comfort to us that he suffered our kind of disappointment at crucial stages of his development. It means that if we cannot hope to share his successes we can at least be one with him in failure; and both of these important trials were failures. His old friend Brearley fired him out at Lord's for 2 and 9. Remembering their past exchanges, it was rash of him to try to hook Brearley in the early overs; it is hardly likely that the ebullient Lancastrian let the occasion pass without comment. In the second innings he got a touch on one that went away steeply, a ball of which Brearley was perpetual grand master. We can see in the mind's eye the nicety with which, in later years, he would have dropped his wrists and compelled the bat away from the danger. At the Oval he did little better, being l.b.w. for 5 to his own particular creeping menace, Johnny Douglas, and being caught at the wicket for 19 off his clubmate Crawford in the second innings. *Wisden* was kind, concentrating on the fully-deserved honour of his appearance in the matches rather than on the failures. He does not seem to have desponded unduly. He soon got out of the rut with an admirable 72 against Lancashire (who were minus Brearley), and after a ruinous failure at Blackheath he collected in successive matches 135 against Hampshire and a masterly 166 not out against Worcester, who remembered him well from the year before. On the first day of the Worcester match his wife gave birth to their first-born son; and a fortnight later came a letter from the secretary of the M.C.C. inviting him to be one of the party to tour Australia in the winter.

Right up to this major culmination in his cricket career we find him visited with this curious element of chance. His first innings in a proper match had been for Jesus College choirboys, when he made up the team because they were one short. He played on Parker's Piece against Tom Hayward's County XI because the local side were one short. He appeared in his first match at Lord's against the Cross Arrows because Tom Richardson could not play. He fitted neatly and immediately into the position of opening batsman in the Surrey eleven not only on his own obvious merits but because Abel had at that precise moment of time dropped out. It is assuredly one of the essential concomitants of genius to have the happy knack of being in the neighbourhood of the right place at the right time. He now took advantage of the biggest slice of luck (one conjectures) that ever came his way, saving only the presence of Sir Berkeley Moynihan in Leeds in July 1921. Possibilities are hard to gauge fifty years after the event; no one can tell what might have happened if, or if not, something else had happened that failed to happen. If he had scored a century in the Gents and Players match at Lord's he might have played for England that season, but he tried to hook Brearley and did not. He left himself, centuries and excellent batting record and all, on the outer fringe of the selectors' minds. It seems likely at this stage that he would not have been among the fifteen or so first choices for Australia. What is historically certain is that he was not asked until the M.C.C. had received at least four separate polite refusals from more solidly established players. Hayward and Tyldesley, Hirst and Lilley, had demurred to the terms offered and could not see their way to go. Once more, and perhaps for the last time, Hobbs was invited because somebody else had dropped out.

In the perspective of history these defections appear as a crippling blow to England's prospects. Their best wicket-keeper, their best all-rounder, and their two leading professional batsmen, all removed at one fell swoop. There was in addition an unhappy suggestion that C. B. Fry had not been asked at all; that accounted in the aggregate for five of England's key cricketers. And it is in no invidious sense that the side as constituted for departure can be said to have an air of improvisation about it. A. O. Jones was a fine cricketer and a personality of some force; but in a field which contained such active competitors for captain as Fry, Warner, R. E. Foster and MacLaren it is difficult to regard his selection as other than a courageous makeshift. Accompanying him on the amateur strength were F. L. Fane of Essex, the youthful and versatile J. N. Crawford, K. L. Hutchings, the reserve wicket-keeper R. A. Young, late of Cambridge University, and among the professionals a varying collection of talent ranging from genius to

honesty—Sydney Barnes and Wilfred Rhodes, Blythe and Fielder,
Hardstaff of Notts and Humphries of Derbyshire the first-string
wicket-keeper, Len Braund, Ernie Hayes and Jack Hobbs himself.
The team in the eyes of posterity looks a whale of a good bowling
side, but honour compels the admission that in the context of that
golden age of batsmanship with which we are always so ready to
label the Edwardian period the batting looks either promising, or
unsound, or uninspired. The name Hobbs in this list does not mean
what the name Hobbs was to mean on any of the subsequent tours
to Australia undertaken by the M.C.C. It did not mean here one of
the leading batsmen in the world, a match for the best bowling on
the worst wicket, the most flexible and punishing genius of the
century; it meant a young and hugely promising player with three
full seasons only of first-class cricket behind him, who had shown
by his record up to date that he possessed all the necessary capacities for excellence provided that you did not rush him; that he
had the fallibilities of inexperience but a remarkable resolution to
overcome them if given his own time to do it in; a potential, rather
than an actual, world-beater still busily engaged in perfecting a rich
and fruitful technique; a pupil still, not yet a master. Nevertheless
Wisden at the end of the 1907 season placed him boldly in the
front rank, remarking on the increased range of his off-side shots
and predicting for him the brightest future among all the young
professional batsmen. He sailed for Australia at the most apposite
moment when he had brought his county maturity to a working
completion and needed to test it abroad. He spent, as he always did,
the greater part of the voyage with his face turned to the wall,
praying for death; in the whole of his much-travelled lifetime he
rarely failed to be prostrated by a ravaging sea-sickness. At the
end of this his first voyage he was weak at the knees.

It is clear that this misfortune was a factor in a rather unusual
situation which faced the captain and his vice-captain while the
tour was still only a few weeks old. Owing partly to his continuing
malaise he was given a rest at the beginning of the tour, going
straight on to Adelaide and missing the first two games. His first
appearance was against Victoria on 15th November and as he did
nothing of note Jones reverted in the next match to Fane as his
opening partner, an arrangement that had so far answered satisfactorily. Hobbs got a further chance on the last day of November

against Queensland, going in first with Fane but making only 21; and he was omitted again from the last match before the first Test which was to be played at Sydney on 13th December. His late start had handicapped his powers of acclimatisation; and it is well established that a player who for reasons of luck or health misses opportunities in the first State matches on an Australian tour is caught badly on the wrong foot for Test selection, as these are the only matches in which the captain can build his most effective team for the crucial games and he can hardly build it with unsuccessful or absent material. Hobbs' record on this tour up to the first Test was not impressive; and on that fact alone it is not unduly surprising that his name was left out of the published team. No doubt this was disappointing, but it was easily understandable; but there were two other factors which turned the knife in the wound. The first was the misfortune overtaking the captain, who took a severe chill in the Queensland game and went down with pneumonia a day or two later. This may have possibly suggested to Hobbs' mind that the ill wind that had swept Jones out at one end would be almost certain to blow him in at the other; and it would be natural for him to expect to be first reserve for opening batsman. It is little wonder then, that he felt what he has described as bitter disappointment when he discovered that not only had he not been picked, but he had been passed over in favour of a player who was not even a member of the touring team at all. He was out, and George Gunn was in.

George Gunn was not in the original party, but was on a trip to Australia for his health, and an arrangement had been made whereby he could be called upon if needed. Up to this minute he had not appeared in the side at all, though no doubt he was in practice; and his choice over Hobbs' head seems in the perspective of history to have been a particularly pointed and wounding one. The actual responsibility for the team changes at this moment are a little obscure, as Jones was in hospital at Brisbane and Fane was in charge of the side, and whether Jones was in some sort of long-range control is doubtful. Hobbs' omission caused less comment, however, than the dropping of the exemplary Humphries as wicket-keeper in favour of the more inexperienced R. A. Young. The manoeuvre certainly suggests a panic hunt for an opening bat, for Young opened the innings with Fane, and Gunn, who was at that time not a regular county opener, followed at number three. Jones and Fane probably never meant it as such; but a more expressive comment on Hobbs could hardly have been conceived. They were at that point not unreasonably doubtful of him on his Australian form, and it would be most unfair not to grant this to them; nevertheless it hurt Hobbs keenly, and behind his reticence it is evident that the memory of the disappointment is still alive. He has recorded the impression, which at this late date matters perhaps very little, that Jones did not think much of him. This may or may not be so; history has righted the balance. One error of judgment, or tact, in circumstances of unusual difficulty, must not distort our appraisal of a gifted and energetic cricketer.

Thus it came about that Jack Hobbs spent his twenty-fifth birthday running errands as twelfth man, and enjoyed the wry experience of congratulating George Gunn on two remarkable innings of 119 and 74. The match turned out a thriller; it was ding-dong for four days, with England slightly on top at the beginning of the last day, when on a dodgy wicket Australia needed over 200 with Trumper, Hill and Macartney out. Armstrong and Noble set their teeth in a strong resistance, but with seven men out 89 were still needed. Unhappily Blythe was ineffective, and Fielder and Barnes had shot their bolts too early; Rhodes was in his singular transition stage from bowler to batsman, and the England attack buckled before the happy onslaught of three tail-enders, Carter, Cotter and Hazlitt, who punched Australia home amid huge enthusiasm to a famous two-wicket victory.

Hobbs had two more innings, only one of them first-class, before the second Test, and both the matches in which he played were wrecked by rain. In the first-class game, against a Victorian XI, he went in first with Crawford and made 77. In the other, a local game against odds, he made 58. This did not matter, but it gave him practice, and the chance to gain favour in a little private and friendly rivalry between himself and Hayes for the last place in the Test team. Hayes did, numerically, rather better, but Hobbs got the place; and on New Year's Day, 1908, he took the field for England for the first time, the first of 61 appearances in Test cricket.

This second Test was an even closer affair than the first; a beautifully-matched contest, it shifted and swung tantalisingly as the six days progressed. It was remarked at the time how slow the scoring was, how Australia crawled to 255 for 7 on the first day (the fault, no doubt, of those unenterprising stonewallers Trumper and Macartney, Noble and Armstrong; a tribute more lasting than bronze to the restrictive accuracy of Fielder and Crawford). Australia made 266, and Fane, still captaining the side in place of the absent Jones, took Hobbs in with him to open the innings for England. He has said how critical he knew this innings to be, how important in the setting of the match, the series, his development, his reputation and his career; and how he made the iron resolve to concentrate carefully upon defence and to study circumspection. Cotter and Saunders, Noble and Armstrong, Hazlitt and Macartney, assailed him with everything they had, but he would neither be tempted nor disrupted, and in three hours he saw the score to 160 before Cotter bowled him for 83. Fane and Gunn had left early and Hutchings was his chief partner, remaining after his departure to complete a beautiful century. The later batsmen scored consistently and usefully and Australia were headed by 116. This arrear Trumper and Noble promptly cleared off and Armstrong, Macartney and the infuriating Carter all took part in a full-scale revival. In the end England were left with 282 to get; Hobbs and Gunn went cheaply, and overnight four wickets were down for 159. Next morning two wickets went at once, and although there was resistance all the way down (every man on the side but Gunn got into double figures) 73 were wanted when the eighth man was out and the pull was all with Australia. But it was the first Test again, in reverse. Humphries and Barnes most carefully and resourcefully added 34, and in horrifying tension Barnes and Fielder hit off the remaining 39. As they went for the last suicidal run Hazlitt's nerve broke and he shied the ball wide of the wicket with Fielder yards from home; and the second of two fabulous finishes had restored the quivering and perplexing equilibrium.

Hobbs' success relaxed all his own personal tensions. He felt, it seems, happier at the outcome of his trial than ever before. When it is realised that never from this moment was he left out of an England team again except for reasons unconnected with his own adequacy, it can be conceded that he had a right to feel pleased. It is no doubt accidental, and cannot be accorded any portentous

significance, that whereas *Wisden* prints the England batting order
in this match as starting with F. L. Fane and J. B. Hobbs, it starts
it in the third Test, beginning three days later, with J. B. Hobbs
and F. L. Fane. For the time being he had become, as of right,
England's Number One. In this next match he himself performed
moderately, making 26 in the first innings and 23 not out in the
second after having to retire hurt; and England, with the match in
their pockets after getting rid of Trumper for 4 and 0, allowed Hill
and Hartigan, a sick man and a novice, to add 243 and to alter
Australia's prospects from hopeless to commanding. Then they
collapsed before Saunders and O'Connor and the cherished
equilibrium broke. England were one down when with a little more
luck and a little more judgment they could have been three up.

There followed a happy little holiday in Tasmania (where
Hobbs sandwiched a century and two fifties between two inevitable
bouts of seasickness) and prepared for the fourth Test by a crushing win over a depleted Victoria. Jones came back from his con-
valescence to take charge once more, and had a chance of recon-
sidering his reservations about Hobbs, who hit a six and thirteen
fours in his highest innings of the tour, 115. Barnes and Blythe
made rings round the batsmen and the M.C.C. won by 330 runs.
Confidently they faced the Melbourne Test a day or two later; the
skies were blue, the wicket rolled out a treat. Australia won the
toss; Trumper and Hill were removed instantly, the catching
matched the bowling and the bowling was so tight and hostile that
the batsmen were struggling throughout, and only Ransford and
Noble acquired any sense of comfort. Crawford bowled with uncommon skill, exploiting every possible variation of pace to take
5 for 48 on a plumb wicket out of a total of 214. Immediately the
innings ended, down came the rain. The Australians licked their
lips, the Englishmen prayed and swore, the plumb hard wicket of
every batsman's delight was converted before their eyes into a
Melbourne sticky, and instantly 214 began to look a very big score
indeed. Hobbs took his life in his hands and sailed into the bowling
with astonishing defiance. He decided to chase runs while runs
were chaseable; the sun was out and to all practised eyes the wicket
was brewing unimaginable potions. He hit O'Connor off his length,
he disdained Macartney, he was as impolite to Saunders and Noble
as adverse circumstances permitted. He made 57 in an hour before

Noble bowled him, and then watched the rest of the team roll up like a discarded carpet before Saunders and Noble. George Gunn made 13 and nobody else made more than 8, the grand total was 105, and Australia had an hour to bat that night. Trumper was fired out by Crawford for his second duck of the match, Noble and McAlister were out before 30 was up and England ended the day on the crest of a sudden swell of optimism. Unfortunately for their sanguine hopes the ground dried completely over the week-end, the diabolically-inspired wicket rolled out hard and true. Armstrong ran to a circumspect and powerful hundred, and once more Carter scored far more vigorously than his place in the order would seem to warrant. The dispirited Englishmen lost heart. Set nearly 500 to win they went down with barely a groan for 186, earning for their pains a mild rebuke from *Wisden*. Hobbs was out for nothing and probably thought it was all his fault; but nothing can detract from the cavalier courage and execution of his first innings. He remembers it with pleasure and pride after more than fifty years as one of his finest; and it may very appropriately go on record as the first challenging sign of genius in the young Test newcomer, playing in highly adverse conditions the fifth Test innings of his career in such a style and to such a tune that the historian half a century later can recognise and hail the individual touch.

The last Test was also lost, mainly through deadly bowling by Saunders in the vital stages and a supremely lovely innings of 166 by Victor Trumper, who came in when England had the match in hand and turned the fortunes of the game topsy-turvy through sheer force of genius. Hobbs made 72 in the first innings and George Gunn another beautiful century; but in the last calamitous innings only Fane and Jones could defy the lightning for long enough to assist the sterling Rhodes, who by this time was a little further into his batting phase than he had been at the beginning of the tour, and whose 69 kept England in hopes until the end.

So the tourists left for home with four defeats in their bag, when but for a flick of fortune, or character, or skill perhaps, it might so easily have been four victories. Three to two, rather than four to one, was a fair-minded Australian's assessment of the comparative merits of the two teams as shown in the Test Matches. They had been so near to a very remarkable set of victories that, considering the withdrawals, handicaps and casualties to which they had been subject from long before the start, their record and reputation can be set down as an honourable one. The bowlers should perhaps be handed their decorations first; Crawford, Barnes and Fielder had waged untiring battles and had won many of their objectives in spite of the expense. On the batting side no one had done better than the elusive and independent Gunn, one of the unacknowledged and unrewarded masters. Hardstaff and Rhodes scored well in the minor games though less consistently in Tests; but it was generally acknowledged that the one genuine discovery of the tour was Hobbs. I feel it is possible and legitimate to point to two of his innings during that series as of key significance for the future: his 83 in his first Test, epitomising the foundation of courage and resolution that reinforced his growing technical experience: and the astonishing 57 on the dirt-patch of Melbourne, warrant of things most emphatically to come.

The implications of these two years are of vital importance in Hobbs' career. The South Africans had imported into cricket a new and formidable menace, which left the seasoned traditionalists for the moment at a loss. The home summer programme, assisted by the deplorable weather, had tightened and flexed his technique, and the Australian tour had given that technique a stern and exhilarating testing. The man for the moment was in process of completion.

CHAPTER VI

THE FIRST MATURING

IT is not necessary to detail his progress through the 1908 season match by match. He kept up the standard without unusually spectacular highlights, just failing to reach the 2,000 runs that he had achieved in the previous season in worse conditions. A steady consistency marked his scoring, with certain ironic exceptions. Brearley bowled him for a duck in the very first match on Easter Monday, the historic Gentlemen of England game, a match that can be marked perhaps with three distinguishing stones—first, in a Surrey innings of 390, Hobbs and Hayward got a duck apiece: second, the Oval was under snow just before the game started: third, W.G. played his last first-class match, scoring 15 and 25. Later on, in a comparatively high-scoring season, Hobbs played four completed innings against Yorkshire for a total of 33 runs, and fell to George Hirst in three of them. He ended the season with successive scores of 5, 3 and 1, the last being also against Yorkshire as Champion County, a ruefully fitting wind-up to his season's form against them. By contrast he was able to destroy for the time any hoodoo which his other unlucky county, Kent, had been able to exercise over him in the past, making two superb centuries against them, the one at Blackheath being a wonderful struggle against inevitable defeat. Finally, he exorcised the Gents. v. Players bogey; he did little enough at the Oval, but at Lord's he made 81, the highest individual score of the match, hitting 13 fours in a brilliant innings that is now part of the historic tradition of the fixture. For the rest he merely settled down happily into the established routine native to one who knows himself by now to be

a mainstay, playing his full part in Surrey's slight lift in the table
from fourth to third. Hayward bettered him on performance, and so
by a decimal point or two did Crawford; while up among their
company was a powerful acquisition from Australia called Alan
Marshal, an all-rounder and a hitter of mighty attainment, whose
potentialities seemed boundless. Lord Dalmeny had had to hand
over the captaincy to H. D. G. Leveson-Gower, another illustrious
figure in the councils of Surrey and the wider reaches of the game,
and under his benevolent and sympathetic leadership the portents
were consistently bright. A minor regret remains, that when the
Philadelphian touring side came to the Oval in late July, Surrey
rested a number of their key players and Hobbs had no opportunity
of facing the bowling of Bart King, whom good judges have ranked
with Barnes and Tate and whose name is still the most illustrious
in American cricket. (According to *Wisden* he is still happily
living, and nearly 90.) On this two-month tour he took 115 wickets,
and Middlesex, Surrey, Derby, Notts and Kent were all victims
of his outstanding powers. In the Surrey match Marshal hit him
mercilessly; but it would have been of even greater service to history
if we could have watched King's techniques opposed by Hobbs.

The *Wisden* for 1909, embodying of course the cricket season
of 1908, is the one in which he enters in rightful series as one of the
Cricketers of the Year. (The section in which he appears is
quaintly entitled "Lord Hawke and Four Cricketers of the Year",
occasioning in an outsider's mind the subversive question whether
his lordship was distinguished from the others by the quality of
his blood or the quality of his cricket.) The three other mere com-
moners ranked beside (or a little behind or below) the Yorkshire
aristocrat were his fellow county-man Newstead, Alan Marshal,
who got the honour earlier than many more prominent players,
and the admirable and destructive Brearley. Hobbs in his Surrey
cap looks seriously at posterity out of the fading sepia photograph,
large-eyed and unsmiling; the oracle says of him all that it had
said before, and more also, ranks him as the best professional batsman in England except Hayward and Tyldesley, and grants him
keenness, ambition, and the strong likelihood of its fulfilment. Piece
by piece he was conquering his kingdom and establishing its
borders. 1908 was a year of consolidation rather than expansion.

1909 is a curious year. It might so very easily have been a

phenomenal landmark, as 1947 is in the life of Edrich and Compton. It appeared to offer him everything, and for a time he seemed enthusiastically ready to go and take it. He had had a winter's rest, which he was more than ready for; he was faced in May with dry welcoming wickets; and after looking at the bowling with some circumspection in the first match, he went out on the hunt for runs. On the sixth of May he and Hayes punished Hampshire to dreadful effect, putting on 371 in two and three-quarter hours. Surrey made 742, which, when you consider the plumb Oval wicket and the fact that the Hampshire bowling was opened by George Brown and Philip Mead, is not so extravagant as it sounds, and Hobbs and Hayes made over 200 each. C. B. Fry, playing his first game for Hampshire, made 42 and 60, but Surrey won by an innings and 468; following this up in the very next match by overwhelming a strong Warwickshire side by nearly 200, Hayward and Hobbs actually putting up 352 for the first wicket in the second innings. Hobbs' 205 against Hampshire had been chanceless; against Warwick he was overshadowed by a magisterially impressive senior partner with 204 not out, and his own 159 included three catches put down. Never mind; he rested for the game at Oxford, made top score (44) in Surrey's first innings against the Australians in a needle thriller which Surrey won by 5 runs, and then travelled to Birmingham to take it out on Warwick again. He had made 159 at the Oval, so went one better here and reached 160, a rather slower compilation than usual for it took him over four hours. In the second innings he renounced caution and made 100 in two hours dead, hitting eleven fours and getting little support from his colleagues. Surrey failed to force a win, but Hobbs in a couple of weeks had now achieved for the first time two cherished ambitions —one double century, and a century in each innings of a first-class match. He had also, though he did not take a great deal of note of this, made 758 runs by the 22nd May, and when he followed the two centuries with 99 against Essex at the Oval (an innings which he regards as one of the worst he ever played, ended by a catch at the wicket off Douglas which deprived him of a century he did not deserve) he had 857 on the tally and five days left for 1,000 in May. However, at this crucial point in time there were sterner preoccupations in the air.

Once more the Australians were among us. They had come

with some new material, primarily Ransford, Bardsley, and Macartney, that was to fuse itself admirably into the continuing strength of the old; a well-balanced side who for some reason were under-rated during the tour and perhaps played rather more drawn matches than a touring team of that quality should. Under-rated or not, the composition of the England side was, as always during an Australian tour, the chief controversial question of the season. Hobbs must have felt on his Australian record alone fairly certain of a place, and on his May record of the present year certain beyond the shadow of a doubt. He did not know it at the time, but it seems that Leveson-Gower had a strong tussle with MacLaren on the Selection Committee before the invitation went to Hobbs. As it happened it went to fourteen others as well, the English selectors showing a disturbing reluctance to make up their minds; but, although it is clear to the chronicler that all the laurels in Hobbs' career had to be bought with patience and wrestling of the spirit, Hobbs' name was at last confirmed in the residual list.

There was an entirely happy informality about the invitation. When he had been asked to go to Australia, the letter from the Secretary of the M.C.C. had begun "Dear Sir," had gone on with "I have been instructed to invite you to accompany the team . . . terms embodied in enclosed agreement . . . please sign and return . . ." and ended "yours faithfully." All most unexceptionable and orderly to the last degree, with the veiled suggestion that the invitee would forfeit all privilege and avoid the agreement if he filled the form in wrongly. On this occasion the terms of reference were varied. Dated (or rather not dated at all) from the Sports Club, St. James's Square, S.W., the missive ran like this:

"My dear Jack,
    Please be at Birmingham on Thursday to play if wanted for England. I am *so* pleased—no one deserves the honour more than you do.
    A thousand thanks for your wonderful innings last match.
    With very many congratulations,
                    Yours very sincerely,
                    H. D. G. Leveson-Gower."

The charm and generosity of this little letter nourish the heart. It cost the writer nothing, it was possibly dashed off in a hurry, he no doubt thought little of it after he had licked the envelope and given it to a waiter to put in the post-box in the Sports Club vestibule; but it invests a formality with a direct spontaneous pleasure and warmth that reach out over fifty years with a graceful and touching humanity.

When the day came the weather was full of rainy premonitions, and England fielded no fast bowler. Hayward was among those present but omitted—a damaged knee gave him severe trouble all that season—but the batting, which included MacLaren, Tyldesley, Fry, Jessop, Rhodes, Hirst and A. O. Jones as well as Hobbs, hardly seems defective from any angle of vision. Australia showed what they thought of the wicket by sending Cotter, a number 8 batsman, to open with Bardsley when play began as late as five o'clock, and never calling on him for a single ball throughout the match. As it happened there was barely an hour's play that night, as more showers fell; Bardsley and Cotter were both out before the end, and the innings never got to its feet next morning, Hirst and Blythe polishing the whole side off before lunch for 74.

MacLaren and Hobbs, the old classicism and the new, opened for England full of optimism. Once more the laurels withdrew themselves; MacLaren played a maiden from Whitty, and then Macartney promptly got Hobbs l.b.w. first ball. He went back to the pavilion like a martyr to the block. "The rest of the day was a misery," he records, "to be followed by a night of remorse and wretchedness." Let us agree that his terms are pitched a little strong, and would have been a little more appropriate if he had murdered his mother; but all allowances being made we can see his point and commiserate with his depression. He derived no doubt little consolation from the companionship in ignominy of Fry himself who also got a duck and who, along with MacLaren, also fell to Macartney before the side's total reached 20. Tyldesley, Jones and Jessop hit their way bravely out of the slush, but the final total, 121, was little to boast of, the foxy Armstrong proving complete master of the later batsmen. This lead of 47, substantial enough in the tenuous context, was happily reinforced that night by the quick removal of Macartney and Noble, the latter to a catch by Jones that is still alive and electrifying to the mind and is a classic in the history of Test cricket. Ransford and Gregory stayed overnight and carried their partnership to 81 in the morning; after which Blythe and Hirst took five wickets, including the sizeable ones of Trumper and Armstrong, for 9 runs in half-an-hour. Well before lunch the innings had frittered itself away, and England were given 105 to win, with the rest of the day to play with.

MacLaren's acute stroke of generalship is now famous. He looked down the score-card, observed ironically that two of his leading batsmen had registered ducks in the first innings, and commanded Hobbs and Fry to put their pads on. It is difficult to conceive that Fry's confidence or concentration was impaired in the slightest by his earlier misfortune, but the younger man confesses to certain misgivings as they walked out to bat. In the upshot MacLaren was wonderfully upheld. Hobbs played Armstrong's first two balls carefully, and then lay back to the third and cut it crisply for four, restoring his own May form and his own self-esteem together with the buoyancy on which his particular adventurousness always throve. He went for the runs from the start as only the pre-1914 Hobbs knew how. Cotter did not bowl, and Whitty and Macartney took heavy punishment. Hobbs and Fry were out at the pitch of the ball on quick eager feet; they seem never to have looked like getting out. Hobbs played one of his best innings ever; Fry, says *Wisden,* seemed strangely anxious. I find this impossible to believe, unless he was preoccupied with the composition and simultaneous rendering into Greek of a Pindaric Ode on Hobbs' batting. In an hour and a half they had 89 on the board, and Hobbs hit Macartney for three fours in a row by way of return for yesterday's l.b.w. Then Fry came out of his Sibylline trance and swept O'Connor to square leg, the batsmen ran four and the match dissolved in a wild revel of shouting uproarious spectators. Hobbs was 62, Fry 35, a clear clean victory and a warm personal satisfaction. The crowd yelled his name till it was hoarse, and he waved his cap fleetingly from the balcony. Then he went home in a pulsing glow of pleasure and found his wife had gone out shopping and did not know, or to his thinking seem overmuch to care, whether he had made a duck or a hundred.

This was on Saturday May 29th, and there was one more day to play with for the 1,000 in May. He had 919 in his bag, and Surrey went north for Whit-Monday 31st, to play Notts at Trent Bridge. 81 runs was not, in his present form, by any means a tall order, and the Trent Bridge wicket was as easy-paced then as it is now.

Alas for ambition—Leveson-Gower lost the toss. Four slip-
catches went to grass in the first half-hour, mainly off the temperamental Rushby; Jones made a lot, Iremonger made a lot,
George Gunn was his solid and formidable self; Hobbs, contemplating from the deep field his lessening chances of a still very
uncommon record, then watched Payton dig in for a century. Notts
stayed in all day; anti-climax engulfed his aspirations. Next day he
failed in both innings; but the record was gone, and he never came
within measurable distance of it again.

The season's promise flared and faded. England's selectors, playing a curious private game of ducks and drakes, put losing sides into
the field at Lord's and Leeds. Hobbs played in both games and did
little in either, though at Leeds in the second innings his 30 was
top score in a catastrophic 87. As often after a brilliant start, a
check brought uncertainty, his touch temporarily left him. He
played one fine innings of 162 against Worcester, and had time
before the third Test to play two of the four innings that he was to
play that season against Yorkshire for a total of 44 runs. (He was
Haigh's rabbit this year; Hirst only got him once.) Fielding at Old
Trafford in early July he went for a high catch given by Brearley
(always present at fateful crises) and badly tore a fingernail. He
was out of the game for a month, missing both Gents. v. Players
fixtures and the chance of two further Tests. When he got back at
the beginning of August he was some little time settling down again,
though scores of 133 and 59 against Gloucester were happy signs
that form was not far round the corner. Immediately after this
game Kent and Yorkshire swallowed him whole twice, 7 and 12
in the one, 8 and 0 in the other—a curious instance of a persistent
double inhibition that must have had more than pure coincidence
to back it. He ended the season with an admirable aggregate (2,114)
and a creditable average (40); but when one contemplates the
month of May it is with the feeling that Surrey's own disappointments were a little reflected in Hobbs.

The county had met rough weather. They had beaten the
Australians, they had finished fifth, but they lost seven matches
and their broad base of confidence had shifted uneasily under Hayward's lameness and Hobbs' injury. Failure of tact and patience on
both sides, it would seem, led to a disastrous row with Crawford,
who broke with the county and departed for Australia, of all places,

in a manner distantly recalling Alcibiades or Coriolanus. Independ-
ently trouble brewed up among the professionals. Rushby defected
to the Lancashire League, and Marshal ran into disciplinary bother
and was suspended at the height of the season. At this distance of
time these disputes and distresses have abated their urgency, but
the surface of the game's history cannot help being troubled and
distorted by such flaws. As against these losses there should be set
the perfection of Strudwick's wicket-keeping, the promise of Hitch
as a fast bowler, and the consolidation of the handsome and
attractive Ducat as a full forcing batsman. A brilliant young
amateur, M. C. Bird, made such a success of the latter part of the
season that he was promptly selected for the South African tour.

It is this South African tour that conclusively readjusts the
balance of Hobbs' ambiguous year of 1909. Once under Table
Mountain the uncertainties of the second half of the summer
departed from him. It would seem that he was, almost without
being aware of it, squaring himself to the problem that had not
previously been presented directly to him but had had all the senior
traditionalists baffled. When Schwarz and his destroying quartet
had unseated the confidence of England's leading batsmen in 1905
and 1907 there was everywhere in the air an implicit appeal for a
new idea or a new method to counter the new negation.
R. E. Foster's article in *Wisden* cried out for help; not in so many
words, but its tone was unmistakable. And it was in everyone's
mind that the team that went to South Africa under Leveson-
Gower in the winter of 1909 was going to have this problem posed
to it as forcibly as it was humanly possible to pose it—by the four
great South African googly bowlers in their own country, in their
own conditions, with the lift and venom of their own matting
wickets to reinforce their added experience.

It is significant that the Selection Committee chose none of the
great traditional batsmen for this tour. Laudably they adventured
upon youth. There were no MacLaren's, Frys, Fosters, Haywards
or Tyldesleys; for the first time Hobbs led the batting as of right,
and among his henchmen were M. C. Bird, David Denton, and
the young Kent all-rounder Frank Woolley. For opening partner
Fate and foresight and wisdom and good luck attached him for the
first time to Wilfred Rhodes, now a sterling veteran of thirty-two
with unfathomable profundities of experience behind him and half

a lifetime's renewed honour as both batsman and bowler before
him. He had opened for Yorkshire by this time for three seasons
and more, was now triumphantly proclaiming that he was more
than worth his place as a batsman even if he never bowled an over,
and now enters a special immortality as Jack Hobbs' first great
Test partner. The Hayward-Hobbs combination, like the Hobbs-
Sandham partnership later, was wonderfully organised for run-of-
the-mill championship work. Hobbs came to Test cricket too late
in Hayward's career to carry that joint effectiveness much further.
On this tour Hobbs and Rhodes began in earnest the second of
Hobb's' four classic associations.

With Rhodes for partner he beat and broke the googly. Not
decisively or finally; the googly has never lapsed in importance
since that day, but its terrors were eased and familiarised. On this
South African trip he had insufficient support lower down the
order for anything like effective victory, but for his part, relying on
the superb stubbornness of Yorkshire character and watchfulness
at the other end he made himself for the first time in Test cricket
a dictator and a master. He filled out his great reputation into a
living actuality, where beforehand it had been compounded not of
achievement only but of promise and hope as well. His victory over
the googly marks his attainment of greatness; and because greatness is not a synonym of perfection but has variations, this present
greatness should be differentiated from the lordly and almost
absolute command of the post-war years when he became an
imaginative inventor in the terms of his skill. This earlier greatness
was a triumph of science; the later was the triumph of art.

The secret must have been in exceptional co-ordinative powers
of eye and muscle and, particularly, feet. He said once that after
1918 he made all his runs off the back foot. We can cheerfully
assent to this if we will, without believing it; but it seems clear
that before 1914 he was up and down the wicket like an eager
terrier on active feet that positioned themselves miraculously early.
His reactions were so rapid and his instinct so true that it almost
seemed as if the preparatory "spotting" of the googly were comparatively irrelevant; for if he sensed a short-pitched ball he was
back on his stumps in a flash, if he saw the fuller pitch in the early
flight he was yards down the wicket to kill the spin. Whatever the
ball was he was on it, at the precise instant and in the precise

relation to it for administering the correct treatment. He has said
that it is essential to spot it, and having spotted it, play it accordingly, which sounds all very well for him, but what about the rest
of us? Yet he says at the same time that on that tour, when he was
virtually the googly's temporary destroyer, he could not spot
Gordon White's googly. He played, he says, each ball on its merits;
which means with him that the nature of its merits were apparent
to him only an infinitesimal fraction of time later when he failed to
spot the googly than when he did not. He goes on to say that his
method was then to hit the bad ones and keep the good ones out
of his wicket; almost the reverse of the individual but effective
method adopted by that other great opening batsman, Mr. Podder,
in the match between All-Muggleton and Dingley Dell. All in all,
his own written comments on the googly and how to play it are
modest but unhelpful; the perfect and indeed the only textbook
was Hobbs in action, light on active questing feet, instant judgment
assisted by intuitive poise and balance. Hobbs in South Africa in
1909 came to his first magnificent maturity.

Beginning by making the best comment possible (two successive
centuries in his first two innings) in face of the remark of a candid
and hospitable South African newspaper who said that Hobbs
might as well go home for all the good he would do on matting
wickets, he opened the Test series by putting up 147 with Rhodes
for the first wicket. Hobbs got 89, and followed it with 35 when
England, needing 254 to win, failed by 19. The partnership
increased its assets in the Natal match, for they had 207 on the
board without being separated, Hobbs making 163 in two and a
half hours. They had consistent opening partnerships, too, in the
second Test, when England lost by 95 runs against some deadly
bowling by Faulkner; Hobbs made 53 and 70, but nobody else got
more than 46 in the two innings. The firm failed to pay its way in
either the third or the fourth Tests; (in the fourth Hobbs, Rhodes
and Denton made 16 runs between them in the match)—but there
was an irregularity in the third game when Hobbs was badly
affected by the heat when fielding and did not feel well enough to
open the innings. When he did go in, at number seven, he was soon
out, but he steeled himself to a crisis in the second innings, when
England with 221 to win lost four for 42, including Denton and
Rhodes. Hobbs began very shakily, but gradually righted himself

against some extremely penetrating bowling by Vogler, and flowering all round with some of the most brilliant strokes in his armoury, coasted England home with a most courageous and decisive innings of 93 not out. It may be that the most judicious finger would point to that resolute performance as one of the greatest even of his Test career; though numerically and sensationally he bettered it in the last Test, the second which England won against South Africa's three, when he and Rhodes led off with a stand of 221 (a record at the time for Test first-wicket partnerships) and Hobbs himself in three and three-quarter hours made 187, which it is a surprise to note was the first Test century he had ever made. According to *Wisden* he also, not for the first time, opened the bowling, a bizarre state of affairs; and in the second innings he captured the wicket of Schwarz.

The tour was for him a complete success; his first-class average for the trip was 62, his Test average 67; he returned with a reputation deepened and broadened, and he returned with the conclusive answer to the South African bowling menace. The touring team itself, admittedly short of established Test batsmen, had been persevering but erratic; as a constructive experiment it cannot be counted a success, as only Woolley of the new tourists became a regular England player. Nevertheless its tactical value was anything but negative; the South African terror was never the same again. In fact it was remarked that the great phalanx of googly bowlers had already abated their formidable powers. Faulkner and Vogler shouldered virtually the whole of the attack between them; but White bowled little, and Schwarz was a complete failure. He played in four Tests and bowled no more than eight overs; and in the whole tour took only two M.C.C. wickets. Perhaps it was some consolation that one was Woolley's and the other Hobbs'.

Hobbs began the season of 1910 with the full richness of the tour reinforcing his maturity. It was a drenching wet year and Surrey were lifted to second place in the championship almost by the sole efforts of "Razor" Smith, whose off-breaks spun venomously on the green turf and brought him 215 wickets in county championship matches alone. (His total bag was 247.) Bird took over the captaincy and relied for most of his batting on the three H's as before, though Hayward had to miss several matches and Hayes damaged a leg when in excellent form. Hobbs, not perhaps without reason, found run-getting a more uncertain business than he might have expected. The change from matting to turf, and green treacherous turf at that, interrupted the practised fluency of his development and his style. He made nearly 2,000 runs, but his average was as low as 33 and he made three centuries only. It is possible that the vivid progress through South Africa had taken some of the edge out of his cricket.

1911 was a hot dry summer and the omens were more favourable. A winter's rest and the prospect of our Australian tour in the autumn were enough between them to stiffen any man's sinews and summon up his blood. Yet it is curious to have to record that for some weeks his chief success was recorded in the Parks at Oxford where he bowled unchanged through the second innings in the dense tree-heavy atmosphere, and swung seven surprised undergraduates back to the pavilion for 56 runs hit off him. For this feat, Leveson-Gower was moved to present him with a silver inkwell in the shape of Great Tom, an academic souvenir which, it is to be hoped, reconciled his mind to an alien and hostile University; particularly as he had pleased himself and his townsfellows by taking 93 off Cambridge University at Fenner's a week or two earlier, he and Hayward setting all the local alehouse wits aflame by putting up 140 in just over an hour and a half. Yet apart from these re-creative adventures among the schoolmen there was no outstanding success to chronicle. He had few conspicuous failures—in the whole of his career there is a marked absence of catastrophic runs of ill-success such as cut at times across the illustrious attainments of batsmen like Trumper, Compton, Edrich and Hammond—but the season proceeded modestly on its way without the usual number of accompanying highlights. One brilliant exception to this, however, stands up in the long history of the Gentlemen and Players series like a great sea-mark. Piquancy is added to the performance by the fact that after he had been chosen for the match at Lord's, his relatively moderate form induced some tactless individual in authority to suggest to him that he might prefer to stand down. Characteristically he saw what he calls the justice of the request, and said he had no objection; but wisdom prevailed over expediency and he played, in the closing stages of the game, one of the great fighting innings of modern cricket. The Lord's wicket, never an entirely trustworthy factor in even the most precisely-formulated equation, created uncertainties in an otherwise stable world, and in a game of two evenly-balanced sides the Players found themselves struggling. Barnes and Buckenham, bowling with admirable aggressiveness, had been blunted by the courage and skill of Fry, Douglas, Warner and Frank Foster; and the Players had found less resource against Foster and Douglas on a rearing wicket than their very impressive paper strength seemed to warrant. They were 151 behind on the first innings, Fry and Spooner took the lead to 273 before a wicket fell, and it was a mercy that Jessop failed or the 423 they had to face would have been enlarged to the realm of the materially impossible and not remained just a dim improbability. The last innings opened on a wicket devoid of all reason. Foster and Douglas were in fierce fettle when the battle was joined; Hayward and Hobbs met them with the old Oval freedom, letting the pace of their own scoring determine the tactical shape of the innings. The batsmen settled in; the Australian leg spinner Le Couteur came on. Hayward at 56 was tempted and fell, Hobbs and Johnny Tyldesley carried on. Hobbs began to dictate terms, even to Douglas, so that even the sober *Wisden*, confronted with the cold enormity of the 330 yet to make, gave the Players at this point a good chance of winning the game. The second wicket put on 77 in forty minutes (it will be remembered that here we had the two best bad-wicket batsmen of the century, who knew that the only paying stratagem was all out attack). Tyldesley was bowled, Hardinge came in and in thirty-five minutes 57 more were added, Hobbs taking every conceivable risk. He dealt the destroying Foster some very rough treatment; he did the same for Le Couteur. Short-leg put him squarely on the carpet, certain uppish endeavours streaked dangerously through absent or unhandy slips, but coolly and deliberately he went out with his ears back for runs. At 188 the wicket-keeper engulfed Hardinge when Foster made one lift, and straightway the bottom fell out of the Players' innings, in one of those dismal passings and repassings that spell so much of lifted hopes and recurrent despairs. Tarrant, Rhodes, Hirst, Iremonger, capable and prolific batsmen, came and pottered and went. Le Couteur, who the year before had made 160 and taken eleven wickets in the University match, stood on his mettle and spun out the later batsmen with hardly a shot fired at him in anger, except by the perennial Hobbs.

Barnes kept his shoulder against the landslide for a few overs; but when all was over, and Douglas bowled Buckenham to win the match by 130 runs, the cheers and the praise were for the tireless and undefeated Hobbs, whose 154 not out was marked from that moment as the classic of the season and a rare anthology piece for the rest of time.

This was a wonderful innings, the epitome of the fully-flowered Hobbs of the pre-war years. It is an invidious and an impossible piece of discrimination; but it could possibly be ranked as the best innings that English spectators were privileged to see Hobbs play before 1914. Unconsciously tautening his abilities to the major duties, he so often performed at his greatest in Test or representative cricket; and it does so happen that the brightest patches of his wonderful first ten years in the first-class game are his contributions to the overseas tours. Home Tests before the war were fewer, and although there were some in which he gave of his best, he blossomed more consistently away from home. *Wisden* in these years never allows a complaint to disturb the even atmosphere of its admiration; but more than once it remarks that although by no stretch of imagination could Hobbs be regarded as having had a bad season, yet he did not seem quite at the top of his game and always performed better for England than he did for Surrey. Clearly the great occasion tuned him to his finest responses; he delighted in the odds, the adverse balance, the lost cause, like that Gentlemen and Players match, or the last stand of the old guard against the googly. I rank that 154 not out for the Players as the climax of this young batsman's maturity; with this innings he attained the summit. Now all he could do was to take possession, and this, over the next few seasons, at home and abroad, he proceeded to do.

The face of Surrey was changing. Not very perceptibly so, but here and there an old face melted into the shadows, a new name began to be bandied about the terraces. Walter Lees and Fred Holland departed, old links with the early days of 1905; Ducat entrenched himself steadily, Tom Rushby carried on a stimulating running battle with his temperament, dodging periodically into the Lancashire League and out again like the moon going behind fitful cloud, the old Oval tradition of fierce and unremitting pace was taken up and mellowed by the endearing and energetic Hitch.

Alan Marshal went regrettably back to Queensland, leaving behind him a sense of disappointment and waste, a potentially great cricketer *manqué*, who later came back to Europe only to be killed in the war. A very young schoolboy called Donald Knight appeared once, with an enormous reputation, and sustained it. Unobtrusively, and with complete modesty and confidence, a cricketer named Sandham played his first innings for the county, looked watchfully about him, and slipped back quietly into the second eleven. Unresting and unhasting, their fortunes varying with the season but their solid and substantial worth unimpaired, the three H's survived all fluctuation and made the core of the finest county batting side in England a resolute and reliable one. Hayes by this time was a little past his most effective, Hayward at forty was slowing up; only Hobbs looked forward as a young batsman might in those days do at twenty-eight, to a virtually illimitable future. For the present, however, the future was next winter; and next winter meant Australia.

Book Two

HOBBS AND RHODES

CHAPTER I

THE HIGH WAVES

THE 1911-1912 tour of Australia is one of those moments in the history of recent cricket that sends a warm and mellifluous glow spreading about the solar plexus of supporters of English cricket. From our vantage-point in the 'sixties it looks like the culmination of a decade of struggle and setback; it is a stimulating chronicle of sweeping victories and memorable individual performances, it establishes England's side as the most formidable in the world at a time when Australian opinion was inclined to be sceptical about it, and it is convincingly endorsed in the following summer by England's conclusive success in the otherwise unsatisfactory Triangular Tournament. It is all the more surprising, then, to discover that the selection of the team was heavily criticised for feebleness both in batting and bowling. On retrospect it seems as powerful a combination as could have been collected (with the customary exceptions of Fry and Spooner, who for a variety of inhibiting reasons never left these shores) and the younger hopefuls who were tried out for the first time on an Australian tour included F. R. Foster, Woolley and J. W. Hearne, as successful a set of experiments as even the M.C.C. ever devised. The experienced Warner had Johnny Douglas to assist him as vice-captain and to share the attack with Barnes and Foster; Bill Hitch had his pertinacious energy on the Oval wicket rewarded by selection as the only genuinely fast bowler on the side; and George Gunn and Mead joined Woolley and Hearne and the lesser lights of Kinneir, Vine and Iremonger in an impressive satellite-orbit of batsmen around the central planets of Hobbs and Rhodes. Strudwick and "Tiger"

Smith of Warwickshire shared the wicket-keeping; excellent
wicket-keepers both, though Smith, who *sub specie aeternitatis* is
never regarded by history as being quite in Strudwick's class, got
the pull in this series and kept in four of the Tests, mainly on the
very understandable strength of his practised brilliance in taking
Foster.

The batting clearly centred upon Hobbs and Rhodes; for
Woolley and Hearne in 1911 were not the forces that they were to
be ten or fifteen years later, and one can never entirely dissociate
from the name of George Gunn a lurking savour of instability.
Warner, of course, was a most accomplished county batsman, and
so was the enigmatic Mead, whose solid triumphs were of course
in the future; but Douglas and Foster's potential value with the bat
would have to be subordinated to the huge task of bowling which
they were going to undertake, and Kinneir, Vine and Iremonger*
had still (and, unhappily, still have) to prove themselves as Test
batsmen. The heavy responsibility resting on Hobbs and Rhodes
does not seem to have affected them in any way. Rhodes would
have been indignant not to have had it; and Hobbs' even temperament was never one to be overborne by the oppressive shape
of things to come.

In the very first match of the tour they obliterated South
Australia without their two leading batsmen putting in more than a
token appearance. A total of 563 was a magnificent encouragement
to a team only four days off the boat; Gunn played an innings of
106 of cultured skill and beauty, Foster drubbed the exhausted
bowlers in a most exhilarating 158, and Warner stayed five hours,
watchful and confident, for a tally of 151 which must not only
have delighted him personally, but have reinforced his estimate
of his own capacity to fit valuably into a constructive scoring
machine. When South Australia batted, Barnes and Foster jolted
them immediately, Hobbs at cover made two lightning returns and
ran out two batsmen, including his old friend the transplanted
J. N. Crawford, and in spite of holding tactics by Clem Hill the side
could only manage 141. In the second innings it was Douglas who

---

*Iremonger had a dismal tour, with few opportunities and the
minimum of success in exploiting them. He has, however, one strange
and esoteric advantage over his more fortunate fellows; in that he is the
only first-class cricketer mentioned in James Joyce's *Ulysses*.

was the destroyer, and he clean bowled four men, including Clem
Hill, in an innings which only Mayne and Crawford made into a
fight. Warner left the field a contented man, for his three main
bowlers had all performed their tasks to a nicety, the only real
failure among the batsmen had been Rhodes, who was bound to
make up for it soon, and the catching and fielding were of a very
high order. It was a happy and yet poignant contentment; for on
that same night Warner, who through a long life has had to con-
tend with the worries and discomforts of uncertain health, was
seized with sudden and severe illness, and never played again on
the tour. For a time he was very seriously ill, and he was not even
able to watch his team in action for nearly seven weeks.

Douglas succeeded to the captaincy. A man of determined fibre
and resolute courage, he took some while to settle into his new
authority. The upset communicated itself to the team, who went
ragged on him and only beat a moderate Victoria by 49 runs.
Douglas bowled well, and Hobbs made 88 in spite of an attack of
cramp, but knowledgeable Australians, looking at the erratic fielding and Douglas' unsure handling of the attack, prophesied cheerfully that England would not win a Test. Rain spoiled one or two
of the succeeding State matches, though Foster and Barnes had
time to fire out Queensland, and the first Test arrived with Douglas'
touch hardly found. The match, as it turned out, was all Australia's.
Foster and Barnes were sorely expensive in the first innings, and
Douglas, though bowling tight, could not penetrate. Trumper
made his last century in Tests against England, batting with a
foreign sedateness that did not veil his complete mastery; Hill and
Armstrong scored well, and Roy Minnett in his first Test made a
brilliant 90 in less than two hours. The Englishmen, facing 447,
started on the wrong foot. Warner's absence let in a reserve batsman, Kinneir; and maybe because he was uneasy away from the
opener's position, he went in with Hobbs, and Rhodes dropped
down to number four. Cotter, bowling very fast, found the edge
too frequently for comfort, Kinneir and Gunn left in quick succession and Mead was in trouble with Hordern, a tall rangy dentist,
probably at this stage in history the steadiest and best googly
bowler in the game. Curiously, Hobbs was never settled, and
Rhodes and Hearne shaped most confidently against the insidious
menace. Hearne, not yet 21, played an admirable innings of 76 in

this his first Test, but even a graceful 39 by Woolley could not prevent a deficit of over 100, and the Australian second innings slowly and methodically increased the lead to nearly 450. Hordern's googlies decided the issue. Gunn and Hearne played with courage and resource, but Kinneir was all flash and edge and Hobbs, after a brilliant beginning, flicked Cotter to the wicket-keeper. The innings did not exactly fold up; but when Carter behind the wicket said he couldn't spot Hordern's googly, who were the Englishmen to assert the contrary? Woolley, Mead and Hearne all said they could see it plain as plain; but he got them just the same. He took twelve wickets in the match for 175; it was the old South African bogey over again, with the comforting reservation that apart from Cotter he had only moderate support. Hobbs and Rhodes, it is to be noted, remained silent; and it may be observed that Clem Hill, visiting Warner in the nursing home after this match, struck one shrewdly curious note amid Australian jubilation. He said that after this game he was less certain of winning the rubber than he had been before it.

The second Test at Melbourne was the turning-point. Right at the start Australia's batting was torn wide open by Barnes, who, in perhaps the most penetrating spell of bowling ever achieved in Test cricket, swept five leading batsmen out in eleven overs for six runs. Before this tall, menacing, medium-pace swinger, who added to perfect length and late swing a practically unplayable fast leg-break, the wickets of Bardsley, Kelleway, Hill, Armstrong and Minnett tumbled to destruction, while Trumper was beaten and bowled by Foster. Six wickets on a plumb pitch went down for 38, and though Ransford, Hordern and Carter revived the innings a little and heaved the total to 184, the damage that had been dealt to Australian confidence was, in the end, irreparable. Even the costly gift of Hobbs' wicket, presented to Cotter with his score at 6 as he flicked him for the second time in succession into Carter's gloves, did not detract from England's moral advantage; and next day a fine partnership between Rhodes and Hearne, though inadequately supported by the later batsmen (Horden again), saw England to a lead of 81, which was instantly and healthily reinforced by the immediate departure for the second time in the match of Kelleway, Bardsley, Hill and Trumper. Armstrong and the tail hammered back courageously against Barnes and Foster with their tails up; and in the end England had to get 219.

The fifth ball of Cotter's first over is the ball we have to watch. There were forty minutes to go before lunch; this England side was by no means a certainty for 219, or even 119, if their various vicissitudes of the early part of the tour are considered dispassionately; the partnership of Hobbs and Rhodes, brilliantly proved in South Africa, was here in an untried and indeterminate state; Hobbs had failed in the first innings. At this crucial moment in this crucial match of this crucial tour, Hobbs and Rhodes, alone in the middle, were shouldering the sky; and the fifth ball of Cotter's first over whipped viciously back off the pitch and beat Hobbs all ends up.

If it had bowled him there is no knowing what would have happened. The disaster might have tipped the quivering equilibrium of the match and the tour, and even brought the batsman himself face to face with a disturbing and even demoralising crisis. As it happened it missed the leg stump and everyone gasped; and from that moment on the batsmen were in quiet command. It was not a great or even memorable partnership, but it established the batsmen and it helped to re-establish the side in the confidence of which Warner's illness had seemed to deprive it. In the nervous period before lunch, forty minutes of tension during which in these days a Test opening pair would feel happy to make 10, Hobbs and Rhodes made 52; and although Rhodes was caught at the wicket at 57, the necessary stability had been achieved. Most intelligently, Douglas sent in Gunn to follow, and not the more orthodox Hearne; and Hobbs and Gunn virtually won the match, adding 112 by brilliant opportunist cricket, the most forceful and imaginative batting that the tourists had yet displayed. The best cover-point in the world, Ransford, was there in his place; but Hobbs and Gunn ran singles to him with breathtaking assurance. This time Hobbs punished Cotter without mercy, his square and late cutting being precise and powerful; and he played Hordern with the tactics that had broken the South African spinners, by hunting him down the wicket or by slipping back and turning him for runs off the base of the stumps. Gunn for his part wandered up the pitch to both the fast and the slow bowlers, driving with apparent nonchalance from half-way down the wicket. This was

a most exhilarating partnership, which called out in response to
its brave batsmanship equally keen and bellicose bowling and fielding; and when Gunn was out for 43 and Hearne joined in to see
Hobbs past the century and England home by eight wickets, the
great demolition work had been accomplished. Hordern had been
plundered for 66 in 17 overs; and he never again fully recaptured
his dominion. Hobbs made 126 not out, by every standard a great
innings and in the context of this tour one of the most important of
his life. It was his first century ever against Australia in a Test;
and he carries to this day a silver cigarette-case that the England
scorer gave him in commemoration of it. He batted throughout
with the toothache, and next day he went to a dentist and had the
tooth out, taking care no doubt, in intelligent avoidance of
reprisals, that the dentist was not Hordern.

England were on their toes; and in the next Test they drove
their advantage home. Just as Barnes had seized the first few
minutes of the second Test to punch a hole in Australia's defences,
so in the third, at Adelaide, the initiative was instantly exploited
by Foster. The weather was fine and the wicket was perfect; Hill
won the toss, and Foster, bowling very fast and accurately to a
predominantly leg-side field, swung the ball in very late to the
cramped and worried batsmen and never allowed them to hit their
way out of trouble. He bowled his first eleven overs for eight runs
and the wicket of Kelleway, and after lunch broke up the dangerous defences of Armstrong and Hordern and clean bowled Hill
and Minnett in a wonderful short burst of destructive attack.
Australia tottered helplessly before this barrage; and if their batsmen got down to the other end they found they had to face Barnes.
When the innings ended for 133 Foster had bowled 26 overs and
his five wickets had cost only 36 runs, a superbly sustained piece
of hostile bowling; and Hobbs and Rhodes batted out the day with
controlled circumspection, cheerful in the security that their
bowlers had bequeathed them.

Next day, in a roasting heat, the Australians wrested little joy
from the situation. Hobbs and Rhodes for the first time were
shown in full flowering. The taste of successful collaboration,
savoured in the second Test, was returned to and relished; Cotter
and Hordern were met and discussed and dealt with; the two batsmen blossomed under the heat and were checked in the pace of the

scoring only by Hill's carefully-placed outer ring on the off-side boundary. The score reached 147 before Rhodes played late at Cotter and was l.b.w.; Gunn in his most peripatetic mood played both Cotter and Hordern, as before, from half-way down the wicket; and Hill tried six wearying bowlers as the score mounted. Gunn helped Hobbs to add 59, Hearne was with him for 54, and Mead saw the score well beyond 300 and to the very verge of the day's end before Hobbs, half-dead on his feet with an exhaustion which had already trapped him into a number of chances, was finally caught for 187 and retreated thankfully into the shade, having made it once and for all perfectly clear to the Australians who was now ultimate master. He had clearly been foremost of the England batsmen in quashing the implicit danger in Hordern; and with that deadliness destroyed, Hordern's colleagues were themselves deprived of much of their terror. This innings of 187 was no classic, like the 126 not out at Melbourne; but it helped perceptibly to release England from much of her imagined bondage.

Next day England reached 501, a vast and on the face of it unsurmountable total; but the Australians with immense courage and tenacity forced themselves back into the fight. Foster, Douglas and Barnes strove all they knew, but Bardsley and Hill in particular, not to mention the presumptuous Carter (who never learned throughout his honourable career that a wicket-keeper is not required to make runs), battled against their attack with great consistency and success. Even without Trumper, who had injured a leg, they refused to wilt before the obvious; and they hit over 100 runs each off Barnes and Foster, and employed terrible savagery upon Hitch and Hearne. In the end England were left with 109 to get; and had Trumper been able to do more than come in last with a runner, there is a chance that the match could have gone to a tense, and for England, unfavourable, finish; a speculation which troubled the repose of English supporters when Hobbs was immediately put out by Hordern for 3. Still, Rhodes and Gunn guided the ship with few qualms to port, and England, breathing evenly again, were one up in the series.

In the interval before the next Test the team sailed to Tasmania, leaving Hobbs on the mainland, to his great content. His vacation debarred him from the pleasure of Frank Woolley's 305 not out, but no doubt he was philosophical about it, feeling that to avoid

two bouts of sea-sickness he was even happy to forgo that. When
the team returned to Melbourne he opened with Rhodes in the
return match with Victoria; neither did anything unusual, leaving
the high scoring to Hearne and Douglas, who were principally
responsible for taking 106 runs off the bowling of a twenty-year
old fast bowler named E. A. Macdonald, appearing in his only
first-class match before the war. Hobbs and Rhodes dealt with him
with indifference, playing in the present rather than in the future;
and bided their time for the Test Match to begin three days later
on the same ground.

By this time Australia were tensed and edgy; and the atmosphere was not eased by an internecine dispute between the Board
of Control and a number of leading Australian cricketers which
was raging throughout this phase of the season and had at least
two highly regrettable culminations—one, a reprehensible and un-
dignified fight with fists between the then captain of Australia's
Test Team and one of the selection committee, and the other the
refusal of six of Australia's most illustrious cricketers to make the
trip to England for the Triangular Tournament. Details of this
deplorable dispute are hardly relevant in this place; but they are
important as a factor in the barely perceptible but slowly effective
disintegration of the Australian cohesion, which ironically coin-
cided with the impressive co-ordination of the English talents into
an organic whole.

The first day of the Melbourne Test was fine and sunny, but
two or three days before it had rained with most prolific abandon,
and people who knew Melbourne sniffed at the wicket with the
utmost suspicion. The convalescent Warner had half his team with
him prodding it before the start, and in conclave with Rhodes and
his bowlers he recommended Douglas to put Australia in if he won
the toss. Sure enough he did, and in the Australians went; and
Warner from the pavilion had some qualmish moments, when he
saw Barnes pitching short and Foster well below form, so that the
openers found that driving and square-cutting brought quick and
useful runs. Fifty was up before a wicket fell, but after the lunch
break Barnes and Foster tightened up and broke through, and
only a plucky and adventurous 56 by Minnett in the latter end of
the innings atoned for the comparative or complete failures of
Trumper and Hill, Armstrong and Ransford, the old guard melt-

ing away in the press of battle. Foster and Barnes, shooting the
bolt home, had four for 77 and five for 74 respectively, and just
after five o'clock Australia were out for 191.

Forty minutes from the close of play Hobbs and Rhodes walked
out into the evening sunlight. There is a snapshot of them in one
of Warner's graphic books of this tour, coming from the pavilion
gate into the hard brightness, the light on the George and Dragon
crests on their caps, their faces in cool shadow; Hobbs slim and
serene, Rhodes sturdy, resolute, observant. They come out on to
the grass from the gay milling buzz of the crowded stand behind
them, every eye in the concourse on them, the welcoming applause
(you can sense it) rising in intensity as the whole of the great crowd
hails their arrival. The caption below the photograph is "Here
they come, Hobbs and Rhodes!" and the popular crude simplicity
of the phrase epitomises the very essence of the expectant murmur
that runs through such a crowd when a famous pair of batsmen
come out to them through the gate. For all I know, that snapshot
in Warner's book perpetuates this very moment that I now record,
as Hobbs and Rhodes came out for the last forty minutes of the
first day of that Melbourne Test. Here they come, Hobbs and
Rhodes; walking side by side, two men much of a height, sun-
flecked and cool, out of the thronged pavilion into the perpetuity of
the record-books.

In that last forty minutes they scored 54; no need to elaborate
on the contrast between this and the likelihood to-day of 20 being
beyond reach; and they scored it with free and attractive stroke-
play and the nicest judgment in quick running. Warner notes, without comment, that the Australian bowling looked easy. That can
well be imagined; in their present form Hobbs and Rhodes would
have made Foster and Barnes look easy. The devil had dried out
of the wicket, the roller laid the surface flat and innocuous, and
the next day's resplendent sunlight gave the two batsmen a wonderful setting for their task. For nearly four hours of the second
day they scored with freedom and safety, Hobbs' strokes in particular flowing out all round the wicket with an almost indiscriminate ease, though as often at this stage of his career the
square cut predominated. He gave a chance of stumping just after
his hundred went up, and a very hard hit to short-leg an age later
must be registered as a flaw; but the first-wicket Test record had

long been outdone when at 323, after four and a half hours of rich and memorable batsmanship, he turned Hordern's googly off his body and Carter caught him close up on the leg-side. His superb 178 included twenty-two fours. Rhodes next day beat his score by one run before Carter caught him too.

This was the peak performance of the Hobbs-Rhodes collaboration. They batted together many times in the future, but never with such enduring and destructive power. This day at Melbourne was their day of supreme efficiency, the dawn of real mastery in a great Test batsman coinciding with the full maturity of a remarkably reliable and shrewd one, who in not very many years would decide to relax his batting powers and concentrate once more upon the bowling art which altogether outmatched them. This was their great day, the day of their prolific and masterly brilliance—evidenced not only in the certainty of their strokes, but most particularly in their infallible instinct for the quick run. Hayward and Hobbs, ever since that first day in April 1905, had been ready and eager for the single; in later years Hobbs and Sandham were the most accomplished run-stealers in county cricket, and Hobbs and Sutcliffe made a new reputation of their own for the cool judgment of their running; but even to this day Hobbs has a special word for Rhodes. "Wilfred," he says, "would *always* come; nobody with whom I ever batted excelled him as a run-stealer." It seems that with an unusual blend of instinct and implicit reliance, Rhodes would be yards up the wicket as Hobbs put bat to ball, ready with complete confidence to back his partner's uncanny judgment. They scored in their time together hundreds of singles which it would barely have occurred to other batsmen to contemplate. The effect on a fielding side was devastating.

The great pair won that Test Match and that rubber as surely as Barnes and Foster won it with their bowling. Gunn, Foster and Woolley took the stunned attack and shredded it; the 323 was raised by hearty leaps and bounds to 589, also in those fair times a record Test score. Australia were expected to retaliate as they had so bravely done in the previous game, but Barnes and Foster took an early wicket apiece and the backbone cracked; Douglas, in a most lively and destructive spell of bowling, demolished the middle batting and the match collapsed about him, not without a fine and defiant little innings from the infuriating Carter.

Two matches only remained to this exhilarating and exhausting tour. In the first, against New South Wales, the insatiable Rhodes made a century in each innings; Foster was unplayable and took 7 for 36 in the first innings; and Hobbs, who did nothing memorable with the bat, took 4 for 25 in a second innings of 403. (As his victims included Kelleway and the young H. L. Collins, the occasion should not go without record.) It should be noted, too, that the touring side won by eight wickets; but all real interest was reserved for the last Test, at Sydney. A well-contested game, it is highlighted in history by Frank Woolley's first Test century, a honey-sweet confection of grace and latent power. Barnes and Foster lost the destroying habit and had to work hard for their wickets, which came in the long run but not for the asking; and the Hobbs-Rhodes combination was disrupted early in the first innings and in the second, while going strongly, was terminated by a magnificent catch at short-leg which cut Hobbs off at 45 and the partnership at 73. Woolley took three glorious catches in the slips, one of which, though nobody was to know it, dismissed Victor Trumper from Test cricket for ever. Hobbs ran out Hordern by a terrific throw from cover, his fifteenth direct run-out of the tour, and Foster happily and appropriately cleaned up the tail to win the match by 70 runs.

The tour was a triumph. No previous touring side had won as many as four Tests. They had in fact played eighteen games and won twelve of them; their only loss being Hordern's Test match. Douglas had accepted and endured a task of horrific responsibility. He of all men had the temperament to carry it through; but without the gifted and tireless team he would have been as helpless as the invalid Warner. There is no need at this stage to repeat to wearying point the necessary praises and acknowledgments; they are implicit in the barest account of this brilliant series. Foster took 32 Test wickets, Barnes 34; Hobbs made 662 Test runs with an average of 82, Rhodes 463 with an average of 57. Until the later years brought Tate and Bedser and Bradman and Hammond, these figures stood as minor symbols of major feats of character and pertinacity and skill that had not been surpassed.

Warner's personal disappointment had been counteracted in the best possible fashion. The victory was no doubt the best tonic that his recuperating tissues could have desired, and it is pleasant to

think that he throve and, God bless us, still thrives, on the success
of his team that winter. He is, and has been for so long, such a
father-figure in the game that all his accounts and pronouncements
on the cricket and the cricketers of whom he was such a keen
observer carry the unspoken implication of an admonitory or pos-
sessive relationship, as if they were all his boys playing in the sun
under his benign and approving patronage. He wrote of these men
as if they were his own sons or his own pupils; he gave them com-
mendatory reports. So shrewd an observer cannot have failed to
realise, though his very natural delight modified his expression of
it, that our victories were at the expense of a Test team in a period
of awkward transition. The great stars of the old Australia,
Trumper and Hill in particular, were perceptibly fading; the newer
lights had hardly attained their proper lustre, and some who had
previously seemed assured were on this occasion found to falter,
like Bardsley and Ransford. The promise of Hordern and Minnett
was to remain, for various reasons, a promise only. The one
impressively great player of the next generation, Macartney, fusted
unused for some inexplicable reason for most of this series. Only
Armstrong remained impassively static, a formidable piece of the
past to be projected minatorily into the yet hidden future. The
Australian selectors were bewildered men, to whom the inexcusable fisticuffs of Clem Hill were unconstructive but pointed indica-
tions of a dangerous lack of confidence. The Triangular Tournament, following hard upon this humiliation, must have come to the
Australian selectors as an embarrassing burden. As the M.C.C.
team sailed for home, they had these things to consider. Experienced men among them, happy enough at the present taste of
victory, were as aware as the outsider of cyclical variations in form.
If they were wise, they took a hint from George Robey (also a
cricketer, we remember), and tempered their hilarity with a
modicum of reserve.

CHAPTER II

TOWARDS THE VERGE

THE season of 1912 gave them no serious occasion to retract their high optimism, and at the end of it England's supporters must have felt that they could now sit back happily and luxuriate in the possession of the champion cricket team of the world. In the cold perspective of history the season of the Triangular Tournament wins no especial commendations from the connoisseur; the brave and ill-omened experiment failed, and nothing but cool and final dismissal has been considered appropriate for it. It was an ambitious and not unattractive scheme, this steering of two visiting teams simultaneously about the counties, a brilliant and bewildering pattern of colourful fixtures punctuated with no less than nine Test Matches. Even allowing for the regrettable ruin that the scheme necessarily created in the county programmes, the heightened excitement of the régime could have made the season of 1912 a most exhilarating and memorable one. A wicked combination of bad luck and bad management destroyed the hopeful project almost in its inception; and the experiment, which had been pushed and cosseted and frustrated and revived for three years and more, primarily by the South African gold magnate Sir Abe Bailey, was roundly damned and, as best as could be, forgotten. It is unlikely ever to be repeated.

Three factors conspired to its undoing. The first was the regrettable but perhaps not unnatural failure of the South Africans to perform as formidably as they had on those memorable days when they had fluttered to violent and fatal distraction the stability of the greatest English batsmen. Vogler did not come; Faulkner

95

had partly, and Schwarz wholly, lost the necessary knack. The
bright particular spot on their horizon was a youthful batsman
named H. W. Taylor, who in at least one classic innings of 93
against Australia at Lord's proved himself at least the potential
rival of the two most brilliant batsmen in the other two camps,
Macartney and Hobbs. Apart from him and Dave Nourse, the
batting was nerveless and uncertain. Against Barnes and Foster
on a dirty Lord's wicket, it crumpled like paper. The truth was
that South Africa was at this time in an unhappy transition, and
did not regain confident stability for a generation. Meanwhile they
collect, unfairly enough, a good share of the blame for the failure
of the Triangular Tournament.

The second factor was the avoidable weakness of the Australians.
The rights and wrongs of the lamentable schism that split
Australia's resources length-wise that year are buried too far for
profitable recovery; all that can be said is that it must have been a
truly weighty matter of principle that excluded Trumper, Hill,
Ransford, Carter, Armstrong and Cotter from what was supposed
to be a representative side. The second XI did their best, and the
new opportunities offered him threw up one batsman of genius,
Macartney, into his rightful place in Test cricket at last. But the
batting went to pieces on tricky wickets, and the bowling, entrusted
largely to Whitty and Hazlitt (Hordern for private reasons was
unable to come), can only be described in this kind of context as
good Senior House stuff. They were adequate enough to crush
South Africa twice; but in their depleted state, and with England's
weapons sharpened on victory in the winter, they could not match
their hosts. And the other factor that they could not surmount
was the third agent of the Tournament's destruction—an English
summer flowing with storms and floods, a grey drifting miasma of
a season, ruinous with the butt-ends of uncompleted matches.
Anyone can see with half an eye who held the advantage in these
conditions; Woolley when the wicket was soggy, Barnes and Foster
when it bit and lifted; and on the rare days when it was hard, Hobbs
and Rhodes and Fry and Spooner; and when it was soggy, Hobbs
and Rhodes; and when it bit and lifted, Hobbs. The common factor
of adaptability to all these kinds of wicket told in the end, as it
always does; and in a lean and scrappy season and a lop-sided and
unsatisfactory   tournament   certain   of   England's   batting

performances stand out clearly as triumphs of control in adversity, model exemplars of opportunism and imagination in conditions that gave no favour. England's success in the tournament—she collected four wins in the six matches and the two other games were indeterminate ruins in the swamp—was due mainly to the shattering breaches blown by Barnes in the opponents' defences, and his 39 wickets out of the 84 that fell to English bowlers; but also to the supreme daring and brilliance of the exploitation (by Hobbs and Rhodes at Lord's and the Oval against Australia, by Spooner at Lord's against South Africa, by Rhodes at Manchester against Australia, by Fry at the Oval against Australia, and by Hobbs at Leeds and the Oval against South Africa) of the English improvisator's way with an adverse wicket. All these batsmen realised that the only answer to unpredictability was attack; and Hobbs' wonderful 107 against Australia at Lord's, and his 66 and 32 on very difficult wickets at the Oval, would stand out in any recital of famous bad-wicket innings were it not that he has, before and since, surrounded them with so many of their own kin that discrimination and preference have become invidious. Fry's 79 at the Oval, his last Test innings, a blend of defiance and technique, is in every respect a worthy companion to these great displays; and Woolley's signal contribution to Australia's final defeat, by scoring 62 and taking in the match ten wickets for 49 in 17 overs, admits him at last to the place in the Test hierarchy where he properly belongs. This is a book about Hobbs and not about Test cricket; and the value of the Triangular Tests and the dim unsatisfactory season of 1912 in the context and progress of his own career is perhaps to be appreciated slightly differently from their value in the developing history of the international game. It would not be far from the mark to say that whereas the Australian tour just past left Hobbs potentially the most resourceful batsman in the world on plumb wickets, the season at home proved him now beyond question the most accomplished performer on the bad ones. Now that Trumper and Fry and Tyldesley had ceased to play Test cricket, though not all of them knew this, Jack Hobbs, though perhaps he did not know it either, had moved in to take their place.

One single instantaneous reaction of his, too, highlights his corresponding supremacy in the other half of the game. When in

the second innings of the Australian Test at the Oval, Bardsley cut
Barnes square and took off for a brisk but comfortable run, Hobbs
picked up on the turn at deepish point and threw down the bowler's
wicket in a single action. The fact that Bardsley did not think that
he was out (being reinforced in his opinion, according to *Wisden*,
by "several famous cricketers" in the pavilion, who might have
been in the Vauxhall Bridge Road for any value their views on the
matter might have) does not detract either from the dismissal as
recorded in the score book or from the accurate brilliance of the
fielder's promptitude and aim. It underlines the fact that had been
growing steadily more apparent for some seasons now; that the
slow-footed youth of 1905 was now the best cover-point in the
country. Warner in his record of the Australian tour had spoken
of Hobbs' fielding in terms which even for that extravagant stylist
bordered on the idolatrous. "The equal of any fieldsman in that
position I have ever seen ... not even Jessop at his best is his
superior ... wonderfully quick in moving to the ball ... neat with
his feet ... hands always in the right place ... beautiful and fast
return ... underhand throw deadly ..." The admiring encomia
pour out, the felicitations of the keenest and most appreciative of
all cricketers flow on like a river. By the time Warner gets to his
batting he confesses that he has run out of adjectives. It is well to
remember this; that in the eyes of one who in all his boyish
enthusiasms never relinquished his shrewdness, Hobbs' fielding
was in the same class as his batting. Those of us who remember him
at cover, and most of us now remember him rather in his long later
years, call up the vision of the canny strolling figure on the verge
of activity, hinting rather than spelling menace, passive and receptive rather than active and destructive, who temperately controlled
the opportunity and was master by implication. In his younger
days, as also in his batting, he not only controlled the opportunity,
he actively and electrically manufactured it, moving like a streak to
the ball, gathering and throwing with a patented underarm swirl and
flick of which the beautiful vestiges remained with him to the end
of his playing days. He fired in his throw like a rifle-shot. His old
friend Strudwick, partner for the best part of sixty years of his life
and his leisure and his memories, knows better than any living
man the feel of the sprung-steel throw-in rammed home into his
gloves at stump-height that had so many batsmen out, and what

is far more satisfying and enduring, so many spectators thrilled with delight. For years and years young Australian batsmen, after repeating nightly their usual creed beginning "I believe in Victor Trumper" and ending with the customary appeal against the light, were solemnly adjured on rising from their mother's knee, never, never, on pain of excommunication and total destruction, were they to attempt to run a single to Jack Hobbs.

The season of 1912, rain and the Triangular Tournament assisting, was a moderate one for Surrey, who dropped down to seventh place and exuded an air of pained disappointment. "Razor" Smith was injured for much of what should have been for him an ideal summer, and this is the year when *Wisden* remarked of Hobbs, a little edgily, that he played much finer cricket for England than for his county. He made one magnificent hundred at Old Trafford and a number of other characteristic innings were scattered, a little thinly perhaps, up and down the championship matches. Strangely, his most vivid recollection of that patchy season apart from the Tests is an almost holiday affair in the Gents. v. Players match at the Oval. Foster bowled him for nothing in the first innings, and as soon as he had got off the mark in the second, the devil entered into him and he went for everything regardless, clouting the accurate inswinger Greswell again and again over the short-legs for four. "I'd made 49," he recalls pleasurably, "before Wilfred had scored." In the end Greswell caught him for 54. He had made his runs in just over 20 minutes. Next day he received a letter.

"Swanker,
    You thought yourself very clever for getting a few fours off Greswell, and you only did it to pander to the Oval mob, which you are always doing. They applaud anything *Surrey* there, even if Hobbs, Esq., misfields a ball! You had not so much side on Friday when Foster bowled you for a duck!
    England would fall to pieces without you—I don't think."

The modest recipient of this little billet charitably assumes the writer to have been a schoolboy. Whoever he was, his independence and spirit can be applauded, if not his manners. Let us hope he tempered both in the fires of experience and mellowed his enthusiasms in later life. At least he was no shameful conformer. Perhaps Hobbs' modest 1912 record, the result partly of the gruelling Australian tour, and partly of the Triangular distractions, gave him malicious pleasure. One should be indulgent, for he had precious few occasions for it during that long career.

The bedraggled season dried out into a warmer 1913, a year of recoupment and expansion, a home season without the distraction of visitors blending happily into a South African tour at the back end. The hot summer bred runs on the iron Kennington wickets, Surrey climbed up to third place and if "Razor" Smith had been fitter would have challenged Kent and Yorkshire more dangerously than they did, and Hobbs came back into the runs with a relaxed contented certainty that had in it a happy contrast to the rather febrile achievements of 1912. His successes this season were a routine matter; his execution more resourceful than before, his growing mastery no longer a wonder but an accepted axiom. Yet in his brilliance he must for a moment make way for Hayward, whose prime powers were not perceptibly fading and who had, during the whole time of his young partner's rise to power and fame, been as steadfast and prolific in the forefront of the Surrey batting as he had been for years before he plucked Hobbs off Parker's Piece to go in to bat with him. Portly and solid, the senior N.C.O. of the Surrey eleven still guarded and guided the junior professionals with implacable discipline; in provincial hotels for away matches every Surrey pro knew at what time he was expected to present himself in the dining room for meals, or answer embarrassingly to Tom Hayward for his defection; more than one illustrious skylarker on a midnight landing had to scurry for his life before the menacing appearance of Hayward in his nightshirt, frowning at his bedroom door with a candle in his hand. Mr. This or Mr. That could captain the side and be welcome; but Tom Hayward was the boss, and upon his imposing figure was concentrated the awe and admiration of his juniors and the excited affection of his public. In this season of 1913 he and Hobbs beat the standing record of century opening partnerships; and at Worcester in August they actually opened the game by scoring 313 in three hours and ten minutes, a full hundred an hour. The younger man scored with immense energy and rapacity, but Hayward was no lagger, and he was out first for 146, a supremely competent display. But Friday 27th June was his signal occasion; when after fielding out for a day and a half while Johnny and young Ernest

Tyldesley with 320 runs between them saw the Lancashire total
to 558, Hayward, with his colleagues failing to consolidate, battled
for four and three-quarter hours for 139 and achieved his
hundredth century in first-class cricket. Since his day this feat has,
if not lapsing into commonplace, at least foregone some of its
uniqueness—three other participants in this very Surrey and
Lancashire match all got there in due time—but at this moment
it had been performed once only before, and that by W. G. Grace.
Tom Hayward, with his brown seamed face and his chocolate cap
pushed back off his forehead, drove with phlegmatic dignity to
this triumph and stood acknowledging the cheers for minute after
minute as the Oval crowd gave him back in waves of delighted
applause their congratulation and their joy. Hobbs was to surpass
this feat and more also; but he never outlived his friendly envy of
Tom Hayward's good fortune at arriving at his great target before
his own folk.

Hobbs that season hammered eight championship centuries,
and crowded on an aggregate of 2,605 runs. He made 23 in his
last innings of the season, and Philip Mead made 43; and by so
doing the Hampshire man got to the top of the batting averages
by the skin on the end of his nose, registering 50.51 as against
Hobbs with 50.09. Hobbs good-humouredly resigned himself to
the common fate of never being top at all; if in this season when
his hundreds had blossomed as the roses he could not outdistance
all pursuit, then he could not possibly hope to do it another time,
as conditions would never be so favourable again. He shrugged it
off as unimportant; happy for Hayward, happy for Surrey, happy
in the prospects for a South African tour. Of his innings that
season none gave him more pleasure than one that hardly makes
the record books at all—an undefeated 72 in the Gentlemen and
Players match at Lord's which saw the Players precariously home
when given an hour and three-quarters to get 123. First Rhodes
and then Tarrant supported his busy attacking methods on a
wicket still uneven and treacherous after rain, and by the time they
were both out the score was 87 and there were forty minutes left.
With Woolley coming in it looked a cake-walk; Hobbs drove Foster
twice for four to bring up the side's 100 and his own fifty, and
then when nothing seemed more formal and foregone the game
closed up like an oyster and the Players were suddenly bankrupt of

scoring strokes. Foster and H. L. Simms gave nothing away; Simms in particular, who a week earlier in the Oval fixture had taken eight wickets and had bagged another six in the first innings of the present game, kept an unimpeachable length and bowled cripplingly tight. Time slid through the Players' fingers like sand. Even Hobbs was nailed to his crease by Simms' supremely judged length and spin. At 109 Woolley went out and drove Simms with the desperation of cornered genius, and Simms caught him low down to his left in a manner that is still remembered. Hobbs and Hearne had to dig the runs out of the living earth in the last horrifying minutes; the mastery of Simms was palpable and infuriating. At last Hobbs winkled a single out of him to tie the match, and in the very next over, releasing his pent-up frustration, lay back and cut Jessop for four in the grandest of all winning strokes, with the clock hands five minutes off time and the crowd on their feet with excitement and relief. "Very few batsmen," said *Wisden*, "would have given such a display on the same wicket." It is a dreadful frustration to be able to do no more than read such a masterly display into a few lines of print.

The season ended and the team under Johnny Douglas set out on their South African tour. This 1913-1914 venture has been somehow overlaid in history; the 1911-12 Australian tour and its resounding glory have taken some of the native shine out of it, and the grimmer events to come have perhaps thrown a lengthening shadow over its progress as we recede from it. It is a tale of practically undimmed success from the instant of disembarkation, a triumph of talent and co-ordination, a series of displays of irresistible brilliance that unhappily found the opposition wavering and uncertain. England's cricket had not been so healthy for years; nine of the tourists were happy veterans of Warner's great campaigns, and they completed their strength with the adventurous amateurs Morice Bird and the newly-fledged Lionel Tennyson, the very capable Sussex all-rounder Albert Relf, and the Yorkshireman Booth (whose parents, no doubt consumed with admiration for their namesake General William B. of the Salvation Army, and desirous of commemorating their reverence in the Christian names of their son, had faltered with diffidence at the font and invested the child with a lower rank by christening him Major William). In Hobbs they had the best batsman in the world, in Barnes the

best bowler; Rhodes, Mead, Hearne and Woolley formed a scarify-
ing bodyguard; Strudwick and Smith alternated behind the stumps.
It was as good a side as ever left England, Foster being the only
conspicuous absentee—he had tired considerably in 1913 and did
not return to his best form until the last summer before the war:
ironically enough his last season in first-class cricket. As against
the power and concentration of England's resources, South Africa
could muster sadly inadequate opposition. Their great googly
bowlers were dispersed or ineffective; Faulkner had come to live
in England; the fire had died out of their game. It was the beginning
of a prolonged period of struggle for South African cricket that
was not happily resolved for twenty years; for although they frequently held England to tight finishes in their own country, they
were heavily overpowered when they themselves were the tourists.
This season of 1913-14 saw them at their temporary nadir; and
England won very comfortably the four Tests that were completed.
Barnes, playing in four Tests only, actually took 49 wickets in the
series, an altogether exceptional and barely approachable performance, and as nobody else took more than 10, the destructive quality
of this one bowler remains the chief of England's assets on this
tour. Hobbs, almost as pre-eminent in his own line as Barnes in his,
compiled in all matches nearly 700 runs more than any other batsman and had an average of 76; his first twelve innings in South
Africa were 72, 80, 107, 170, 57, 10, 66, 82, 102, 23, 92 and 41,
and one cannot expect a more prolific consistency than that. In
the Tests he failed to get a century, but he was way out at the top of
the batting with a 63 average, Mead coming second with 54. In the
only match of the tour which the Englishmen lost, he was standing
down as he did not feel well. Natal's bowlers found hidden weaknesses in England's usually immovable batsmen, and H. W. Taylor,
the one great positive hope for South Africa's future, added to his
excellent displays in the Tests by making 91 and 100 against
Barnes, Douglas, Woolley and Relf and conducting his side to a
four-wicket victory.

   The Hobbs-Rhodes combination had two partnerships of over
100 in the Tests, and one of 92; and against Transvaal they had
made 211 in the second innings when Douglas declared. Rhodes'
best opening Test stand was not with Hobbs, but with Relf, whom
Douglas sent in with him in the second Test as a kind of rich man's

night-watchman, and who stayed until 152 were on the board. As for the future of the Hobbs-Rhodes collaboration, it is well to note that a small cloud, no bigger than a man's left hand, had appeared on the horizon; Rhodes in the Tests bowled 88 overs. Time and inclination were beginning to turn the great wheel once more. It was not the end, yet there were intimations that changes were round the corner. The Players' innings at both Lord's and the Oval in the following season were opened by Hobbs and Tarrant; Rhodes, who took 110 wickets for his county, did not play in either of the big representative games.

The tour of 1913-14 marks no climax and contains no vital conflict; in the career of Jack Hobbs it marks continuing and unbroken success merely, not an obstacle surmounted or a corner rounded. It fits easily and happily into the account of his wonderful pre-war maturity; but as anything but that it is, historically, a commonplace. He came back to England in the spring of 1914, feeling full of runs and hopes; and noted in his diary was the eagerly-anticipated date of his benefit match; Surrey v. Kent, last year's Champion County, at the Oval, Monday, Tuesday and Wednesday, August 10th, 11th and 12th, 1914.

The dry bright summer of 1914 is compact of all the ironies. They cannot be escaped, but in a chronicle of this kind it would perhaps be unwise to emphasise them. Too much has been thought and said and written of that fateful year already, and very little of what has been recorded is concerned with cricket; why should it be?—nevertheless there is a slender parallelism that links the sunny midsummer of that year with the high deceptive waves of gay secure complacency on which Europe sailed to the brink in those last years and months. In long perspective they both have an active brilliant prosperity about them that accentuates the fearful shock of the ruinous catastrophe to which they were the prelude. The summer of 1914 is as much the end of the golden age of cricket as it is the last afterglow of Edwardian ostentation and success. Rupert Brooke, in a curiously prophetic descriptive piece written from America in the previous year, has a purple patch on the waters above Niagara Falls which in our context can stand as appropriately for the last pre-war years as for the waves, for the cricket of that last season as for the years. "The waters seem to fling themselves on with some foreknowledge of their fate, in an

ever wilder frenzy. . . . They prove that Greek belief that the great
crashes are preceded by a louder merriment and a wilder gaiety.
Leaping in the sunlight, careless, entwining, clamorously joyful,
the waves riot on towards the verge."

The hastening inevitable processes of this last season took Surrey
once more, for the first time since Hobbs had been with them, to
the head of the championship. Or rather, Surrey was left there,
nemine contradicente, when under stress of urgency, expediency
and decorum, the championship was abandoned at the end of
August. Small things are swallowed up in great; but it was a pity
that this fine team should have had, as it were, the ceremonial
rewards thrown at it in haste, by default, as a preoccupied afterthought. They won the championship by energetic and unremitting merit; and by that time nobody cared, for everyone was
over the verge together. Jack Hobbs was never again in a side that
won the championship. The honour did not come to Surrey, after
that truncated August, for another thirty-six years.

It is of course a truth hardly worth uttering that Hobbs' batting
was one of the prime factors in this most welcome triumph. We
can look at it more closely in a moment; for the present let
us remember, as he himself would be the first to remind us, that a
team won the championship and not one player. Bill Hitch, the
cheerful grunting fast bowler, was this year faster and better than
he had ever been before or would, in spite of his immense popularity in the 'twenties, ever be again. Backed up manfully by the
talented but unpredictable Rushby, he was splendidly reinforced
by a new and brilliant importation from Sussex, a striking and
unusual original named P. G. H. Fender, lanky, multifarious, un-
restingly intelligent, a cricketer of unfathomable potentiality and
erratic attainment, who in this first full season at the age of 21
took 82 wickets and made 740 runs for the county. The prodigious
Donald Knight came late into the side after the Oxford team, a
complete classical style already perfected at twenty; Ernie Hayes
was as reliable and prolific as he had been when Hobbs first tied
with him for top score or rivalled him for last place in the England
eleven; and the young free-styled batsman Ducat came back fresh
and capable after a year off for injury and scored 1,300 runs.
Inevitably and unforgettably there was still Tom Hayward, who
after a tentative start found his old touch and his old form in the

tense prodigious July and ended the season's work in a crescendo
of honour and glory. Only "Razor" Smith's touch faltered; had he
enjoyed the health and capacity of his great seasons the side would
have been downright invincible. Even so, it was a superb side, controlled with a quiet competence for the second year in succession
by a modest but by no means negligible performer named C. T. A.
Wilkinson, an excellent club cricketer who compassed the transition to the first-class game with honour and mild distinction, and
continued (and for all I know still continues) to take wickets and
score runs in club games to an unbelievably advanced age.

Hobbs led the batting with an average twenty points ahead of
the next man, and if we discount his first four games or so batted
throughout the season with a prodigal, not to say royal, ease. Out
of touch for a week or two, he clicked neatly into position in the
away game with his old bugbear Yorkshire; it was a tooth-and-
claw contest in which all hackles were up and the best was wonderfully extracted from everyone. Rhodes made 89 and took eleven
wickets; George Hirst made 48 and 55; Hayes made a most skilful
125; and Hobbs in the first hour and a quarter of the game hit
five sixes and eleven fours to make exactly 100 out of a breathless
151. Surrey forced a lead of 33 and in the second innings Hobbs
made 74 with even more punishing brilliance, in the course of
which he landed a ball from Drake with shattering violence into
the face and hands of the clock on the football stand. Surrey then
slithered a little; Yorkshire, set to make 223, lost eight men for
106, but Hirst found a partner in Birtles and in face of a triumphant Rushby and Fender added no less than 82 and made a needle
finish of it. Surrey edged home by 28 but it was anyone's game.
Hobbs' success mounted inside him like sap; on the very next day he
began an innings against Warwickshire which ended with himself
183 and Surrey on the way to 541; and a week later he re-opened
Essex's old wound by scoring 215 not out in what was at that stage
the highest score of his life, accentuated by the failure of any one
of his team-mates to make more than 27. In the next match, when
Hampshire came to the Oval, he defied a heavy thunderstorm and
made 163; and on the following Saturday, after being caught for 4
in the opening overs, sat watching for the rest of the day while
Hayward, Hayes, Harrison, Ducat and Wilkinson hammered over
500 off a powerful Middlesex attack. His failure in the midst of his

and his fellows' plenty was just a casual phenomenon, not an omen; even though on the following morning Gavrilo Prinzip shot the Archduke Franz Ferdinand at Sarajevo.

It is to be doubted whether this literally world-shattering event affected his present concentration, but it may be noted in passing that his next seven innings contained three scores of under ten and one of only 11. To redress the wobbling balance he took 64 off Lancashire up North and a beautiful flowing 142 off them at the Oval, having tucked in between these innings a matter of 156 which was the highest score he had yet made for the Players against the Gentlemen. Surrey, high on the top line, had struck a winning sequence; Lancashire were obliterated twice, and Hampshire and Sussex as July wore on went down to them as successive unwilling victims. Portsmouth on 23rd July may have been outwardly normal; the Home Fleet, back from a courtesy visit to, of all places, Kronstadt, was not yet mobilised for anything more ominous than manoeuvres; but rumours of Balkan simmerings can hardly have failed to invade the Hampshire v. Surrey match, where Hobbs, acting as an involuntary barometer to extraneous atmospheric pressures, was stumped for 3. Moving into a tenser week, Surrey scraped the Sussex victory by one wicket, with little credit to themselves; there were ultimata and rumours of ultimata in the air. Churchill at the Admiralty sent the Fleet to sea, electric sparks flicked to and fro between the embassies. It is difficult to see how anyone, even cricketers, could keep their undivided minds on the job.

On July 30th Surrey went to Blackheath for their customary humiliation. It was seventeen years since they had last beaten Kent on a Kentish ground, Blackheath was a dirty word, and Kent were running neck and neck with Middlesex for second place. Nearly all the long hot Thursday Surrey perspired in the field while Kent made nearly 350; Hayward and Hobbs went in for forty minutes at the end. On the next morning, while the British Foreign Secretary was asking Germany for an assurance that she would respect the neutrality of Belgium, Hayward and Hobbs under a sweltering sky took the early measure of Blythe, Carr and Woolley and began to render them harmless. For the whole pre-lunch period and for some of the afternoon the two great batsmen methodically dealt out the vengeance for which they had been waiting for seventeen years. 234 was on the board before they were parted; and when they left, for 122 apiece, Donald Knight's first century for Surrey made the Surrey supremacy unmistakeable. (Surrey's innings of 509 not only deprived Kent of their customary Blackheath victory, but also, lamentably enough, of their famous googly bowler D. W. Carr, whose none for 134 and terrible battering from Hayward and Hobbs so discouraged him that he asked to be excused from appearing for the county again that season, which, in the historic circumstances, meant for ever. This same ill wind, however, compensated ironically for this defection by blowing in as make-weight a young second eleven bowler named Freeman.)

The tensest Bank Holiday in history dawned bright and warm. Between the Surrey team's parting at Blackheath on Saturday evening and their foregathering for the usual Notts fixture at the Oval the international screw had turned many points tighter. Germany had declared war on Russia, her troops had violated Luxemburg, the crowds thronged along Whitehall and outside Buckingham Palace. Miles away over the North Sea the first of the German cavalrymen approached the Belgian frontiers. It would hardly have been surprising if the Oval had been deserted; as it was, whether through indifference, ignorance, distorted values, bravado, courage, philosophy, sang-froid or what, over fifteen thousand people came in that morning through the turnstiles. The ground was tolerably well filled, the pavilion was crowded, Surrey won the toss. From the high deck of the pavilion the Westminster towers dominated the background, an incessant reminder; but Hobbs and Hayward, walking out into the hot noon-day, were able to dismiss all irrelevancies from their thoughts.

Surrey stayed in all day and made 472 for five. Hobbs, batting with the fluent ease that characterised all his play in that high summer, achieved a further advance on the highest score of his career. He notes it almost without comment in his autobiography; "I made 226, with never a thought of war." I must believe him, I suppose. I cannot accuse him of callousness or indifference; I can only commend him for the single-mindedness of his concentration on his job, that protected him from the distractions of a universal tension. Among the 15,000 that milled in through the turnstiles to see him, who delighted all day in his lovely artistry, who sat in their shirtsleeves or under straw hats while Grey spoke in the House of

Commons, who bought up the successive editions of the evening
papers and tried with varying degrees of success and failure to
shut the doors of their minds upon the unknowable horrors at the
gate, must have been many who went from the Oval that evening
and the next to stand in Whitehall or in the Mall to feel themselves
somehow nearer the living heart of the tension, who maybe were
there in the congregated midnight mob with Osbert Sitwell when
the Lord Mayor's coach lumbered under the Admiralty Arch on
its fatal and decisive visit to the Palace, and he heard "the great
crowd roar for its own death". How many of that 15,000 ever
came back to the Oval no one can tell; that the last sight of cricket
that some of them ever had was a double century by Hobbs may
have been in more than one instance a memory disproportionately
precious. For their sakes only it is an admirable thing that before
the veils descended he should have treated them to this superb
last performance, untroubled in his mind by externals, happy in the
supreme exercise of his art.

Next day he was given disturbing news about his benefit match,
due to begin in a week's time. The Army had requisitioned the
Oval, and hurried arrangements had been made to transfer two of
Surrey's matches to Lord's, where the usual August School fixtures had all been cancelled at once. The Surrey Club gave Hobbs
the option of taking his benefit at Lord's or of postponing it until
after the war, whatever that might mean. He thought for a bit and
elected to have it at Lord's. This severely restricted the takings
from collecting boxes, which are forbidden in the sacred precincts;
but there was a kindly relaxation of the rules in his favour. Nevertheless, as anyone could have guessed, the result was a failure. In
a low scoring game Kent were overcome in two days, in spite of a
wonderful farewell performance from Blythe; the beneficiaire himself did nothing of note, and the takings were laughably inadequate.
The Surrey Committee very handsomely offered to wash the whole
thing out and to re-stage the benefit after the war. They would
retain the gate-money, but would keep the subscription lists open.
This very fair offer he had no hesitation in accepting.

The strange twilight season guttered to an indeterminate end.
Hobbs had followed up his record score on Bank Holiday with a
fine hundred at Worcester, and after his unsatisfactory benefit he
had pride of place in a magnificent win over Yorkshire, who came

to Lord's with eight successive wins under their belts and were crushed by an innings. It was the last century partnership with Hayward, and they made it a memorable one, for they put up 290 in just under four hours. Hayward's 116 was his 104th and last century; Hobbs' destroying 202 was his tenth of the season. Hayes made 134, and Surrey's 549 for 6 (declared) gave them the victory by an innings and 30, Hitch cleaning up the opposition with nine wickets in the match, with Rushby eager in support. Three away games followed; Gloucester and Warwick were beaten, Middlesex held to an even draw, another Lord's fixture in which Hobbs made two fifties. The end came on the last day of August; the Oval was released again by the military authorities and staged a county match for the last time before the stress of preoccupation and public opinion, reinforced by a classic letter to *The Times* from W. G. Grace and a public speech by Lord Roberts, closed down the cricket season for good. Surrey in this last game met Gloucestershire, while overseas the Marne battle was preparing, Paris was menaced, the Allied commands were bickering and non-co-operating, and the life ran out of the pre-war world like saw-dust out of a stuffed doll. Gloucester, owing to enlistments, had only ten men. Hayward and Hobbs came down the pavilion steps together for the very last time, though perhaps they did not know it. Hayward was caught at the wicket for one, but Hobbs kept it up to the very end. 141 in three hours was his last offering before the dark descended; Surrey wiped up their opponents in two days, Hayward appropriately ended the game by catching the last man off Fender, and soon the Oval was left for the best part of five years to nothing but the sunlight and the sparrows to counteract the memories and the forebodings of its one-time frequenters.

*   *   *

So petered out, in violence and ruin and pain, the Golden Age of much more than cricket. The war is a part of cricket history as much as it is a part of all other activity that it disrupted; and it has to be recorded here as a factor in the Hobbs story. It was naturally so much more than that that it would be inexcusable to omit our awareness of its profounder significances; and if it is necessarily treated here as little else than a tiresome interruption

in the career of a talented games-player, that is only because for
the moment it is the games-player, and not history or society or the
human condition, that is our theme. It is not that he is apart from
these; but sport is an art not close enough to the fundamental
realities to be disturbed by the forces that most assail them. It is
part of its charm and its weakness to be interrupted only, and not
transformed, by tragedy or revolution.

Jack Hobbs' career was cut by the war into two clearly-defined
blocks. We have just seen him to the end of his tenth English season
and his fourth overseas tour. He had by this time the completest
technical equipment of any batsman still in the game. *Wisden*
named him at the end of the 1914 season as pre-eminently the
batsman of the year, and with the natural decline of the vintage
batsmen of the early 1900's there could be no contemporary rival
to his supremacy, though Warner did express in print the conviction that J. W. Hearne would be in a few seasons the best batsman in England. His time was not yet, although he was to have a
very successful and honourable record most unfortunately be-
devilled with illness and injury; and although he had a nearly
perfect technique, health and temperament denied him Hobbs'
creative genius in its employment. Hobbs at 31 was in the full flush
of his most prodigal gifts; the season of 1914 denied him much
bad-wicket opportunity, which always screwed him to impossible
heights of skill, but gave him royal occasion for his superb agres-
sive opportunism. By the end of that season he had scored in first-
class cricket something like 27,000 runs; and he had made 65
centuries. A cricketer in mid-career subjected, as he was subjected,
to a four-year slice cut out of his active life, could have been
excused for failing to survive the operation. At the height of his
most prolific powers he was abruptly cut short; when events permitted him to begin again he would be on the wrong side of 35, a
middle-aged cricketer, one whose place in the game would be precariously at the mercy of the ambitious juniors to whose preferment
he would be an ossifying obstacle. What he hoped for, what he
expected of the future one cannot at this stage know with any
certainty; yet even his resilience and adventurousness can hardly
have foreseen that his second phase would be even more glorious
than his first; that he would double the number of his centuries not
once, but almost exactly twice over; that the place accorded to him

in the game before the war would be as nothing to the honours that his skill and success would earn him after it; that the very considerable achievements already his were a flat foundation merely for the structure of artistry and beauty that he was to build in the years of his pre-eminent greatness. In 1914 we say goodbye to the young Hobbs with the delicate features and prominent contemplative eyes, the dark thoughtful student with his modest grace and adventurous brilliance that retained through the dizziest triumphs a quality of self-effacing decorum and quietness. The man emerging on the other side of the war would still be modest and decorous; but now he would be the Master.

Tom Hayward: Hobbs' first great partner

*Photo by courtesy of Surrey
County Cricket Club*

Surrey XI, 1905,
Hobbs' first season

Back row: Strudwick,
Baker, Jackson,
Holland, Nice, Hobbs,
Davis.

Front row: Hayes,
N. A. Knox, Lord
Dalmeny, Hayward,
Lees.

Jack Hobbs

Hobbs at the close of his career

Photo: Central Press Photos Ltd.

Wilfred Rhodes: Hobbs' second great partner

Photo: Central Press Photos Ltd.

Surrey XI, 1914:
Championship
Winners

Photo by courtesy
of Surrey County
Cricket Club

Hobbs and Sandham: third great partnership

Photo: Radio Times Hulton Picture Library

Hobbs leading
the Players out
to field; Players
v. Gentlemen,
1924
(left to right:
Kilner, Hendren,
Howell,
Duckworth,
Tyldesley (E.),
Hearne, Freeman,
Tate, Hobbs,
Sutcliffe.
The camera
missed Woolley.)

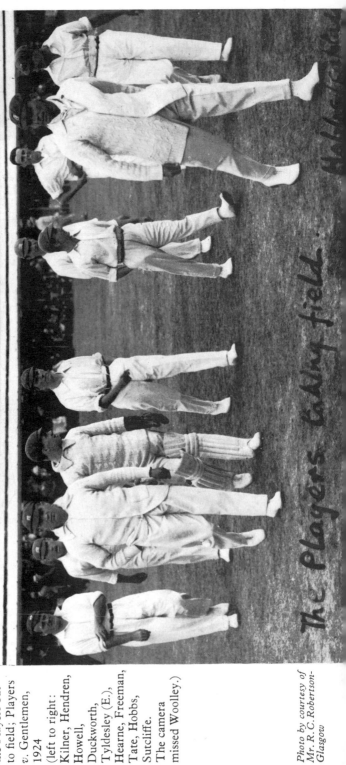

The Players taking field.

Photo by courtesy of
Mr. R. C. Robertson-
Glasgow

Hobbs completing
his century,
Players v.
Gentlemen, 1924
(M. D. Lyon
keeping wicket,
R. C. Robertson-
Glasgow at slip.)

*Photo by courtesy of
Mr. R. C. Robertson-
Glasgow*

Hobbs and Sandham's record stand: 428 for the first wicket,
Surrey *v.* Oxford University, 1926

The England XI that regained the Ashes, Oval, 1926.
Back row: Larwood, Tate, G. T. S. Stevens, Geary, Sutcliffe, Hendren.
Front row: Strudwick, Hobbs, A. P. F. Chapman, Rhodes, Woolley.

Photo: P. A. Reuters Ltd.

Hobbs and Sutcliffe: fourth and greatest partnership

Percy Fender
Hobbs' Captain most frequently

Errol Holmes
Hobbs' last Captain

Herbert Strudwick
Hobbs' oldest and greatest friend

Hobbs in his greatest season: July, 1925

Photo: Radio Times Hulton Picture Library

Hobbs in his last Test series
First Test *v*. Australia at Nottingham, 1930

Photo: Central Press Photos Ltd.

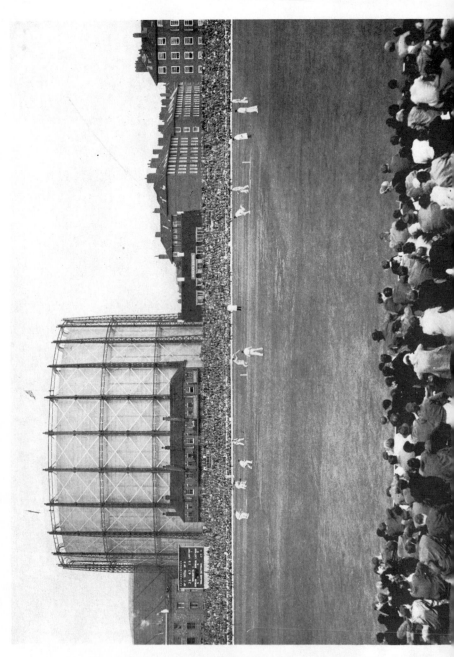

The Oval

Photo: Central
Press Photos Ltd.

Book Three

HOBBS AND SANDHAM

CHAPTER I

NEW BEGINNING

In company with many other more important activities, cricket
struggled up into the light again in 1919 with no very clear idea
of its place or its direction in the changed surroundings. It is not
surprising, with the old world about it in ruins, that it took time to
settle down. The season of 1919 has in many ways the appearance
of a hastily-improvised picnic; it does not seem possible, looking
back at those matches through the thickening mists of forty years,
that all of the players, all of the time, were taking the games with
the deadly professional seriousness that later and staider campaigns were used to exact from them. That the county matches
were of two days only gives a country-house flavour to the season
to begin with; the games were elongated from dawn to dark and
the players and umpires found them a harrowing strain on the
muscles, and complained that the routine was not only crippling
them, which was poor, but cutting into their evenings, which was
worse. A fantastic proportion of matches was drawn; Surrey, one
of the most enterprising of the counties that year, drew ten games
out of twenty. This might have been foreseen. Whether it was or
not, the effects were too obvious to ignore; the experiment was
very properly discontinued.

Nevertheless, cricket was still popular. And the season of 1919 is
not to be despised for its faults; let us remember it for its invigorating virtues, its adventurousness, its gaiety, its air of relaxation and
refreshment. I do not think we should carp at its shortcomings.
It represented for so many desperately weary people a dawning
consolation and a delight for which they had hardly dared at times

to hope to see again. For everyone it spelt in a measure the end of the night. It was high summer again, and the sun winked on the fresh paintwork at Lord's, and there was the smell of new-cut grass on the light wind; and the war was over.

There had been too many deaths, but the soul had learned in those days to grow skin quickly over a wound. Some had died who meant more to the watcher than their bare presence, for when they died their departure over-clouded the once-happy past. Blythe and Cotter, Hutchings and Booth, Gordon White of South Africa, were among those whose deaths reached back and took some of the savour out of the memories of the great pre-war Tests. Every county, too, had its roll of honour, though Surrey were more fortunate than most. And Nature, as well as War, had been as active as ever in her arbitrary condemnations. 1914 had removed through illness R. E. Foster and A. O. Jones; and 1915 went two better and laid fatal hands on the greatest of them all, W. G. Grace and Victor Trumper. W.G. had been ageing and ailing for some while, venerable and patriarchal, though still far away from true old age. Jack Hobbs had, as we saw, played with him on many occasions and absorbed sufficient of his personality to be able to communicate some of its essence to a later generation. The old man had attended a war-time charity game not long before his death and had moved the younger very much by his very evident desire to single him out and speak with him. It is a memory that has refreshed him for the rest of his life; in Jack Hobbs' genuine veneration, the enormous personality of the magnificent old rascal is reflected and re-created. As for Victor Trumper, there are still Australians who cannot speak of this unusual man's early death unmoved. In this game an inspired and transcendent artist of the most delicate and brilliant nature, in life a character it would seem of an exceptional gaiety and integrity, Trumper is still for nearly all Australians and a very high quota of Englishmen a cricketer without any parallel, concentrating upon himself an emotional affection equivalent to what an Englishman might feel for a blend of Woolley and Hobbs and Ranji, with an additional injection of the kind of frustrated regret that many others feel when contemplating the life and death of Keats. With this lamentable withdrawal had gone Jack Hobbs' only possible rival for the role of leading batsman in the world.

Wisden, wagging a rather schoolmasterly forefinger at Hobbs, crisply rebukes him for over-adventurousness at the start of the 1919 season. *Wisden* has at all times been prodigal in his praise; and yet one feels inclined on this occasion to adjure the old yellow-backed troglodyte to have a heart. The most aggressive batsman in the fifteen counties, itching from head to toe with the ugly deprivations of the last four years, could surely have been indulged a little. He had played a little league cricket, and later, when in the Air Force, a number of service games; but naturally his time and his energies had been absorbed first in his munitions work and then in his service duties. When he was demobilised in January 1919 he slipped straight back into the routine without a falter, and, perhaps injudiciously, thought to go on where he had left off at the end of August 1914. This brought him a couple of hundreds in a not very exacting trial match, and scores of 64 and 86 against Somerset, and 88 and 92 against Warwick; but it was truly enough noted that he was over-fond of turning (or in bad moments, trying to turn) the straight ball to square leg. It is equally true that scattered up and down the list of his high scores that season are a number of failures; but there are not enough of them to call for adverse comment. To one of his judgment equilibrium is not difficult to restore; and when he had for backing such a powerful and experienced batting side as Surrey turned out to be, it was almost certain that his failure would be balanced by somebody else's success. Hayward, alas, had allowed the war to dictate the time of his retirement; but a genially-relaxed Hayes was back from the Army as an amateur, and played at least one innings with all his characteristic power and aggression. Ducat had improved and matured, a fine athletic player who always looked as if he was due for the highest honours but through injury and vicissitude somehow failed to reach them; in this year of short-time matches he made two colossal scores, one of 306 not out against Oxford University and one of 271 against Hampshire, and there seemed no limit to his free potentialities. To add to the richness J. N. Crawford had returned from Australia and made his peace with Surrey; and although he played by no means regularly his batting had abated none of its glory. The difference to English cricket had Crawford been a regular player throughout his career can hardly be measured in the imagination; and Surrey must have welcomed this renewal of dynamic force with a strange mingling of delight and regret. Above all, there was D. J. Knight. He had gone back to Oxford when the war ended, and was therefore unable to appear for Surrey until July; but when he did come, and this was his great year by which everyone remembered him for the rest of his life, he performed with such a brilliant and resourceful mastery that he overshadowed Hobbs; and who, having once done this, can complain of comparative obscurity thereafter? He had one terrific week in July when he made 71 and 124 for the Gentlemen at Lord's and 40 and 101 not out for Surrey against Middlesex at the Oval, while a few days later he collected two centuries in a match against Yorkshire. He was, in the opinion of good judges, the more attractive half of the Surrey opening partnership. Having achieved this distinction in the days of which I speak, there could surely be no crown more that a man would covet. In 1919 Knight looked as if he could go anywhere; and though accident and his chosen career muffled his subsequent performance, which never quite did him adequate credit, his style and grace and precision were assets that not even time could annihilate while people were alive to remember and record them. He remains the most brilliant and the most evanescent of Hobbs' great partners.

There were other young batsmen, too, Harrison, W. J. Abel, a newcomer called Tom Shepherd, thrusting forward for notice. Prominent among them was the composed neat figure of Andrew Sandham. When Hobbs got his two hundreds in the trial match, Sandham was his opening partner, with scores of 81 and 70; and Hobbs and Sandham walked in to bat together for the first time in a championship match when Somerset came to the Oval in May. This year was not yet Sandham's year; for although he batted at all times with a compact competence that was evidence of an unusually vigilant concentration, he was discarded in mid-season to make way for Knight, and even when he played he was not invariably sent in first. This great and under-rated batsman had a long and testing apprenticeship; it was a measure of his character and his quality that in a side stuffed to bursting-point with batting talent, and playing their home matches on the Oval wicket, his courage and skill reacted to frustration and delay by improvement rather than by impatience. Sandham was the first junior partner to be guided by Hobbs to classic stature; in these early unsettling seasons the imaginative example and encouragement of the older man created for the newcomer the relaxed security he needed. Another season and he was established; one more, and he took on fate and fortune single-handed. There is more of Sandham to come.

If Surrey's bowlers had been half as effective as Surrey's batsmen, the side would have been frankly invincible. Hitch and Rushby toiled until they dropped, but they had no shadow of support. Fender was away injured all the season, and Crawford's bowling had not come back with his batting. They had to be content to imagine that they could have won in three days the matches they could only draw in two, and to yield their 1914 laurels to Yorkshire. The ensuing decade, in ever-intensifying degree, would repeat this pattern to the point of exasperation.

The celebrated Australian Imperial Forces team, a formidable collection of talent new and old from which the nuclear centre of Armstrong's frightening combination was ultimately to be hewn, voyaged most happily in this year up and down the counties. The spearhead of their attack was the young loose-limbed fast bowler J. M. Gregory, tall and active with a predatory leap at delivery that scared the vitals out of all but the most practised batsmen. Since Knox had fluttered the Players' dovecotes in 1906 nobody had seen such unpredictable pace; and even then it seemed that he had barely warmed up in 1919, and that when he and Macdonald let all hell loose about the ears of English cricket in 1921 he was a yard or two faster still and this time had a partner who in artistry and accuracy was far his superior. With 1921 in the background of our brooding fore-knowledge, it is ironic to note that Hobbs played all through the Surrey first innings against these Australians and made 205 not out. Fast bowling, particularly indiscriminate fast bowling, was to him like horses and dogs to the gentleman in *David Copperfield* who bred Suffolk Punches by wholesale, namely lodging, wife and children—reading, writing and 'rithmetic—snuff, tobacker and sleep. He battered the destructive Gregory without compunction, and Gregory took 2 for 119. Even more ironic is it to note that in the second game later in the season Gregory was submitted once more to most fearful punishment, this time by the upstanding Crawford, who hit a six and eighteen fours in 144 not out, mainly by hard straight drives banged back over Gregory's head. To point this double anecdote it has to be recalled that when the 1921 Tests came round, and Gregory and Macdonald were limbered up, Hobbs was injured or ill and Crawford was no longer playing; and while I do not wish to go in for premature anticipations, it may be noted that George Gunn, who in 1919 also made a nonchalant 100 off Gregory as if he had been an inefficient mosquito, was not in 1921 invited to play for England.

Sufficient unto 1919, however, be the evil thereof; it was too full of life and promise to warrant forebodings. For Hobbs it was a season of happily high scoring after his first shaky patch. He scored over 2,500 runs and got eight centuries, one each in the three Gents. v. Players matches, which is a little pocket record of his own. If he had ever had any misgivings during the dead years, he could put them away now. His skills had all remained; and when cricket began again in earnest, after the tentatively festival atmosphere that had characterised this first thrilling renewal, he would find himself elevated and enlarged, as he had never been before the war, into the great representative cricketer of his age.

His final triumph that season was the last game that Surrey played at the Oval, the Kent match set aside after such a long delay as the benefit he had earned and been baulked of five years before. This time no extraneous forces imposed their alien patterns, unless you count the compression of the fixture into two days, about which Hobbs might have grumbled but I am quite certain did not. Kent batted first and were led by 90 on the first innings; and drudging away late on the second (and of course last) afternoon were nearly 100 ahead by six o'clock with three wickets in hand. Even when the tail crumpled suddenly before Hitch and the last three batsmen fell over each other coming and going on the pavilion stairs, the time element seemed far too oppressive for any result to be thought possible; and as Kent walked out to field at a quarter to seven the clouds banked up over the gasworks, the evening dimness spread murkily about the stands, and a spatter of rain blew across the greying Oval. Spectators that year, when matches went on until 7.30, had a disconcerting habit of getting up and going home when it was supper-time; it was particularly noticed that they did not do so that day. It was, after all, their hero's benefit; and on top of that they sensed the possibility of a fight. That Surrey had forty-five minutes only, and had to get 96 mortal runs, was an obstacle which given the occasion it seemed possible could be surmounted. And when they saw that Knight (who was captaining the side) had overlooked his own superb form and sent in Crawford with Hobbs, the possibility became suddenly a consuming excitement. As the batsmen walked into the roar of welcome, the steady drift of drizzle came in at them over the housetops.

Blythe was no more, but Fairservice and Woolley were both deadly accurate on their day and they set the field tight in the gloom. Crawford challenged at once, half-blind with the rain on his glasses; he went down the wicket and drove, and there was no loitering between wickets. In fourteen minutes 35 were up; Crawford had 27 and they had twice missed him in the murk. Half Surrey's eleven, padded up, clustered waiting, in case. The tempo speeded up, the batsmen ran twos for a normal single, threes for a normal two. Neither of these men was far short of forty, but they ran their runs like schoolboys and in their choice of aggressive strokes they hit not wildly but with the ingrained skill of years of Test cricket. Twenty-five runs came in the next seven minutes; and Hobbs got going at last. It was not slogging; it was scientific aggression intensified.

Calm in the midst of this unparalleled whirlwind, Hobbs saw Surrey home with Crawford in precisely 29 minutes of one of the most coolly-conceived and effectively executed pieces of attacking cricket that the Oval has seen this century. With 15 minutes to go Hobbs made the winning hit; they cut and ran for the pavilion as the rain drifted down in clouds behind them, and they, and the generous Kent men, and the hungry rewarded spectators, were mixed in a swingling melee of damp and ecstatic humanity glorying in as triumphant a schoolboy finish as a benefit match has a right to expect. Hobbs 47, Crawford 48; Surrey 96 for no wicket in one minute under the half hour. Hobbs, chaired home to the pavilion gate by his enthusiastic supporters, found half his batting glove mysteriously abstracted and a pound note as mysteriously substituted. It was an admirable climax to his benefit; and when the net takings were handed over he got £1,671 more, which in the terms of those days was considered a big success. That winter he used it to start his famous sporting outfitter's business, which he shrewdly established at the expense of a coaching appointment in South Africa. From that time on, he always looked twice at winter tours before accepting invitations to join them.

Hobbs moved into the 'twenties on confident feet. As often after a war—it was the same in the late 'forties—the bowling took longer to restore to full powers than the batting; and a succession of hot sunny summers accentuated his complete mastery. Only accident and illness interrupted an almost monotonous productivity once the three-day championship matches were installed again; a hundred by Hobbs was a weekly expectation and in fact on the average a fortnightly actuality. The Hobbs of 1920 contains perhaps the last authentic glimpse of the questing pre-war adventurer who was oftener out of his crease than in it, who pirated runs with a swift predatory relish and cut all bowlers to his own convenient lengths. After 1921 a cricketer's middle-age compelled recession; but through the rich happy season of 1920 he led Surrey's batting as of natural right, dominating on the good wickets and inspired to special genius on the bad ones. He had for the most part the opening co-operation of Sandham; in the first match they put up 190 against Northants in an hour and a half, and late in the season the very much stronger Kent fielded out to 196 before Hobbs left for 132; but the partnership was not yet an established unchangeable truth, and at various times Miles Howell or Harrison or Donald Knight opened with him even when Sandham was in the side. Knight unhappily was badly injured in August and never showed his 1919 form; which may have been unlucky for Knight and for Surrey, but gave Sandham at last a regular opportunity to take the place that was his right for the next fifteen years. Hobbs' own cricket did not suffer; he crowded on the runs this season irrespective of who stood at the other end. As in 1914 he totalled eleven centuries; he had five up before the middle of June, and in one productive spell he had four in succession, including a brilliant 112 in the Yorkshire match at Sheffield, in the second innings of which he infuriated himself by being out for 70 and missing his fifth consecutive hundred.

He looks back upon one of those centuries as one of his ripest, as it was played at Leicester on a wicket that saw the match off in a day and a half and maimed three batsmen (all, ironically enough, Leicester men). Fender, winning the toss with an air of gloomy prognostication, observed bleakly that he did not wish to have to bat twice; and Hobbs took the hint and played one of his special emergency innings, plundering all the runs he could before the top tore off the wicket and the undertakers had to move in. *Wisden* does not know where to look for the appreciative adjective; he himself enjoyed it, and enjoyed remembering it; he scored 134 in just over the hour and a half, was out well before lunch, had a brief rest and was there at cover while Rushby and Reay committed systematic double murder on the appalled home team. Fender, hurrying back on the second afternoon after having had an urgent business call to London, heaved the biggest possible sigh of relief when he found the ground deserted and Surrey victorious and unbruised.

Fender was now in partial command, as Wilkinson's availability became uncertain; and in the next match he showed an early hint of his invigorating flair. Surrey moved from the battlefield of Leicester to the more level and reliable sward at Edgbaston; and somewhere between the one abiding place and the other the incalculable Rushby got lost. A cricketer of high value, he was blessed with an erratic individuality of temper which was apt on occasion to make a causeless enemy of circumstance. He had slightly slipped a muscle in the Leicester carnage, and when the time to start at Birmingham arrived, very late, owing to rain, and Surrey found themselves with ten men and a great silence, it was surmised among the survivors that once more the temperament of this admirable bowler had overcome his never very positive discretion. The defection was explained if not excused when on the very verge of taking the field the captain was handed a telegram; which bore for the general enlightenment and satisfaction the gnomic legend, "Rushby ill. Rushby." Restraining the almost overwhelming impulse to reply at once, "Fender displeased. Fender," the captain searched the depleted ranks for an opening bowler, and whether in hope or despair it cannot be certain, threw the ball to Hobbs. This bowler then proceeded to improve the damp Saturday evening by taking five of the first six wickets that fell. The pitch was soaked and the air hung heavy; and he exploited both swing and spin in an unexpectedly destructive manner, bowling seven maidens out of fourteen overs, hitting the stumps of three men and even getting Willie Quaife, of all people, first ball. He finished with 5 for 21 and Warwick were put out for 70; after which Hobbs, like A. E. Housman after a celebrated lecture, went back with relief and thankfulness to his proper job and made 101 with all imaginable ease.

He made half of his county's 16 championship centuries that fine summer, and made big scores in nearly all the extra games in which he played outside the competition. This was of course the year of Plum Warner's great farewell, when Middlesex, far down the table at the end of July, won nine matches in succession in a historic racing spurt and came up deliriously at their very last chance at Lord's to beat Surrey by 55 runs in a match which in its own right is one of the classics of the game's annals. In one glorious swoop this snatched the championship from Lancashire (who far away in Manchester that afternoon had already begun on the champagne) and relegated Surrey to third place, leaving them only with the memory of a great game of cricket and an intimate share in Warner's personal joy and satisfaction. Hobbs' own share in the game was moderate, but he watched Sandham play two wonderfully mature innings, and his pleasure in this and in the splendid out-cricket that brought victory to Middlesex and the crowning Boy's Own Paper finish to Warner's playing career entirely outweighed the transitory disappointment. A small satisfaction remains, devoid of malice or vengeance; when Middlesex as Champion County came to play the Rest at the Oval a fortnight later, a formidable phalanx of batsmen belted the hell out of the Middlesex bowling to the tune of 603 for five at a rate of 115 an hour, of which Hobbs made 215 in 200 minutes. Middlesex were happily undismayed and held their own without trepidation (an ominous note in view of the coming Australian tour and the not unreasonable presumption that a bowler who could get wickets would be a handy man to have about the house). So ended a season of great gaiety and excitement, and a few days afterwards off started Douglas for Australia with a large collection of successful batsmen and a slightly less experienced and more experimental bunch of bowlers. An atmosphere of buoyant optimism prevailed; 1920 had been a year of admirable and adventurously-conducted cricket, any feeling that the accustomed joints were still stiff after the four year interruption had been dispersed by the exhilaration of the summer, and the party sailed with great achievements at their back, a strong memory in many of the seasoned members of the grand successes of 1911-12, and a happy anticipation of renewing the old contacts and friendships that the A.I.F. matches of

1919 had done so much to stimulate. Hobbs, with a personal season aggregate of 2,827, was now an even more accomplished attacking batsman than he had been nine years before, and he had to support him not only his old comrade Rhodes but Frank Woolley and the highly prolific Hendren and Hearne. Rhodes was by now a bowler again, and was not designed for an opening batsman on this tour; the partner allotted to Hobbs being the accomplished and aggressive Jack Russell, the best of the Essex batsmen of the 'twenties, who tempered a naturally free and open style with long meditative spells of great patience. Sanguine critics hoped that this fine batting side (which also included the dogged Makepeace, thus offending the clamorous advocates of Sandham and Percy Holmes) might possibly build such a barrier of runs that Australia's greatest endeavours could not surmount it, however ineffective the probable penetrative power of our somewhat second-class attack. These hopes were, as so often such hopes are, reinforced by an early series of clangorous defeats of State sides by huge margins; and a rather disconcerting piece of table-turning by New South Wales, who, set to get in the fourth innings a considerably higher total than any yet reached in the match, calmly and easily got it, did not shake the confidence that the prior successes had happily bolstered. Not until half way through the first Test did the warning note suddenly rise to a pitch of horror. A powerful Australian side were neatly despatched for 267, and England got comfortably to 140 with only three wickets down. At this point Gregory clean bowled Hobbs, and the rest of the side were gone with the wind for the addition of 50 runs. On taking the field again they were there and then subjected to a really terrible drubbing, Armstrong and Collins getting hundreds and nearly everyone else making substantial scores, and before the task of making 659 the English batsmen yielded up the ghost with a token struggle only. The crushing attack delivered by the Australian batsmen was a psychological knock-out from which neither that year nor the next saw them effectively rise.

The tale of the 1920-21 tour from an English point of view is one of steadily deepening depression. Again and again the weak or moderate State sides were plundered for huge totals by the England batsmen; and again and again the concentrated talent of the Australian Test team was stiff enough both to curb the batsmen and blunt the experimental bowling. The bowlers in particular, effective as they were in the minor games, were horribly mauled in the Test matches; the three fastest bowlers, Howell, Waddington and Hitch, had eight Test wickets between them, and the fearful cost of their successes quite overweighted the actual bag of wickets secured by the inventive Parkin and Fender, at once the two most dangerous and least dependable bowlers on the side. In the State and county games the batting figures soared out of this world, all the accredited batsmen making voluptuously huge scores; but in Tests a soberer economy prevailed, and Hobbs headed the batting with the very creditable total of 505 runs for 10 times in and out, and his fellows following in a cluster with averages generally in the thirties. Woolley and Rhodes were disappointing; Russell failed badly as an opener (though he played several excellent innings lower down the order) and Rhodes, brought back as a substitute, never found the ancient touch. Hearne, after a good beginning, was taken ill and played no more; and Hendren, up to his ears in runs in the lesser games, was no more than adequate in the important ones. Hobbs himself was the only squarely dependable batsman on the side, making one classic century on a drenched and drying Melbourne wicket when only he, and for a short time Hendren, had any answer whatever to the domination of Gregory. And in the third Test at Adelaide, when all the England batsmen struck form together and their totals of 447 and 370 would have won many Test matches twice over, he played a wonderful fighting innings of 123 which nearly screwed up his colleagues to an impossible victory. But there could be no kicking against the pricks; Australia, under the highly experienced and still remarkably versatile Armstrong, had a superb blend of maturity and youth which they were busily moulding into one of the most forbidding Test sides in history. Collins, Bardsley, Macartney, Kelleway and Armstrong among the old, blended happily and menacingly with Taylor, Pellew, Gregory and Oldfield of the new; not to mention the rising fast bowler Macdonald and the newest of the Australian googly bowlers, a cheerful and popular comic named Arthur Mailey who liked to buy his wickets dearly but saw that they accrued to him all the same. Shrewd, companionable, wily, he began this season a life-long duel with Hobbs, each one being always perfectly certain that he could get the better of the other and the battle remaining at a constant equipoise for the duration of a happy and indissoluble friendship. He got Hobbs three times in this series, and in fact collared nine Englishmen in one innings of the fourth Test and 36 in the series. A talented and extremely likeable character, a cartoonist above the average and a writer of modest individuality, Arthur Mailey's friendly disposition cloaked a deceptively formidable player. His part in Armstrong's five-Test victory is not far off the most important part of all.

For Hobbs the tour ended on an ominously muted note. In the second match against New South Wales in late February he tore a tendon in his thigh, and as the next match was the fifth Test he injudiciously played again instead of resting. No immediate harm followed, although the injury noticeably affected his concentration when he batted. The game was then lost, and all other considerations were swallowed up in a general wailing and gnashing of teeth.

This is the story of Hobbs and not of English cricket; this is no place, therefore, for recriminations or judgments about this strange and ill-fated tour. The M.C.C. had wished to postpone it, as they felt that our cricket was insufficiently stabilized after the four-year break, but the Australians had been so keen to set international cricket going once again (the slaughterhouse was ready, even if the lambs were a little unprepared) that the M.C.C. gave in, with the results we know. Something of the same figure was re-enacted after the Second World War. The justification of the tour was in its huge popularity; it built up a great Australian team; and it added to Hobbs' Test reputation. On the debit or English side it did no other single individual a ha'porth of good; no player going out with that team for the first time ever went again, except Harry Howell who was hardly a success either time, and Hendren after fearful vicissitudes. It was one of those experiments which no doubt gave plenty of pleasure while it lasted, but which in the light of history seems overcast with a certain gloom. The British public were commendably resilient about it (though I recall myself my first visit to Henry Ainley and Edna Best in *Peter Pan* that winter being spoiled by reading in the evening paper before it of Australia's 582 in the third Test and the utter demoralisation of our bowlers); and when the team came back they mobbed them as if the Ashes had been won and not lost. The touring party returned on the same boat with Armstrong's compact combination, loins girt and amiably challenging, and had plenty of leisure during deck-tennis to ponder on first and last things and the shape of next season.

CHAPTER II

DISASTER AND FULFILMENT

THE shape of the season of 1921 declared itself for Hobbs before the first whitening had flaked off his boots. We may usefully pass over the Surrey trial match, in which he allowed his friend Strudwick to stump him off a lob-bowler, and rest for a moment at Old Buckenham Hall in Norfolk, where a philanthropic gentleman named Lionel Robinson kept a vast mansion and a private cricket-ground, on which in early May he confronted Armstrong's Australians with a team of all the talents. It was as cold as charity and there was a strike on; the Australians had butchered Leicestershire in their first match and were licking their lips for more; and in the freezing spring weather this terrific scoring machine was ignominiously outed by Johnny Douglas for a beggarly 136. Archie MacLaren, captain of the scratch side, maintained stoutly through the hell and high water that engulfed England during the next few months that this, and not the succeeding matches, represented Australia's true quality, and nothing of the horrors to come could persuade him that they were not vulnerable if the proper team to beat them could be assembled. (He vindicated himself at the end of the season by collecting a scratch team of amateurs and doing just what he said he would.)

It is the direst irony of the whole season that this cold afternoon in Norfolk provided the only occasion that year when Hobbs faced Gregory and Macdonald. These two fast bowlers made the ball rear and rip as all England was soon to know; but after Knight's early dismissal Hobbs and Vallance Jupp took quiet and confident charge. Hobbs himself tamed the fast openers and for the moment

129

was the complete and prolific master of Mailey; he batted with the rare grace and control that only a great batsman can command against bowlers who begin with a high psychological advantage; he hit ten fours and made 85, and has himself expressed the modest opinion that in some ways this can be called the best innings of his life. Gregory at one end, with his long bounding run and joyous leap at the moment of delivery; the rippling grace of Macdonald's catlike approach and spring-coil action at the other; and Hobbs, the quick-footed hawk-eyed master, playing them both like fish on the end of a line. It is to be doubted if 1921, during all its blistering iron-hard summer, ever saw a finer concentration of cricket as it did in the depths of Norfolk, for an hour or two, on this cold uncertain May afternoon.

He had made 85 when his thigh muscle gave out on him again. It had clearly never strengthened itself since Australia; and it comes back to my personal recollection that in that Surrey trial game of a few days before he had, to my own insensate rage and frustration, been off the field when I was there to see him; I do not doubt that this infernal leg muscle had been to blame. On this occasion it tore while he and Jupp were going for a quick run; and Jupp, supplying the necessary corroborative detail designed to give artistic verisimilitude to a narrative which is unfortunately only too convincing, declared that he heard it snap as he passed.

What became of the match after that, nobody cares. As it happened, it rained again and it fizzled out. What was deadly important was that this frustrating accident put England's best batsman out of the game until late in June. During the enforced idleness, Gregory and Macdonald stoked up their fires, the English wickets grew adamantine hard under the slow grill of one of the hottest summers in recent record, and a badly-selected, badly-disorganized and not very well captained England was submitted at Nottingham and Lord's to two of the most humiliating defeats that we have ever suffered on our own grounds. Knight and Holmes batted well at Nottingham, and Woolley played two immortal innings at Lord's; but the bowling was dismally innocuous, and England's confidence and the selectors' judgment sank together without trace. Knight went completely, and Holmes virtually, out of Test cricket for good; and there were fearful hints about that the selectors were doing their selecting with a pin.

Hobbs reported fit again in time for the third Test at Leeds. He played against Oxford University as a try-out and made 49; and appeared in his first championship match on 25th June against Yorkshire, where he assisted Surrey to a very fine victory with a chanceless 172 not out. This put him on top of the world, and a failure in the Gents. v. Players match at the Oval worried him very little. The selectors hailed his recovery with a great sigh of relief; it restored their spirits if not their acumen. He duly presented himself on Saturday, July 2nd, to play for England for the first time this season.

He had felt off colour for a day or two, but thought little of it; on the way up to Leeds the dull pain which had begun to trouble him developed a positive identity. On Saturday morning he felt worse. It is difficult at this stage to understand why the selectors allowed a clearly unfit man to play; but he was prevailed upon to turn out, certainly against his inclination, probably against his better judgment. Australia won the toss and he stuck it in the field till tea-time. Then exhausted nature declared its unwillingness to be driven, and he had to give in. After a day's rest he felt a trifle better, but on the Monday the pain came back, and the selectors advised him to return to London.

It appears that if he had taken this advice he would have died on the train. As it was, a most fortunate chance suggestion put him in touch with Sir Berkeley Moynihan, the very eminent surgeon, who was right there in Leeds. Sir Berkeley took one look, and with very little preliminary argument persuaded him to be operated on there and then. Before England were all out—and this speaks much for Sir Berkeley's dexterity and despatch—Jack Hobbs' appendix was out, too. It was the culmination of his, and England's, bad luck. Again, it hardly seems to matter what happened to the devastated game. Australia easily won it, of course, their eighth in succession, in spite of the injured Tennyson's fabulous performance in making 63 and 36 against Gregory and Macdonald with his right hand only. England were dead and demoralised; their bowling was in shreds, their best player was in hospital, their batting order was in ruins and they lay wide open to change and chance. Nevertheless it is helpful at this moment to remember one obscure and interesting historical fact; it does not mean much, but it may call to despondent minds in this and other contexts the inscrutable imponderabilities of the great wheel of fate; and it is this—that when the Australians had at their ease completed this entirely deserved victory, they had scored their last win over England in England for almost exactly nine years. This bare statement had admittedly a misleading ring; but it proffers to the saddened responses a note of regeneration and hope. The last two Tests of this baneful series were dreary and weather-spoiled draws, enlivened at Manchester by a tremendous row over the technicalities of a declaration and at the Oval by a record score from Philip Mead and the famous spectacle of Armstrong perusing a newspaper in the long field. They proved nothing but the inadequacy of a three-day limit when bowlers were stale and batsmen improving in confidence; and the least cherished of all Test series dribbled away unmourned, leaving Armstrong's invincible bodyguard to meet a double Waterloo in the autumnal festival games at the season's end.

The deprived Surrey, it must be recorded, barely noticed their loss. The baked brown Oval resounded to their tremendous scoring; as many as twenty-four centuries were hit for them in a year when their greatest century-monger was restricted to one alone. The reliable and unworried Sandham came into his own, with two scores of over 200 and an average of nearly fifty; he had a wonderful August, and it won him an England cap, which he wore with the unassuming neatness that was characteristic of one of the most capable and circumspect batsmen who have ever played. Ducat got a cap too, but not without justice thought he was lucky; an admirable county player but without the final international *cachet*, he gobbled runs on these dry wickets, made his own two double centuries, and was above Sandham in the averages. Leading them both was the honest moon-faced Shepherd, who also got a couple of 200's but got them in successive innings, a delightful square-framed hard-driving batsman with a placid and unruffled temperament, or rather no temperament at all, who for more than a dozen years sustained the middle batting of the finest batting side in the competitions. A tall auxiliary amateur named Jeacocke was one of the most prolific scorers for several seasons; and Jardine and Miles Howell added spasmodically their skill and their Harlequin caps to Donald Knight's already well-established reputation. Knight, unhappily, never regained the wonderful form of 1919; but the others consolidated themselves with ease and authority into

the centre-piece of the great edifice that was the Surrey eleven in
the 'twenties. How formidable, how overwhelmingly formidable,
that batting side could be is easily gauged by the recollection that
that terrific array of seven high-class batsmen who scored most of
Surrey's runs for them in this run-greedy year does not contain
the greatest of them all. That year the Surrey batting was frightening enough if it began with Sandham and Knight, Sandham and
Jardine, Sandham and Jeacocke; but in all the other years of this
great decade, they began with Hobbs and Sandham. And it was
remarked by someone with a fine and exact sense of the true value
of a phrase that bowling to Hobbs and Sandham on the Oval
wicket of the 'twenties was like bowling at God on concrete.

Surrey were baulked of the championship in the last match of
1921, just as in 1920; and just as in 1920, they were worsted by
Middlesex at Lord's when they looked as if they had the match
and the championship in the bag. The honours they carried away
from the season were ones of general competence and effectiveness
rather than of pre-eminence; being primarily those of cumulative
run-making. The fact that they scored 616 for 5 against Northants
in one day was enhanced in interest by the fact that the season
before they had scored 619 for 5 against the same county, at
Northampton. Ducat was the only batsman to make over 100 on
each occasion, but Hobbs scored only 3 and Shepherd only 9 and
4; these fantastic totals were spread lavishly among Sandham,
Jeacocke, Ducat, Peach and Fender. These two scores, against
bowling which was admittedly below standard, show how wide in
the team the mantle of productive batsmanship spread.

In 1922, when Hobbs returned to the team, the pattern of this
impressive and enigmatic side formed itself into an inevitably
recognizable picture of strength and weakness. It is against the
background that is now forming itself that the great public figure
of the Jack Hobbs of the 'twenties is most characteristically seen.
He had had ten years at the Oval before the war and three after it,
and was now, by undisputed right and justice, by far the most
illustrious figure proper to those sordid but endearing surroundings. Now begins in earnest and in general—although in particular,
no doubt, it had been anticipated years earlier—the great age of
the schoolboys' worship, when the steps he descended or the
ground he stood on were revered from near and from far and his

down-sittings and his uprisings were chronicled and published to all believers. It would be incorrect to regard his England record and his England appearances as irrelevant in the eyes of these young admirers, for they intensified the avid affection that they felt; but the Hobbs of their adoration was primarily a Surrey Hobbs, who lived and had his true being at the Oval. He himself, nearing forty, was now ripe for veneration; he had assumed an avuncular maturity which the rather shy, wide-eyed diffidence of his youth could never have compassed. He moved with all the old grace and with an added assurance; his eyes had retired behind humorous and contemplative wrinkles, his pale, dark, slightly feminine features had tanned and weathered to an alert liveliness, he looked about him with an air of amused anticipation. If he was aware that he was the centre of a seething idolatrous hero-worship, and he could have hardly escaped noticing something of what was going on, he never showed it. He was too readily concerned to do his part for the Surrey team in their perennially-frustrated snatches at championship honours to worry much about his own potentialities or performances as a pin-up. He was the leading batsman in the most talented batting side of all the counties; and if championships could be won by batting alone, as they most patently cannot, that fabulous team of masters would have carried off the honours for a solid decade.

As all the world knows, Surrey in the time of her great classical batsmen went gravely short on bowling. In the field they were as accomplished as any side but Yorkshire, Hobbs, Hitch, Sandham, Miles Howell and Ducat being of first-rate quality, Fender being a slip-fielder of unusual agility and retentive capacity, and Strudwick being regarded by a number of very experienced cricketers at that time as the best wicket-keeper in the world. Unhappily the bowling declined and the stuffing ran out of it just when the time and the place and the *Zeitgeist* demanded that it return to the old standards of Lohmann and Lockwood and Richardson. For years they had to take the field on the plumb Oval wicket without an adequate fast bowler; Hitch was thickening up and slowing down, Rushby had (no doubt by telegram) announced his decision to play no more, Peach was a lively enough mover of the new ball but a rather generous gift on a hard wicket to a good batsman in form, and a quick glance at the first-class averages will indicate that in those unhampered days there were very many of these. Shepherd kept his chocolate cap on and wheeled steadily up and down, compact of goodwill if not of penetrative power; and apart from an odd amateur playing an occasional game, there wasn't a slow bowler in the business. Except, of course, Fender.

Percy Fender, tall, angular, beaky, balding, surprisingly reminiscent in appearance of Groucho Marx, looked about as unpromising material for an all-round cricketer as could be conceived. He looked decades older than he really was, and his large horn-rimmed spectacles on the long inquisitive nose over the assertive tufted moustache gave him the air of a fierce cashier peering angrily among the ledgers for a lost sixpence. Yet for a dozen years he was one of the most vigorous and successful all-rounders in the game, a merciless hitter of all but the tightest bowling, a predatory slip-fielder and a bowler of remarkable variety of talent who could behave in the course of twenty minutes or so like a seam bowler, a spin bowler, an off-spinner and a googly merchant, varying the mixture with an occasional and deliberate high full toss to upset the batsman's concentration. With all this he was perhaps the most actively intelligent and hard-thinking captain of any country side then in the championship; and if there were ever any very cogent reasons why he should not have captained England both on his merits as a player and his astonishing capacities as a captain, then they have been concealed from the interested world both at the time and since. Fender throughout the 'twenties held Surrey poised between overwhelming victories and ignominious defeats, coaxing his bowlers into performances beyond their powers, shuffling them to and fro like greased cards in a pack, taking time off during the Surrey innings, when his batsmen preserved him from worry, to plan campaigns of preternatural ingenuity for when Surrey should be in the field and his bowlers should preserve him from complacency. That Surrey cut such a prominent figure in county cricket in the 'twenties, on that celebrated Oval wicket that was the breath of life to her batsmen and the kiss of death to her bowlers, is referable to the administrative genius and tireless inventiveness of Percy Fender. Jack Hobbs, Percy Fender and the Surrey team; on a postcard; two pence. As a monument to skill, ingenuity, courage and endeavour, cheap at the price, two pence well spent indeed; a team of varying but sometimes surprising

talent, who might one day score 500 and dismiss their opponents
for 60, and yet be kept in the field for a day and a half in the second
innings and fail to press for victory. Yet no county took them
easily, whether at the Oval or elsewhere; for however gaily Surrey's
opponents might riot among the runs, there was an unsuspected
flair of genius in even their mediocrity that might skittle half a side
in half an hour; and when the opponents with runs in plenty on the
board came out optimistically to field, the bowlers who were to
bowl on that iron-bound wicket could never avoid the sudden
qualm of misgiving as they turned to pace out their run and saw
Hobbs and Sandham, cool and relaxed and mildly appraising,
advancing over the grass to begin Surrey's innings.

It is in the context of Surrey cricket that we see Hobbs' almost
monotonous progress through the two or three seasons that followed
his return after the disappointments of 1921. From this moment
onwards he seems, surprisingly enough, to have stepped on some
kind of accelerator. The operation shook him, and for a season or
two he became easily tired; it seems that from this phase dates his
famous habit, not invariable but noticeably frequent, of getting
himself out when he had achieved the hundred. Nevertheless it
was an accelerator and not a brake. Baulked by nature of the necessary endurance for very long scores, he compensated in the most
satisfactory manner possible by making more of them but keeping
them generally short. In 1922, when he might well have been
expected to be shaky and tentative, he helped himself to ten centuries. It is no enhancement of the variety of this narrative to
chronicle them all. These years are his years of high harvest;
mellow fruitfulness is the appropriate phrase. The sun was always
shining at the Oval, and Hobbs was always batting. Summer time
meant Oval-time, and Oval-time meant Hobbs. These were the
days that gave birth to these jingles and to the enduring legend.

One date in 1922 has to be noted; it was late in September, and
the county games were done with. An M.C.C. touring side had
been picked to go to South Africa. Naturally Hobbs had been
invited; for the first time he had declined, thinking of his business
and his family and possibly of the greater need for a winter's rest
that the aftermath of his illness had bequeathed him. Never again
was he to tour with the M.C.C. to any other country but Australia.
He was nearly forty and he felt the need for moderation. So the

team was chosen for South Africa, and he was not among them;
and on 11th September at Scarborough the M.C.C. touring side
were faced by a strong scratch team got together by Mr. C. I.
Thornton. Thornton's team were captained by Douglas, and he
won the toss and batted; and Jack Hobbs and Herbert Sutcliffe,
opening the innings together in a first-class match for the first
time, put up 120 before the first wicket fell. The moment passed,
and the not very important match passed, and the occasion is all
but forgotten as it lies in the record books unnoticed; but it seems
unfitting not to celebrate as we come up with it the modest and
obscure beginning of the association of the greatest opening pair
in the history of cricket. Later on it will occupy the foreground of
the story; at present it is a presage merely.

1923 was showery and unpromising, and it ranks as one of his
least prolific seasons. Let us put it down to the effect of wind and
rain on the joints, to the prolonged business of reorganisation
of his gay youthful technique against the onset of illness and middle
age, and to the fact that in the winter he had passed forty.
Nowadays it is quite a rarity for a leading batsman to continue
for more than a year or two after this age; it is sufficient comment
on the modern practice of retirement at forty to note that Jack
Hobbs made 99 centuries before he reached that age and (wilting
visibly) only 98 afterwards. No similarly productive late middle
age is known to the game's annals, except perhaps W.G.'s; and
here at a moment when modern batsmen think of forming themselves into a limited company and retiring into the business world,
we are on the approaches to the second half of a career which in
many ways is more extraordinary than the first half.

It was in the lovely Georgian setting of Bath that he reached,
in the early days of May 1923, that most gratifying half-way house,
his hundredth hundred. He had gone into the winter with ninety-
nine, and had, no doubt, kept the great memories of his old
associates Grace and Hayward much in his mind, the only two who
had reached that milestone before him. In his bones he knew well
enough that given freedom from accident or Act of God he was
bound to do it; but plums never fell readily into Jack Hobbs'
mouth, and it was of the essence of his greatness that he had to go
for his prizes and not wait for them to come to him. A drifting
misty rain came in over the hills that Saturday when Surrey played

Somerset, and postponed play until five o'clock. Then when Surrey
batted they could only face three overs before play was washed
out for the week-end, Hobbs and Sandham not out 0 each. Some
of them caught a train back to town, and were asked in all innocence
by a fellow-travelling parson whether Hobbs had made that century yet. Hobbs, still incognito, gave it as his opinion that he would
never make one against Somerset. When they revealed their
identity the surprised and delighted parson wished them well and
departed let us hope to his prayers; which for the moment availed
them little, as on Monday Hobbs and Sandham got a duck each
and Surrey were bundled out for 91. The wicket at Bath, however,
always deals out its destruction with an impartial eighteenth-
century cynicism and before the shades fell Somerset were all out
too; a little more generously blessed with runs than their
opponents, but not much, 49 being the limit of their lead. Hobbs
and Sandham, walking a little delicately on account of their first
innings record, were in again before the close, and I regret to report
that Sandham was out again for 4 on the stroke of time. The unshakeable Hobbs, 19 not out overnight, put his troubles to bed and
went to the theatre—the title of the play is not recorded—and rose
next morning to a day of responsibility and, as it turned out, destiny. He began it in the least promising manner possible, being
intimately, and I fear culpably, concerned in the immediate running out of none less than Ducat and Shepherd. Feeling less than
happy about this, he apologized to the incoming Fender (also 0
in the first innings) who replied crisply, "Can't be helped," not a
reassuring remark, and himself sent Hobbs back in the next over
when he was three parts of the way up the pitch. Here were
amassed for all to see the stock ingredients of a grave situation;
three good batsmen out, the star survivor apparently demoralized,
and the home team's total as yet not passed; and a few moments
later out went Fender, making everyone's day.

In this unpleasant impasse it was the uninhibited Hitch who
administered steadiness to Hobbs' shifting confidence. It is possible that he was the angel designed by Providence to answer the
clergyman's prayers. Sturdy and unperturbed, he ignored the
general panic and bludgeoned his way out of trouble. So often it
happens, in this context and in others, that at a moment of crisis
the finer sensibility is sustained and encouraged on the knife-edge

by the less sensitive but equally valorous companion lucky enough
to have been born without nerves. On this day at Bath Bill Hitch
led the revival by belabouring everything he could reach, overhaul-
ing his partner in no time, taking no notice whatever of a number
of hair-raising escapes, and bombarding the whole surrounding
city from Beechen Cliff to the Royal Crescent with the violence of
his attack. Inevitably the tension eased; Hobbs at the other end
found his confidence flooding back to the rescue. No calculation
can tell how much of his hundredth hundred he owes to the
admirable Hitch, who carved his way to a glorious 67 and then got
out, leaving Hobbs a few minutes later to walk into fame alone.
The scoreboard at Bath did not show the individual scores; and
his worst moment of horror came when Strudwick signalled from
the ringside that he had six more to get. Cavernous apprehension
possessed him; six runs seemed more even than the 94 that had
preceded them. He dug three singles superhumanly out of the
deadly accuracy of the bowling; the ordeal closed round him like
something palpable and hostile. Then he pushed one to cover,
scampered, turned, saw the return go wide and ran liberatingly for
two overthrows, and the whole of Somerset broke out into the
relief and rejoicing of congratulations and cheers.

He spent the rest of the day in a pardonably elated daze, thinking
of his successes, his family, Tom Hayward, his father, his happy
fulfilment. He almost overlooked Fender's adventurous declaration,
and Somerset's scaring chase for a win. Ultimately Fender's
instincts and Fender's hunch prevailed, and Surrey won by 10
runs; let us be pardoned for subordinating the result to the
individual incident of a great and difficult century, worthy the
struggling for, and when at last achieved a landmark and a legend.
The more so that in that lean season he had to wait two months for
another one.

It is as well to leave 1923 on that note; it is the one memory that
he cherishes of a niggardly year. Let us think of it primarily as a
reculement pour mieux sauter; an almost unconscious process of
complete reorganization under the press of years and circumstance;
a retreat from which in the next season of 1924 he emerged to
begin his fantastic Indian summer that never rightly or traceably
died out from him. From 1924 there seemed to accrue to this
already matured and experienced batsman, who by all normal

standards was now bringing a wonderfully successful career to a temperate and unobtrusive close, an access of energy and skill which can only be called by the name of genius. It would have been quite outside all predictable reason to envisage it; but this forty-year-old cricketer, hampered by the after-effects of a severe illness and compelled accordingly to husband his natural energies with some care, who had already to his credit more centuries than any other batsman but two who had ever played first-class cricket, was yet before he retired to add to his existing total of centuries more than C. B. Fry had made in the course of his whole life. He still had nearly 25,000 runs to make. He had still, when he scored his hundredth hundred, batted only once with Sutcliffe. He had still never improved on his highest score, that memorable 226 scored on the sunny Bank Holiday before the August crowds in 1914; he would beat that, in a few years, twice or three times over.

The long rainy months of the 1924 season feasted the country with runs; Surrey's great batsmen gorged themselves again at the Oval. The admirable Sandham, plagued by a sharp attack of pneumonia early on, came back in full force in mid-season and ended with both an average and an aggregate above those of his senior partner. In August he hardly ever seemed to get out; he was by now at his prolific peak, an assured neat stylist with a calm restfulness at the heart of his batting that chilled the ardour of the keenest bowlers. Sandham's poised and circumspect confidence was an incalculable assistance to the burgeoning adventurousness with which Hobbs graced this first of his great renascent years. "Less audacious than in his younger days," observed *Wisden*, "Hobbs never inspired greater confidence." His method, as we have seen and will continue to see, was more guarded, but so perfected was his attacking ability that the runs came not a whit more slowly. Sandham collected six hundreds for Surrey, four of them in the welcome heat of August; Hobbs had four, and their county averages were in the sixties. The great partnership reaped this year some of its most splendid rewards, and Shepherd and Jardine backed them bravely; but Surrey's bowling, as always, failed at the last jump, and the superlative scoring could get the county no nearer the head of the table than third. They could press no more than nine wins when Yorkshire at the head managed 16; though it may be parenthetically remarked that in that August an honest fast-medium bowler named Sadler had his great day and Surrey won a terrific game with the champions in the last few minutes of extra time.

But 1924 is more, in the story of Hobbs, than the tale of his happy normality at the head of Surrey's magnificent batting strength. In 1924 there toured this country what must regretfully be labelled a weak South African side; and this weak South African side took a very heavy pounding in the Tests. The most experienced batsmen in the team, Taylor and Nourse, were assisted by a spasmodically brilliant newcomer, Bob Catterall, and such sterling auxiliaries as Susskind and Commaille, but they never struck convincing form and after being disastrously routed by Lancashire in May, lost all but the most tenuous hold on their confidence. As for the bowling, it showed no signs at all of shifting the dauntingly formidable English batsmen. Taylor called on everything he had, including cricketers not even selected for the tour, Aubrey Faulkner for one, but to no very evident purpose; and they lost three Tests, the first two funnily enough by the same margin, an innings and 18 runs. England won the third by nine wickets and weather washed out the other two.

These not very satisfactory Test Matches are chiefly to be noted for the inception in Test cricket of the partnerships of Hobbs and Sutcliffe. They had batted together less than half a dozen times before this season; an early Test trial gave them no particular success; and the first Test at Birmingham was their first full-dress ordeal in the highest class of cricket. It might have been a very unpleasant one, as the sun was shining on a wet pitch and Taylor put England in. A year or two later, eyeing this particular opening pair, he would sooner have cut his own throat; and on this occasion he could see after a couple of overs that he had sold himself, bound and gagged, down the river. The batsmen walked into Taylor's indifferent bowlers with frightening ease; by lunch time they had over 100 on the board and there seemed no weakness in their fluent technique; at 136, scored in two hours and ten minutes, a yorker removed Sutcliffe for 64. Hobbs made 76 and Woolley and Hendren carried on where their forerunners had left off; and next morning when the innings closed for 438, Gilligan and Tate had the whole of South Africa out in three-quarters of an hour for 30, with every attendant circumstance of ignominy and disaster.

They gallantly struck back in the follow-on, but their gallantry could not save them. Hobbs and Sutcliffe, Gilligan and Tate; the two great twin reputations were built on the solidity of the achievements of this single match.

The game at Lord's still further emphasised the inequalities. The South Africans, fighting back after a dreadful start, gave this time an air of reasonable respectability to their first innings total. Catterall made his second successive Test century, and an exhilarating one it was, and the angular Susskind supported him most efficiently. Nevertheless, 273 did not look a lot; and it looked less in the evening light as Hobbs and Sutcliffe jogged comfortably to 28 in the last twenty minutes of the day. Taylor, leading his discouraged team into the field on the Monday, and listening to the crowd as they roared a welcome to their own batsmen, must have thought of Birmingham and made his qualms as secret as he could. They were shared publicly enough by lunch time, when the astonishing pair had in two hours and a half added 200 to their overnight score. The pace of the scoring, the fluent certainty of the stroking, demoralised a bowling side which was partly unused to first-class cricket and almost wholly designed for the mat and helpless on turf. They ran unbelievable short runs without any appearance of haste or danger. Their defence was impenetrable, their attack as commanding and assured as if they had no wickets behind them to lose. When Sutcliffe pulled a ball on to his wicket at 268, the crowd cheered him home, long and loud, for his brilliant 122; and the weary South Africans, lying exhausted among the ruins of their aspirations, looked at the pavilion gate and saw Frank Woolley coming in.

One might have expected the ageing Hobbs, about 140 not out and 41 years old, to be a little leg-weary. As it was, he and Woolley occupied the next hour and twenty minutes in adding another 142 runs; the pace was too hot and furious to describe. Hobbs got his 200 and began to hit at everything; at 211, sublimely careless of the fact that one more run would have given him the highest Test innings ever played in England (knowing no doubt in his bones that whatever he did about it Bradman would be sure to beat it sooner or later) he lifted his head and gave an easy catch. In his great 211 were fifteen fours; but, more significantly in the annals of this unusual veteran, there were 85 singles. The unfailing machine never faltered; Woolley and Hendren went on until Gilligan told them to stop; and next day the bowlers brought victory home.

Once more the great opening batsmen had made a historic beginning; their reputation was now firmly in existence, the talk of cricketers. Hobbs and Sutcliffe were climbing up beside Hobbs and Rhodes, as Hobbs and Sandham were now ranked in eminence with Hayward and Hobbs. In this glamorous access of joint fame they arrived at Sutcliffe's home ground at Headingley for the third Test, walked out to bat to the deep all-embracing approving welcome of 30,000 Yorkshiremen, and in the first over of the match were involved in a nightmarish misunderstanding in the middle of the pitch. All order and principle vanished in a moment of expanding horror and agony; the two batsmen slipped and floundered for what seemed a cavernous eternity in a No Man's Land of danger; and Hobbs saw the length of the wicket stretching between him and safety as the fielder with the ball poised himself to throw. If he had lobbed it to the bowler Hobbs would have been run out by many yards; but he slammed it in hard and wide, and the bad moment ended. They added a somewhat chastened 72, and Sutcliffe made an admirable 83; but the shock had unsettled them and they hoisted no more records together that season. In the very next game, which was the Gentlemen v. Players at Lord's, they struck one of those fearful early-morning Lord's wickets when the ball reared and spat, and Johnny Douglas in particular bowled in his opening spell as venomously as any bowler breathing. Hobbs was beaten to the wide three times in the first over; Sutcliffe was hit sickeningly on the body. The Players began to feel that the toss might with advantage have been lost. Nerve and intelligence prevailed, and though Sutcliffe was unseated early, Hobbs and Hearne, playing with extreme caution, to which the crowd in their infinite and experienced wisdom saw fit to object, piloted the Players through a dangerously ugly period and out into the uplands of easy and abundant scoring. Hobbs' 118 was perhaps his best century of the summer; the Players made over 500; and Freeman and Kilner spun the amateurs out twice at a very low cost.

The season declined to winter, and the touring team made ready, with feelings of mingled confidence and doubt, for their first encounter with Australia since the time of the Armstrong humiliation. Hobbs, of course, was a certainty; but it is interesting and a trifle disturbing to remember that on first being invited he begged to decline, being unwilling to leave his family and his business for the winter. On the strength of this refusal he was left out of the fourth Test, which was designed by the selectors for tourists only. This situation he accepted without a murmur. About the same time he was approached by Lionel Tennyson and asked if he would join a privately-sponsored tour to South Africa that was being financed by Mr. Solly Joel, the terms in this case including a free trip for Mrs. Hobbs. This looked a possible offer; and the M.C.C. when they heard of it made an instant suggestion to him that he go to Australia instead and take his wife with him. This, after chafferings on both sides, was finally and amicably arranged, even though the M.C.C., not being Mr. Solly Joel, could not see their way to paying Mrs. Hobbs' expenses. Never mind; he was happy, the M.C.C. were happy, Mrs. Hobbs was happy and we who knew nothing of what was going on were too happy in our happiness. On such small contentions does history hang. Gilligan took the team out after all with Tate in it, and with Hobbs and Sutcliffe to open; and we who were left in the dark and cold faced the winter months with unwonted hope.

Book Four

HOBBS AND SUTCLIFFE

CHAPTER I

SEASON OF MELLOW FRUITFULNESS

GILLIGAN'S tour of 1924-25 is a kind of Dunkirk; a comprehensive defeat which the perverse and conceited English persist in regarding as a triumph to be celebrated for ever. They lost four Tests and two other games as well; all their bowlers but one were comparative failures, and in the Tests at least only Hobbs and Sutcliffe preserved unjaded the batting reputations with which they left England. In other matches Hendren and Sandham scored heavily, and Woolley played several big innings; but the combination was uneven and too many admirable cricketers did too little for their money or their pleasure. Nevertheless they fought the Tests as they never fought them in 1920 and 1921; the fielding, the enthusiasm, the tension under Gilligan was back where it was in pre-war days; and Tate's wonderful bowling, that put him in the Barnes category without a Foster to back him, brought him 38 wickets in the series and raised him to the level of the most dangerous bowler in the world. Unhappily Gilligan himself had not fully shaken off—in his whole happy and attractive career he never really did—the effects of the blow over the heart he received in the summer of 1924 just before making a beautiful hundred for the Gentlemen at the Oval. It slowed him up and damped down the fire of his aggressive energy. Up to July 1924 he and Tate were the best successors to Barnes and Foster in the business, and superbly destructive too. After that date, though they played together for many seasons to come, Tate went it alone. The 1924-25 Tests were admirable evidence of his ability to do it with relish.

But he could not get the embattled strength of all Australia all out on his own every time; and far too often England had to begin their innings (Gilligan being apparently congenitally incapable of winning the toss) after running about in the field for anything up to two days. In addition to bowling deficiencies, it always seemed that when mishaps were dealt out in the field they were dealt out to the bowlers; Gilligan, Tate and Freeman were all off the field together at one crucial stage, and it is an informative fact that among England's Test bowlers were perforce included Hobbs, Hendren, Chapman, and Whysall, and that Chapman and Hendren with one wicket each were as successful as Johnny Douglas and more so than Dick Tyldesley.

Hobbs and Sutcliffe were the rock and foundation of the batting strength which hoisted us so near to victory; on this tour Sutcliffe came finally into his own especial kingdom. Here is the fourth of Jack Hobbs' great partners; a Yorkshireman of infinite patience and tenacity, with less than the normal bluff and sturdy complacency that characterizes most of his fellow-countrymen, and with more polished and suave sophistication in his appearance and method. If his batting had exactly matched his personal appearance it would have been easy, compact and tailored as few other batting styles have been; but rather curiously it did not, for with all his trim elegance he had an angular stance and an unexpected stiffness of movement that possibly disguised, while it never hindered, an attacking power (particularly in the drive, the pull and the sledge-hammer hook) equalled by only two or three other batsmen in the game. Temperamentally quiet, confident and unshakeable, his mien had a reserve and competent deference about it that always suggested him to me as the exact living model for P. G. Wodehouse's incomparable valet, Jeeves. But do not be blinded by this perverse analogy into thinking of Hobbs and Sutcliffe as master and man. The unresting willowy genius of the one complemented exactly the rooted and reliable oaken genius of the other. As opening partners, of course, they were already far gone in wisdom before they ever went in to bat together; for the watchful unfailing Sandham had by this time let down all the sure anchors by which the Surrey partnership held for so many years, and in Yorkshire Sutcliffe played indispensable foundation to the brilliant and stylish Percy Holmes. It was the fate of these two to live out their Test expectations in the shadow of their two great

superiors; late in time Holmes did partner Sutcliffe once or twice
for England, but a baleful and unrewarding Providence deprived
Sandham for ever of the corresponding honour. And it would not
be doing justice to a number of other excellent opening batsmen
of this decade, Hardinge, George Gunn, Bowley, Whysall,
MacBryan, Hallows—the list goes on for ever—to forget that had
they flourished at any other time they would have been conspicuous
adornments to Test cricket and been welcomed there regularly
with open arms. It is perhaps fitting here to pay a belated tribute
to the unfortunate Jack Russell, a batsman of all the requisite
offensive and defensive powers and a cheerful and prolific performer in all kinds of cricket. There were clearly efforts in 1920
to train him on as Hobbs' standard partner, but a few failures
alienated someone's sympathy; nevertheless when Hobbs went sick
they were glad enough to call Russell back, and he did not often
let them down. On each of the last two occasions when he appeared
for England in England he made a hundred; on the last occasion
when he appeared for England anywhere else he made two hundreds in the match, a feat not lightly accomplished. On the last
occasion when he partnered Hobbs in the Gentlemen v. Players
match at Lord's Hobbs got a hundred in the first innings and
Russell a hundred in the second, so there seems to have been no
fatal or reciprocal distrust; and yet when Sutcliffe came (and who
can say that there was any reasonable alternative?) Russell was
bundled unceremoniously into the shadows. The lesser performers,
so good in themselves, too often go unrewarded not only by their
own fortune but by posterity as well. All cricket-lovers of goodwill
should be glad to remember the excellence of Russell, and of these
other men whom greatness unhappily obscured.

The illustrious partners began the tour modestly enough; there
were a number of minor games interspersed with the major State
matches, and nearly all the five or six regular opening batsmen on
the side had a turn at going in first. Before the Tests began, however, they had hoisted the hundred together twice; and when the
first all-out contest came they rose to it magnificently. Australia
took eight and a half hours to make 450 and then England's openers
coolly put up 157 together, Hobbs making his seventh Test Match
century. England were put in immense good heart, but the depressing pattern of most of the coming series was cut almost at once,

with the middle sliding dangerously out of the batting and only two others reaching 10. The tired and mediocre English bowling failed to back the increasingly valorous lone hand played by Tate, whose eleven wickets in the week-long match for 228 were only a partial reward for his wonderful skill and courage. Australia again reached more than 450 and England were set 605 impossible runs to win. Promptly Hobbs and Sutcliffe answered the challenge; 100 went up once more without a wicket; Arthur Mailey, buying his wicket at a great price, got Hobbs for 57 when the score was 110, and went on to be terribly punished for it by Woolley, who avenged a first-innings duck with a most beautiful and fluent 123. The unshakeable Sutcliffe stayed for a hundred of his own and England's fighting 411 was at that time a record for the fourth innings of a Test. Their defeat was substantial enough; but there had been bravery and independence in their fight, and 1920-21 was clearly far behind.

Within a few days they were at it again, and Gilligan once more lost the toss. Exhilaratingly Tate struck at once, and Collins, Bardsley and Arthur Richardson, beaten and demoralized by the whip and spit of his break back, were all defeated in one way or another before the total reached 50. Then the crushing strength of the home batting prevailed, Ponsford and Taylor wore down the persistent attack and Victor Richardson made fritters of it. All the later batsmen joined in the riot; the innings lasted ponderously and productively to the very end of the second day; and before Mailey was hilariously out the total had reached the then gigantic total of 600. England, nursing sore feet and pondering upon the impenetrability of matter, resigned themselves once more to ignominy.

This Melbourne ground thirteen years before had seen Hobbs and Rhodes about their methodical record-making and had generously rejoiced with them in their triumph. Now it saw Hobbs and Sutcliffe come out to chase 600. It was Saturday, it was as hot as the flagstones of hell, the ground was packed to the outer turnstiles. Hobbs and Sutcliffe stayed in all day; they blunted the fiery edge of Gregory, were circumspect but uncompromising with Kelleway, and did what their whimsy pleased them to do with the flotsam and jetsam served up to them by Hartkopf and the friendly persistent Mailey, sardonic and appreciative. Woolley and Hearne sat tensed on the balcony in their pads from dawn till dusk; from

dawn till dusk the incomparable partners displayed supreme con-
solidating powers of defence to the dangerous bowling, equally
supreme contemptuous powers of dismissal to the looser stuff,
and throughout kept cool heads and light feet for the ever
demoralising quick single. At the end of the day 283 was on the
eloquent scoreboard; and Hobbs and Sutcliffe, and the rest of the
England team, and the whole of England away on the other side of
the world, went to their week-end rest content.

Alas for resurgent hope; Mailey's second ball on Monday hung
longer in the air than the bowler meant or the batsman expected,
and bowled Hobbs on the full pitch. Woolley, pitchforked into the
arena at a split second's notice after an eternity of tension, was
promptly yorked by Gregory; and the avalanche poised, slithered
and came down with a roar, leaving only the impeccable Sutcliffe
unmoved. His 176 was a classic of patience and defiance; after
Hobbs' 154, nobody else got further than the thirties, and there
were some cavernous failures among the more resounding names.
479 was a fine enough total; but not with the memory of that
wonderful opening stand so fresh and so poignant in the consciousness. Yet the amazing Tate nearly overset the balance; he whipped
three of them out for 27, and it looked for a time as if England,
holding on, could at last shape a match to their own design. If
Taylor had not stayed, life for us all would have been very different
that hard winter; but he and the tail-enders saw 250 hoisted before
Tate and Hearne between them finished the job. Tate's 6 for 99
was one of the bravest efforts in a brave series; and the task set
England, a matter of 372, looked at least a possibility. Too much
rested on Hobbs and Sutcliffe to make their personal responsibilities easy to bear; and this time Mailey trapped Hobbs l.b.w. for
22, and not even the trumpet-tongued roll-call of names, Woolley,
Hearne, Hendren, Chapman, Douglas, could avail to sustain the
end that the perennial Sutcliffe was compelled to leave to someone
else. Sutcliffe's two centuries made this one of the great matches
of his life; and mainly through him our defeat by 81 runs seemed
not only as honourable as a victory, but marginal even when
regarded as a defeat.

There was a curious mathematical progression about the Test
results that winter. The Adelaide match, a fluctuating struggle of
the tooth-and-nail order, brought equilibrium within hard

breathing distance. Tate scared the hide off the opening batsmen before the plague of injuries that made this match notorious struck all the England bowlers one by one. Even then six were out for 119, but the tail cut loose and scored heavily against a second-line attack, Ryder making 201 not out and even Mailey achieving 27. Against a total of 489 England changed their batting order on the second evening to keep Hobbs and Sutcliffe for the broad daylight. Hobbs went in next morning at third wicket down; Sutcliffe soon joined him and they stayed together for two hours. Later Hendren scored with freedom and confidence, but without Hobbs' splendid century it would have been a scrappy enough performance. He was removed in the end by the unpredictable Mailey, who according to the tale had arranged that on the first ball of a certain over he would bowl a googly while Jack Gregory at slip would whip behind the unsuspecting batsman and take the catch in the space he would believe unoccupied. Mailey bowled and Gregory moved, as arranged; but the story goes that Mailey forgot to bowl the googly and that Gregory realized this, clamped on the brakes and got back to slip in time to receive a catch off a normal leg-break. Mailey tells this well enough to convince the devil; but to those of us mere fallibles who have fielded at slip and been glad to snatch a blur out of the air and be thankful things were no worse, it is of the order of tall stories that you may believe or not as you please. What is inescapably clear is that Hobbs was out.

England were again over 120 behind, and that night the earlier Australian batsmen led by Ryder spat on their hands and gave the tired and injured bowlers hell. By close of play 211 were on the board and only three wickets down; the triumphing Ryder 86 not out. I and my contemporaries heard the news as we assembled for the opening of the new school term; it made depression even more depressing. Nobody reckoned with a night of rain, which descended in bucketfuls and left the wicket wide open to the only two English bowlers who were able to stand up. Joyfully Woolley and Kilner whaled into the attack, enjoying quite precisely one glorious hour, sixty literal minutes, in which they removed seven inadequately prepared Australians for 39 runs. Once again the fourth innings pattern was laid down; once again too much burden was laid on Hobbs and Sutcliffe. They scored 63 together before Hobbs turned an inswinger into short-leg's hands; but for once the break-through did not immediately follow. Sutcliffe, Whysall, Chapman, all scored over 50, Kilner, Tate and Woolley all had 20's; Gilligan and Freeman with immense courage and tenacity lasted until the next nerve-racking morning, when England needed 27 to win with two wickets to fall and the ground was thrown open to the public free. Red-eyed and sleepless, Gilligan battled on in the teeth of crisis until he over-drove Gregory and chose the wrong fielder to drive to; and Strudwick joined Freeman for the electric end. The ubiquitous Mailey, who had spent the previous night, as was customary with him at crucial moments of his life, playing poker or dancing in his tails, found energy enough to run one un- expectedly away from Freeman's bat, Oldfield performed his duty, and England had lost by 11 runs; after which a messenger was deputed to fetch Sandham, who had fled from the agonizing ordeal of reality into the depths of the nave of Adelaide Cathedral, and to tell him he could come out now, for it was all over.

The story of Hobbs on this tour is primarily the story of the Tests, for it happens that by accident or design he played no cricket of any kind save Test matches after the 16th December, when he had celebrated his 42nd birthday by taking 4 for 15 against a team of Juniors. Thereafter his record was accordingly sparse but hugely impressive; and he began the fourth Test, when Gilligan at last made a good guess, by putting up 126 for the first wicket with Sutcliffe, who himself stayed in all day for 141 not out. Hobbs with 66 and Hearne with 44 were the only two wickets to fall on the first day; and nearly everyone followed up with good runs on the second. England's 548 was a tremendous relief to the weary loyalties of her supporters, and so were the two mediocre and collapse-ridden innings of the Australians, whose displeasure at being beaten by an innings was overlaid by their very genuine and generous delight that their old rival had once more dictated terms to the end. But theirs was the last word; for at Sydney in the last match they clangorously overturned all the tables on to England's confusion and discomfiture, winning a not very high-scoring game by a very wide margin indeed, and hoisting into prominence at a surprisingly late stage in life a wizened painter and decorator of the name of Grimmett, who had the whole side helpless against his round-arm leg-spinners and took eleven wickets in the match for 82 runs. Tate took nine himself, and these two bowlers share the

top honours of an otherwise undistinguished match. Hobbs and
Sutcliffe, collecting 35 runs between them in their four innings,
took no personal joy out of the game; unless Hobbs' native mag-
nanimity could bear to extend itself to the aesthetic pleasure in the
contemplation of Oldfield's miraculous dismissal of him for a duck
in Gregory's first over of the first innings, when Hobbs glanced
Gregory firmly down the leg side and Oldfield made yards to his
left for one of the greatest catches in the history of Test cricket.

It was Sutcliffe's tour rather than England's; and it was also
Tate's. The triumph of these two great cricketers outweighed any
sense of defeat or injustice, if even any injustice were felt. And by
Sutcliffe's side the achievement of Hobbs gave deep satisfaction.
His 573 runs in the series for an average of 63 would have been
phenomenal in itself had not Sutcliffe's 734 at 81 an innings
been there to obscure it. These records were not long for this world;
but while they lasted they were good to contemplate, and their
supersession by others takes none of the initial achievement away.
The arrival of Hobbs and Sutcliffe, as an entity (not Hobbs, not
Sutcliffe, but Hobbs and Sutcliffe, just like that), is a great landmark in the history of batsmanship. In this great Australian season
we see them for a short while at their very finest. They were better
in adversity than in prosperity, as a rule; they were fond of an
obstacle to surmount, a record to break, an impossibility to overcome. There is a great deal more of them to be seen yet; and their
finest moments were still at this stage in the future. For nearly ten
years the cricket world offered Hobbs and Sutcliffe as one of its
prime adornments on the twin levels of art and attainment; and
those of us who were lucky to live through those years held on
grimly to the experience while we had it; for the very satisfaction
that we took in it made us the more conscious of its inevitable
evanescence. They are an enduring part of cricket history; but no
more than anything or anyone else could they outlast the short
term of playing years that their advancing age allowed them.

Sutcliffe, full of honour and wearing it with the elegant restraint
so typical of his whole career, signalized his return by being clean
bowled for 0 in his first innings of the season. Hobbs did nothing
so conspicuous at the outset. He felt particularly fit after his enjoy-
ably strenuous winter, and when May came in fine and warm he
flexed his muscles approvingly, feeling half his age. There were

no touring sides to bedevil the happy routines; the sun shone on the Oval and the wicket was made for runs. Australia had given him ample and valuable practice. He walked out against Hampshire in his first match at the age of 42 to the greatest season of his life, though naturally it made him aware of it by degrees only. Hampshire were lucky to get him out twice under fifty, but in the next game he indulged in a sudden onslaught on Gloucestershire and made a hundred before lunch. (In this game the young Walter Hammond, batting at number two for Gloucestershire, made two noughts; it is sufficiently rare to make a sardonic note of it.) This was on the thirteenth of May; it was early June before Hobbs played through a match in which he did not score at least one century. Glamorgan, Warwickshire, Essex all felt the whiplash of his early form; he had over 600 by the end of May (he had not batted until the ninth, and he missed the Sussex game owing to a slight strain) and by the first of June he had topped 800, giving Notts a prodigious Bank Holiday belabouring in an innings of 189 in something over three hours. Leicester and Lancashire contained him within reasonable limits (in this most prolific of his seasons he was to collect 41 in four innings off Lancashire) but the thirteenth of June saw the beginning of what can only be called a goloptious fortnight in which in the space of four matches, the first three at the Oval, he helped himself to 798 runs. The rational mind dizzies at the thought of this high summer and its enrichment by this batsman, and most of us not there to see it. To think that had he scored just another thirteen in his second innings against Essex (he was caught and bowled for 87 after one hour's incandescent batting, flawless and unbelievable) he would have had six mortal centuries in a row; 107 and 87 against Essex, who had still inadequately atoned for that primeval wrong; 104 and 143 not out against the striplings from his home university who were grateful for the precept and showed it by making 427 for 4 in the last innings and beating a dumbfounded Surrey; 111 against Somerset, since he now had acquired the happy knack; and to ram his point home, 215 against Warwick with a miserable 31 in the second innings to spoil everything. Here he was by the end of June with about 1,700 runs in the bag, in the lordly height of his great maturity, with an answer to every move and more than one to most, the uninterruptible Master at the perfection of his personal art. Typically, he faltered against Yorkshire, who in championship games got him three times that season for a total of 50, and after a splendid though short display for the Players at the Oval he came up against Lancashire on the same ground on a blazing hot Saturday and made 3 and 5, an ignominy which for some reason has irked the marrow of my youthful sensibility from that day to this. He recovered all his prestige in the next week by putting up 140 in an hour and three-quarters with Sutcliffe for the Players at Lord's, though it ought for the record to be admitted that the partnership ended with a run out. (I believe this happened only twice in its whole history.) Hobbs stayed to make 140 on his own, and followed this by contributing a fine 105 to the very satisfactory punishment that Surrey were able for once to deal out to Kent at Blackheath. The date was the 21st July.

Up to that moment he had been to the wickets that season twenty-eight times. His aggregate at this stage does not matter— it was over 2,000—but it is a pointed fact that twelve of these twenty-eight occasions had been centuries. Nor had it escaped the notice of the vigilant that the century against Kent was number 125 in the canon. The mystical figure of 126 had been worshipped for so long wherever Grace was said that as Hobbs gaily and insatiably handed himself hundred after hundred that flaming June and July the religious excitement grew more and more fervid every match. Not only the cricket-lovers knew about it—that was an admirable thing, it was their province and they deserved it, and the batsman in his joy and success was as glad for their sake as for his own—but the papers and the outer public were made to be aware of it too. In our expressive latter-day manner of understatement, a thing was made of it. Spectators who had watched Hobbs all their lives began to be joined, and embarrassed, and not seldom impeded, by cameramen and news sharks and publicity-hounds and all manner of sensation-mongering layabouts who had to ask, as Surrey's openers came out to bat, which was the one they had been told they must come to see. Droves of these creatures began to move with him from match to match; they pestered him for his autograph, his photograph, for anything that was his; they rang him up and asked what can only be described as damn silly questions; they converted the pursuit of a somewhat obscure sporting record into a nation-wide man-hunt with bloodhounds. Those of us who were simply followers of the game and admirers of the greatest living player of it wanted this record as passionately as he did, because in a curious primitive tribal fashion he was doing it for us and we were helping him do it. Our good wishes as he went in to bat must have seethed round him until he felt them physically. We ached for him; and the publicity-mongers, seizing on our instincts for hero-worship, curdled up the whole nerve-racking situation into a vast simmering stunt, as alien to the cricketer at the centre of it as to his lifelong admirers round the grounds.

After that Kent match Fate roasted him for weeks at a slow fire. The weather broke, to begin with; this perhaps slightly unsteadied his almost mechanically perfect technique. Almost certainly he must by now have been prone to a mid-season staleness; and the artificial zinging-up of the natural nervous tension fretted his concentration. When the whole circus went to Brighton to see him do it, he was out for 1; and for match after match after this a malicious disaster time and again whipped the trophy from his grasp. He could not be said to fail; following the Brighton debacle, he played seven innings for 250 runs and one not out, an average of over 40 an innings, which would lose nobody his week's money; but these fifties and forties and thirties frayed the irascibilities of the gentlemen of the Press as if he had made a formal promise which it was a point of honour to keep, and had deliberately broken it. The classic poster was "Hobbs Fails Again," the evening after he had made either 54 or 49, I forget which. He has not said so, and it is like him to keep silent about it; but it must have played the devil's own tune on tired and jangling nerves. Neither did it ever seem to occur to anyone at the time, though it occurred to him, that this almighty fuss was being made about a putative innings that would equal a record, not beat it. He himself could do little about this, but bear himself tranquilly and withdraw his mild gaze from the yellower Press; and renew his hopes each time he went to the wicket, with a modest proviso that when success came it would be very gratifying if it could come at the Oval.

The match that brought him the prize is a classic by now; a classic on account of it, and the fine questing struggle that grew up round it. One of cricket's finest writers happened to be playing in it; and R. C. Robertson-Glasgow's gay and admiring account in his autobiography of the setting and the drama that was played out in it makes it superfluous for anyone else, especially one who was pronouncedly elsewhere at the time, to utter a single word on the subject. The Surrey v. Somerset match at Taunton on 15th August 1925 is as well known as any cricket match in recent history; but as this is Hobbs' story, and Hobbs' story would be incomplete without a word on this game, the familiar contours of its progress must at least be lightly traced once more.

The Taunton ground was bung-full on the Saturday morning, and the inevitable film-men were creaking about on the tin pavilion roof to the accompaniment of generally-voiced hopes that they would fall off it. Somerset postponed immediate tension by winning the toss, but not for long; Surrey had them out for 167 by tea time, and the professional spectators busied themselves with the preliminaries. Hobbs started, for him, shakily enough. Someone caught him at cover in the first over, off a no-ball; one or two shots went unexpectedly in the air. The bowling was, as it should be, methodically savage. Hobbs played himself gradually into safety. Donald Knight, joining him when Sandham left at 50, flowered almost at once into his 1919 form. It is a deprivation not to have seen that lovely batsman at his best; and he and Hobbs that evening displayed two facets of beauty for all who cared to enjoy it. For once Hobbs was inhibited by circumstance, and Knight was not.

They had added 96 when Hobbs laid the ball dead at his feet and moved into a run. Wilfred Rhodes would have responded on the dot; Sandham or Sutcliffe would have given him the denial in the necessary split second. Knight did neither; he hesitated, said "No," and realized Hobbs was almost upon him. The fielder had the ball in his hand. Either way it was a dead loss. Knight with exemplary promptness ran himself out; Jack Hobbs has never forgotten this. All men of good will applaud Knight's chivalry without reserve; but look for a moment at the cavernous alternative. He made the right choice, for there was honestly no other. Hobbs survived that night, 91 not out, the Somerset authorities happy for financial reasons that he had not reached the hundred before the close.

After a barricaded week-end, with reporters skirmishing on the outskirts and every train from London bringing reinforcements past his hotel window, he took up the delayed struggle on the Monday morning. Even then the turnstiles could not get the fighting millions into the ground by the starting time, and play was held up at Somerset's diffident request until the last homuncule had been packed in. The enormous throng buzzed like bees; Bridges and Robertson-Glasgow were refreshed and keen, searching for evidence of tension, trying for the fast yorker, giving no insulting quarter. Three inched singles got him to 94; then Robertson-Glasgow, putting the extra venom into a yorker, bowled a no ball. No catch this time; a spectator threw it back, 98 up, two to go. He turned another single off his legs to bring him to face Bridges' next over, and once more Somerset rang all its congratulatory bells as he played Bridges wide of mid-wicket and Jardine ran through with him to make the single and the century complete. The cameras whirred and clicked and the boys jumped up and down on their seats, the Somerset men crowded happily around to shake his hand. The record had been equalled, not beaten, but the crowd and the Press were satisfied; Hobbs handed to a ground-boy a prepared telegram for his wife, and in the midst of the excitement Fender was observed advancing from the pavilion with a celebratory bottle and glass. With this the hero toasted the crowd, the liquor being variously reported in the Press as champagne and whisky, and later by Hobbs himself as ginger ale; after which noxious draught it is no wonder that he only added one more run before the wicket-keeper caught him, and he came back to the most needed relaxation of his career. Normality returned with a palpable rush; Errol Holmes went in to bat; and nearly all the vast crowd got up and went home.

The later Surrey batsmen, led primarily by Fender, saw the side's score with excellent consistency to 359. History would have been significantly different if Somerset's second innings had been as flimsy as their first, but MacBryan and Young played with great skill and courage and MacBryan's beautiful century got good support from the later batsmen. Somerset prolonged their innings until lunch on the last day, and Surrey were left, a little to their surprise, with as many as 183 to make to win.

Everyone had gone home, the Press had folded up its tents, there were no cameras on the stands, the world was on holiday. It was I think an entirely admirable thing that whereas the whole publicity world took the febrile impact of Hobbs' 126th century, it was the handful of cricket lovers, the unassuming faithful, the un-

vociferous, the dedicated, who were privileged to enjoy the
master-spectacle of the decisive, the important 127th. Hobbs
dropped all his cares and played with the Somerset attack until,
all but White, it disintegrated before him. He hunted down the
wicket like the Hobbs who batted with Hayward, he let his hair
down and exploited his skill like a conjurer at a Command Performance. It was a display to bedazzle even the elect; and as indispensable aid to glory there stood well out of the limelight at the
other end the unrewarded and selfless Sandham, judging to a nicety
his chosen part in the business of the day. He diagnosed it to an
inch; Hobbs got the hundred with nine runs still to win, this wonderful display brought him the match and the triumph over Grace
and his fourteenth century of the season (another record this), a
bagful of golden return for two-and-a-half hours' work—and for
ever after he has never thought of the struggle and stress and
success epitomized in this one famous fixture without coupling it
in honour in his mind with the name of Sandham, who shared the
burden but would not share the glory.

There were a few more moments to 1925; the disappointment
that he could not have broken the record at the Oval being partly
allayed, first by a congratulatory message from Buckingham Palace
and secondly by a magnificent welcome given him by the Surrey
members and spectators when he next appeared to bat on his home
ground. Then a week or two later, the highest score ever, 266 not
out, in a Gentlemen and Players match, this time at Scarborough,
and his own highest ever too. Then a hundred against Yorkshire
the Champion County at the Oval, bringing his centuries for the
season to the record number of sixteen; and in the second innings
the attainment for the only time in his life of a total of 3,000 runs,
and his rightful place, never before achieved, at the top of the
batting averages. He was getting on for forty-three; and if ever a
prime was royal, it was Jack Hobbs' in that grand climacteric
season of 1925, the established schoolboys' hero and the perennial
wonder of the whole of the cricket world.

This was the time of his adoption into the common consciousness of England; his acceptance by the whole population, whether
they cared for cricket or not, as a representative figure, a symbol
making do for the game itself in the minds of even the least engaged
individuals. His features became familiar, in newspapers and on

placards and on hoardings, pleasant and mildly contemplative under the England cap with the George and Dragon crest. He became associated in the common mind with a popular brand of cigarettes, which I very much hope for his own sake he did not smoke himself, although a modest addiction to the weed was one of his companionable weaknesses. His sober and unexacting habits were often, during these years of his great fame, made the subject of more or less relevant homilies from pulpits up and down the country, from which he was, deservedly no doubt but I cannot judge with what propriety, held up to all and sundry as an exemplar and epitome of the more attainable Christian virtues. A quiet and self-effacing churchgoer himself, he may have felt that he never courted this, nor such popularity as accrued to him from Wayside Pulpit asseverations of teetotalism.* Yet these extravagances incidental to an inevitable publicity in no way contradicted the true picture of a solid and attractive personality wearing what might have been overwhelmingly encumbering laurels with a natural lightness and grace. He was taken into the home and hearth of the whole cricket world, paper boys and bus conductors, barristers, journalists, peers of the realm and the Royal Family—but that is the prerogative of any public figure who answers a common demand for an idol as a symbol. What was far more to the point was that his friends and colleagues and opponents on the field of their expert play all echoed the less informed praises of the crowd. The verdict of them all has been that they did not know whom to admire more, the batsman or the man, the skill or the character, the technical resource or the unassuming integrity, the expert colleague or the quietly entertained or entertaining friend. The private character of the man, affectionately cherished by all who knew him or played with him, never manifested itself in the public *persona* affected by some popular players; he never projected his own nature into quips and cranks to amuse the ringside; it was not in his nature to show himself as anything but a cricketer playing the game he was there to play. The amazing warmth of the communal and national feeling for him was in general a response to his immense skill and the

---

*A conspicuously temperate man, he never professed or practised total abstinence from liquor. I myself have had the pleasure and privilege of helping him to dispose of a bottle of *vin rosé;* and he seemed to enjoy it as much as I did.

spectacular results of that skill, but was perceptibly heightened by the humane and attractive grace of character which accompanied it and was evident in every gesture and movement. Among his friends and fellow-players he had a warm uncourted popularity; he leavened his natural retiring diffidence with an unexpected vein of humour, dead pan and deceptive, which on occasions took a practical turn and made him a character of whom wise men needed at times to be wary. It must be recorded that he probably needed all his popularity and more to get away with the continual repetition of some of the merry japes the historians father on to him; and let us hope that his celebrated dressing-room performance, contrived at the expense of some preoccupied next man in with his back to the game, afforded the victims as much innocent merriment as it did the joker, who in a pensive attitude would remark explosively, "He's done it!" a simple enough exclamation which on occasion was known to propel a nervous batsman convulsively out of the door under the impression that a wicket had fallen. One great day a wretched dupe, startled into action in this way, was accompanied right out on to the steps and half way to the gate by a solicitous Patsy Hendren, and only found when he arrived on the grass that the game was tranquilly proceeding uninterrupted. It is the constant repetition of such stories, and of those of not-out batsmen when a wicket had fallen being detained in absorbed conversation and being mysteriously without a bat when the time came to bowl the next ball, which convinces the cold-blooded reader of the essential goodness and charm and popularity of the man who could continue to be responsible for these agreeable extravagances and yet not be taken vengefully apart in consequence.

It was this humane artist who gave flesh and blood to the newspaper fame in those days. For his runs and the gay precision with which he made them, we gave him all our youthful worship. We agonized when he was in, with perhaps less reason than with any other living batsman; but youth is illogical in its emotions, and had he not done the same by Hayward? What we never considered, as we watched him go in to bat, was how this massive tribal worship affected his nerves or his play. Could he fail to be aware, almost palpably aware, of this concentration of hope and good wishes? Was not this terrific burden of vicarious responsibility almost too much for one man to bear? When you or I get out, our mistake and downfall disappoint us and perhaps our team; when he got out, he spoiled the day for thousands. It was difficult to know whether he let this disturb him. Later in time, I believe it to have affected Hutton; but Jack Hobbs was less rigidly disciplined. He did not hag-ride his imagination. Thinking of his classic mastery, it is tempting to impute to him a classic imagination, of the Shakespearian order; but I know in all sobriety that this is an illusion; he was merely a great games player with no necessary endowment of any other supreme greatness. It is possible that he had no imagination at all, and that this was the making of him in his craft and his art. Whatever assisted him to it, he gave us in those seasons of his rich plenty; we grew up in the bounty of the maturity of an artist among his own kind, who added to his artistry the natural graces of a friendly and reliable man.

CHAPTER II

THE FINEST HOURS

APART from the milk and honey that flowed so bountifully in the summer of 1925, there are few crucial occasions to mark the progress of Jack Hobbs through the tale of Surrey cricket at the time of his prolonged success in the 'twenties. It is almost impossible to chronicle this rich productive time without either swamping the surrounding country with statistics or seeming unfairly to pass over the recurring centuries as commonplaces. The great years unrolled slowly and inevitably, one cannot isolate one or another with any precision. Between 1919 and 1934 there were two seasons only when his average was less than fifty, and one of those was the last of all when he was 51 years old and playing out of a capacious memory. And he regards 1925 as his best season, but we look down the rows of figures and see that in 1926 his average was 77 (which beat that of his *annus mirabilis* by fully seven points) and in 1928 it was 82, a prodigious feat for a man of 45 by present-day or any other standards. Averages are pointers only, and tell us little of the class of his cricket; yet it is to be hoped that we are aware of this already, and can use the figures with intelligence to grasp something of the energy and consistency with which for season after middle-aged season this multivarious expertise was deployed. There was, as this great period unfolded itself, comparatively little hot news value in a Hobbs century. One of these happened along on the average once every ten days or so during a season, and sometimes they came oftener; one would turn to Surrey's score in the stop press, or switch on the radio, and there it would be, "Surrey 368 for 4; Hobbs 106, Sandham, or perhaps

164

Shepherd or Ducat, 153 not out." Hobbs had made his hundred rapidly and efficiently and departed to give the next man a knock, choosing with deceptive carelessness the bowler he had punished most to give his wicket to. After the fabulous sixteen in 1925, ten came in the following year, seven in 1927 (when he was out of the side for a month or more with a skin complaint), twelve in 1928, again ten in 1929. The list goes on, I do not need to add to it, the point I hope has been sufficiently made. It is of little use to comment that for many reasons this kind of consistency does not occur nowadays. Bowling has developed sealing techniques hostile to ready run-getting, conditions of one kind and another have altered against the batsman's interest, and at present there are no batsmen playing with sufficient inventive genius to overcome these handicaps. I see no reason to suppose that Jack Hobbs, who broke the power of the googly and who never until his late retirement acknowledged any bowler to be too fast for him to play with comfort, could not have met and beaten the present-day challenge.

Scattered about these years were the satisfying landmarks. In the middle of the 1926 season he and Sandham put up a little matter of 428 for the first wicket. The victims were Oxford University; there was an apocryphal rumour that academic representations had been made in an injured tone of voice because Surrey had been in the habit of fielding less than their strongest team to play the aspiring students, and that Surrey acceded to the request by heading their batting order with Hobbs and Sandham, who then duly performed as stated. Hobbs made 261, flexing himself for a Test Match against Australia to begin next day, in which he duly made 119. The other major feat of arms which he performed that year for Surrey was the establishment of the record individual score at Lord's. Up to a year before this had unbelievably been still the property of a gentleman in a top hat named William Ward, who had made 278 far back in the 1820's. Hendren some seasons ago had most tantalisingly been left high and dry at 277 not out; and it was left to the admirable Percy Holmes to thrash Middlesex all over their home turf in 1925 for a monumental 315 not out, and to cherish for himself this excellent consolation prize for his failure to be thought worthy of more representative honours. Poor Percy Holmes, one cannot help being sorry for him; after all that, he was to hold the record for not much more than a year. Hobbs,

after carrying his bat right through Surrey's innings against
Middlesex at the Oval for 176, went many points better three
weeks later at Lord's and carried on to 316, when with the record
in his pocket the innings was very properly declared closed.

In 1926 he was granted a second benefit. Surrey had opened a
testimonial fund for him after the triumph of 1925, but they generously saw that it did not interfere with the greater occasion. They
honoured him with the Notts match on August Bank Holiday
Saturday, an unusual procedure and at that time a gold mine as
well as a compliment. Arthur Carr defied the tonsilitis that had
interrupted his Test captaincy, and Hobbs tossed with him before
an enormous crowd. The game itself provided little of the glamour
and drama of the great Kent match of 1919, and Hobbs failed to
make a century; but well over £2,000 came into the kitty and in
those days that was up among the records.

1927, 1928, 1929—in the combined annals of Jack Hobbs and
Surrey these English seasons merge into a mellifluous sunlit haze,
punctuated by the inevitable hundreds. One week in May 1927
stands out of the background; the story is not all Hobbs, but he is
part of it as he was part of all those seasons. In the cold
early matches of a showery season Surrey led off with a match
against Hampshire on Saturday 7th May. The wicket was wet
and tricky and Hobbs made 112 in his best bad-wicket manner;
and in the second innings when the devil had dried out he put on
152 with Sandham and made 104. The spectators, gorged with
greatness of every kind and style, were alternately being feasted
with honourable and tenacious orthodoxy in the form of two centuries in the same bountiful match from the estimable journeyman
all-rounder Jack Newman. At the end of the game they were almost
too sated with runs to applaud; but those who showed up smiling
on Wednesday the eleventh saw Surrey lead off against Gloucestershire with 557 for 7. Hobbs made only 46, but Shepherd (who, I
forgot to say, had made 120 against Hampshire) made a brilliant
277 not out with the valued assistance of 142 from Ducat. Then,
to crown a week where the prolific extremes of batsmanship would
seem to have been reached already, the thrice happy spectators
were treated to two magnificent hundreds from Walter Hammond,
on his destroying passage to his thousand runs in May. To have
been alive and at the Oval in that week of May in 1927 was the

fortunate lot of comparatively few; let us hope that they appreciated to the full the measure of their luck, and that first and second-generation grandchildren are already being familiarized with the tale.

Yet these middle and later years of the rich decade were enlivened most conspicuously by the two great Test series with Australia, the first in England in 1926 and the second in Australia in the winter season of 1928-29. There is one strangely unfortunate element that seems a constant recurrent in the story of these series; and that is that the two sides never seemed to attain their greatest strength at the same time. Thus Armstrong's wonderful side of 1921 had as feeble opposition as Warner's of 1911 had had; and Chapman's in 1928, a team of genius as well as talent, caught the Australians in a disjunctive transitory moment of uncertainty that righted itself too late. Much later in time, Bradman's unbeaten combination of 1948 were never severely tested; and when Laker decimated Ian Johnson's eleven in 1956 he found no resistance worthy of the name.

The 1926 series might have disproved any general theory which these scattered observations might suggest; for Australia were still compactly formidable both in veteran and newly-tried batsmen and in accurate and menacing bowlers of intelligence and pertinacity. Moreover there was the general feeling on both sides that four to one had been an unfair measure in 1924-25 of Australian superiority over Gilligan's uneven but gifted team. It followed that the 1926 series was awaited, by the English particularly, with unprecedented keenness. Unhappily two factors combined to distort what might have been a superlative Test series. One was the weather, which ruined two of the games beyond repair; the other was the manifest impossibility, which ought to have been realized and acted on as early as 1921, of containing a modern Test Match within three days. With batsmen like Bardsley and Woodfull and Macartney on one side, and Hobbs and Sutcliffe on the other, it only needed one long partnership for each team for the match to be doomed to a draw at once. The danger was recognized in 1926 to the sufficient but revolutionary extent of making the last Test timeless. Inevitably it was the only one finished; the only one where Greek met Greek with no holds barred; and for the first three days it was as withers-wringing a struggle as any story book

could have projected in imagination. It is one of the best-known
Tests of all time, and Jack Hobbs played in its greatest moments
of tension one of the leading parts.

The Nottingham Test had been ignominiously drowned, only
forty-minutes play being possible. Hobbs and Sutcliffe kept their
feet in the slush and scored 32, and that was all. At Lord's the
game was again drowned, but this time in runs rather than rain.
The wicket, in spite of the extravagances of a stray hose-pipe, gave
no trouble, and no bowler could strike either fire or spin from it.
Bardsley batted all through the Australian first innings for 193, his
last great contribution to Test history. Hobbs and Sutcliffe
countered a substantial total by making 182 for the first wicket;
Hobbs was an unusual blend of brilliance and restraint, but he
made 119, and everyone who batted made over 50. Sutcliffe and
Woolley made over 80 each and Hendren's was the second England 100, which all took up so much time that the Australian
second innings, including a most brilliant century from Macartney,
was little more than a formality.

Runs again were the undoing of the third Test after an enliven-
ing opening over. Carr gambled by sending Australia in, Sutcliffe
caught Bardsley off the first ball of the match and Carr agonizedly
dropped Macartney off the fifth. Macartney then made 100 before
lunch and Woodfull and Richardson both made centuries as well.
England faltered in the first innings after the inevitable openers
had made 59 together; but in the follow-on the game was made
safe enough by the same pair's confident and decisive 156. Hobbs
with 49 and 88 bore and wore down the chief menace of the
bowling; but the match like the previous one went to fritters long
before its end. The Manchester Test that followed was virtually a
two-day affair. Macartney got his third Test century running and
Woodfull his second; Australia made 335, and England in the
short time available made a consistent if undistinguished reply,
making 305 for five. Hobbs' 74 was second in size to Ernest
Tyldesley's 81, but his most memorable contribution to the match
was the captaincy of England, an honour visited upon him on the
second day when Carr's illness prevented him from fielding, and
when in spite of the presence of an amateur in the side he was un-
animously agreed upon as the worthiest substitute.

So the question of the Ashes was left to the Oval, as everybody had been secretly hoping it would. The Press and the public seethed with excitement, and nation-wide artificial build-ups were administered to the game, the Ashes, and the contestants for weeks before the event. With the fate of the other run-swollen Tests in mind, it was anticipated that this match would be engorged with vast and slowly-compiled scores and would last somewhere between a week and a fortnight. England sprang two surprises in the selection of her side. Carr was abruptly relinquished and Chapman substituted for him as captain; and Wilfred Rhodes was hurriedly recalled at the age of 49, as being so universally proficient that if he failed in one department of the game he could hardly help making up for it in another. To spice the situation with variety, the bowler who had the best analysis at Manchester, Root, was dropped; and so was the batsman who had made top score, Ernest Tyldesley. To strengthen the batting, George Brown was brought in to keep wicket instead of Strudwick, but an injury prevented this drastic change being made.

The timeless Marathon began before an excited crowd. It was not as vast as had been expected; there were some, and I speak from feeling experience, who were put off from attending this game or any part of it by the fear of being shut out or having to stand all day; I have bitterly regretted this all my life. The spirits of irony were about the Oval that day; the slow and elaborate amassing of runs resolved itself into a series of brilliant and evanescent little Saturday afternoon innings by batsmen who showed they should know better. England were all out for a glad-rag kind of 280; Australia, pinned to defence except for a brilliant little piece of bravura by Macartney, lost four wickets for 60 by the end. Sutcliffe's sterling 76 gave invaluable steadiness to a strangely hysterical innings. Hobbs, continuing to cherish that happy little rivalry with Arthur Mailey, each believing that he is the other's master,* dropped a point in the game by being bowled in the politest way possible and, not for the first time, by a full toss. As he made 37 in under an hour, the set-back undid the confidence of

---

*Mailey has set it on record that he once pointed out to Oldfield, who agreed with him, that Hobbs could not spot his googly. Sir Jack dissents in the friendliest manner; and adds that Oldfield probably agreed with Mailey just to stop him talking.

his successors; and he doubtless felt as much of a fool as he thought he looked.

On the Monday the crowd poured in and the gates had to be closed at noon. Australia cannily consolidated, manoeuvring the initiative away from the buoyant bowlers; Collins, Gregory and a resolute tail eschewed all risk and gained a lead of 20, batting nearly all day in broiling sun. It was admirably intent cricket; the half way stage came as awkwardly for England as could be, but with the balance resting precariously in equilibrium. Their 20-run lead was valuable, and might be more so, depending on the resilience of England's reply; yet the fourth innings drag was Australia's and the disadvantage of this was at that stage impossible to calculate. The match was therefore, at five-thirty on the Monday evening, almost perfectly poised.

Hobbs and Sutcliffe made no bones about the tricky hour's tussle. They batted it out calmly and without hurry, since time in this unusually-planned contest had ceased to be of the essence. Had Australia had the penetrative powers of the Gregory and Macdonald of 1921, the task would have been fiercely intensified; but Macdonald was playing by now for Lancashire, and the Gregory of 1926 retained little of his old menace. He was handicapped by a leg injury, and indeed when this present game began he had yet to take a wicket in the whole series. The striking force of the attack was therefore entrusted primarily to Grimmett and Mailey; and these were not the bowlers on a good wicket to worry the composure of Hobbs and Sutcliffe, assuming that Mailey refrained from bowling full tosses. The England batsmen made 49 that night without stress or strain; and relaxed themselves for the morrow's watchful consolidation. Woolley was to follow them, and Hendren, Chapman and Stevens and Rhodes, batsmen of great attainments; the Oval wicket lay before them unspoiled, and the attack as they well knew had been mastered before and could easily be mastered again. The sleep of the England cricketers and supporters that night was one of reposeful confidence.

That same night the broiling heat broke up in storm. The whole of South London that had sweltered through the Monday in a steamy discomfort was engulfed in a violent cloudburst. The Oval had its share; the fierce rain thrashed across that easy-paced paradise, delivered gallons of moisture into the packed roots. When the spectators began assembling on the Tuesday the wet seats were smoking in the warmth, the ground was ominously green. Grimmett and Mailey surveyed the scene contentedly, practising spin. England players, trying the soaked turf with their feet, looked gloomily at the prospects. The storm had passed, the sun was beginning to come through, the earth was warming as they waited. The feeblest imagination saw that stretch of grass as a potential cauldron of unholy hates. The confidence of last night had gone down the swollen gutters of Kennington.

Hobbs and Sutcliffe, picking their way among the sawdust-patches, were the most imperturbable of all England's elect. This was in fact Sutcliffe's speciality, what later publicists might call his gimmick; he not only revelled in adversity, but took an ostentatious pleasure in pretending an ignorance of it. He asserted that morning to Neville Cardus that he did not know that there had been a storm at all, implying that he cared precious little whether there had or not. Hobbs, taking or affecting a more realistic view, looked down his famous nose at the pitch and declined to commit himself. At present it was less venomous than it would be in an hour or so; he was content to play through it as best he could. Prodding the pitch after the first exploratory over, he remarked to Sutcliffe in the middle, in one of the classic understatements of Western civilization, "Pity it rained in the night."

They settled slowly in to counter the tricks of Mailey, Grimmett, Macartney and the tall medium-paced swinger Arthur Richardson. As the first few overs proceeded, the sun came out and a gentle wind stirred the flags on the pavilion roof. Lovely redeeming Nature, bringing balm after rain, sunlight after shadow; but what of the hell-brew seething up under the turf as the sun shone and the breeze blew and the ground dried and caked? Hobbs and Sutcliffe, watching narrowly, saw one or two early deliveries pop. These they stifled at the pitch or let go. Hobbs in particular knew better when to let a ball alone than any batsman breathing; Sutcliffe was quick to learn and exploit the same aptitude. The tense duel began under the August sunshine. Macartney not many years before could have polished this business off in a few overs, but with age and concentration on batting his power of spin was reduced within the batsmen's ability to foresee and play it. Grimmett, two or three years later, with his infernal accuracy and two kinds of googly would have perhaps worked up a penetrating subtlety to defeat even these two masters. Mailey, who always used the air rather than the pitch for his deceitful effects, gave their vigilance too much time to anticipate his dangers. The serious menace appeared to be Richardson. He bowled with resolute accuracy to a packed leg-field, coming round the wicket at the batsman on to the line of the leg stump; his off-spinners bit and rose, but the wonderful power of wrist neutralized the venom time after time.

He, or Collins the captain, has been criticized since for not bowling over the wicket to a normal field, bringing Andrews at point bang up on to the bat, and relying on the evil wicket to find a groping edge for him. He could retort that with Hobbs and Sutcliffe there were no groping edges; but Hobbs for one was never a hundred per cent free from disaster with the ball that left the bat, and on that wicket the most orthodox delivery was prone to fly every which way. The story goes that Hobbs and Sutcliffe knew this as well as anyone, not having been born yesterday, and that part of their technique was to induce Collins to keep Richardson bowling at them as long as he could be so persuaded. They felt they could play the leg-theory but were doubtful about any other unknown quality; therefore, they argued, we will kid Collins that Richardson is bothering us and may shortly dismiss us; better the devil we can play than the devil we may not be able to. It therefore pleased Hobbs to seem to falter against Richardson from time to time, and to notice that Collins saw him do it. Nowadays he is liable to deny all this and say that he and Sutcliffe stayed there by just playing down the line, and we should listen with respect and keep our own ignorant reservations if we will. By whatever means they weathered this mortal storm, they weathered it; and whenever a loose ball arrived they made runs off it; and they ran those close singles as only they can run them. I have seen a Press photograph taken on this great morning, with the sawdust-patches all over the field and the Australians breathing hard at the batsmen's necks, where Hobbs is off down the wicket and Sutcliffe half way home with the ball killed stone dead within three feet of the bat's end.

At lunch the score was 161; they had added 112 that morning in what *Wisden* describes as rather less than two hours and a half.

At the mercy of this terrible wicket, this keen and menacing attack, these two had scored what today would be regarded as a highly abnormal quota of runs. Hobbs was 97 not out, so near to the first and only hundred he ever made against Australia at his own beloved Oval. The frenzied cheers of the delighted crowd liberated them from their own and the nation's tension as they came happily in. Giving the malevolent wicket a final prod, they unbent and congratulated each other; probably each confessing to the other for the first time, and then in a kind of unspoken undertone, the burden of the ordeal.

Immediately after lunch came the culmination of Hobbs' wonderful hundred; and an over later he relaxed vigilance and Gregory bowled him. The weather and the Australians had been worsted, whatever happened now; and Sutcliffe stayed nearly all day to make a certain thing of it. The persistent Mailey beat him in the last over of the day, when his 161 had become not only the root but the oaken heart of his side's substantial total. Next day the weather spasmodically interfered again, and the Australians, beginning their uphill fourth innings on the wrong foot, collapsed before Larwood and Rhodes and were sunk with surprisingly little trace. Had the body of their resistance been equal to their first innings tenacity the match would have been one in a million; as it was, it remains one in a thousand. And the cheering, milling, stampeding Oval crowd, seething that night round the pavilion and calling for Hobbs and Sutcliffe and Rhodes, knew in their hearts whom to thank for the recovery of the Ashes. There is reason to rate that hour before lunch on the Tuesday, when Hobbs and Sutcliffe outfaced both art and nature, as the finest hour of Jack Hobbs' cricketing life.

There was a strangely parallel performance a couple of years later; and this is the focal dramatic moment of the satisfyingly successful tour of 1928-29. This is Chapman's tour; the tour that ranks in Jack Hobbs' memory with Warner's of 1911-12 as the greatest extended moments in the century for English cricket. It is the last time he went to Australia as a player; and he went with a team of resounding names that still catch at the imagination, a team of great bowlers and great batsmen and great fielders under a popular and inspiring captain; a team from which it was considered possible to omit Woolley, who had made over 3,000 runs in the season just completed. This time Hobbs and Sutcliffe had Jardine and Philip Mead* as well as Hendren in the line of the middle batting to assist their opening efforts; and Leyland and Ernest Tyldesley were an unusually valuable second line of offence. But their chief auxiliary was the man to whom England was destined to look for the next dozen years at least as Jack Hobbs' successor as her premier batsman, and who made this tour peculiarly his own—the great Walter Hammond. Coming to Test cricket a little later than his promise warranted (for in 1924 he was not sufficiently established, there were no Tests in 1925 or 1927, and in 1926 he was out of the game through illness), he arrived with his maturity compact and complete, and with a trial run or two against South Africa and the West Indies, he emerged in his first extended brush with Australia as England's greatest discovery since Sutcliffe and the most powerful forcing batsman in the game. In this his greatest tour he achieved a first-class average of 91 and a Test average of 113; and had there been no Bradman his unbelievable aggregate of 905 runs for the Test series itself would be unchallenged to this day. All reference to the famed 1928-29 tour must pay prime homage to this great cricketer before all others, who made two 200's in the Tests as well as two other hundreds, both in the same match; but Hendren and Hobbs and Sutcliffe had averages of 50 or more too; and with the effective bowling well shared by Larwood and Tate, Geary and Jack White, the finest all round team to represent us against Australia for a generation concluded the series with four victories to one and nothing but the very ominous promise of Bradman to disturb its dreams of the future.

At the beginning of this tour Hobbs' personal touch seemed a little faulty, and though he made runs enough he was reported as being somewhat below form. Immediately overshadowed by extraordinary runs of hundreds by Hammond, Jardine and Hendren, the opening partners took an unobtrusive background place, emerging against South Australia with a century stand and alternately assisting Jardine, when they were split up, to lucrative totals. Everyone made runs in the first Test which England won by 675

---

*Mead had not been to Australia since Warner's tour; and was greeted by a welcoming Australian who said how particularly pleased he was to meet him as he remembered so well seeing his father in 1911.

runs; Hobbs and Sutcliffe, adequately but modestly, got their forties and thirties and were content. In the second Test, another heavy trouncing was administered, Hammond got the first of his double centuries and though Australia fought back against a huge total they only just contrived to make England bat again. Hobbs remembers the match less for his innings of 40 than for the unparalleled reception the crowd gave him on the Saturday, the day before his 46th birthday, when a presentation was made to him during an interval for rain and he was persuaded against his natural diffidence to walk round the Sydney ground. I have the word of a spectator who was there as a small and hero-worshipping boy, that there was never a popular reception like it.

The third Test at Melbourne provided the striking parallel already referred to with the great Oval triumph of 1926. Its early stages were as evenly conducted as those at the Oval for after three and a half days England led by 20, thanks mainly to Hammond. In the second Australian innings Woodfull made one of his cagey hundreds and the young and as yet unsuspected Bradman stayed up the tottering second half of the side with a very fine century on his own account, the first of a very large number in Test cricket. The sixth day dawned with eight Australian wickets down and just under 350 on the board, and, what was infinitely more significant, the very evident traces of a powerful rainstorm on the wicket. The pitch was in fact too wet for play to begin until one o'clock; Ryder, captaining Australia, did not have the wicket rolled; and the hot Melbourne sun came out in full force to bedevil England's chances of making 332—a considerable job of work at the best of times, but now, with a Melbourne special bubbling and spitting under their feet, a vanished impossibility.

Experienced and sympathetic old cricketers, Test men of old, watching critically from the pavilion and assessing all chances, allowed England the bare outside chance of 80 runs on that evil rubbish-heap. There was a transcendent batting side massed in the pavilion, and they knew it; that was why they generously gave them as many as 80. They were of the opinion that an Australian team, faced with a like task, would be lucky to reach 60. But being England, and England at its present impressive strength, they would be prepared to settle for 80.

Hobbs and Sutcliffe paid as much attention to all this as they thought proper. They must have felt, as they went in, that they had been through this kind of thing before, and that given patience and luck they could do it again. The Melbourne turf was more temperamental than the Oval; the ordinary medium-paced half volleys or good-length deliveries not only spun but stood up straight; they were ready for this, playing on the general assumption that a bowler would not be able to hit the wicket if he tried and that a close concentration on avoiding the offer of a catch was all that was needed. Richardson was no longer among those present; neither, to the regrettable eclipse of the gaiety of nations, was Mailey. The chief danger lay in the canny accuracy of Grimmet, the barbed medium-pace swingers of a'Beckett, and the dour off-spinners of Blackie. By these excellent bowlers, transformed by the vagaries of the wicket into world-class menaces, Hobbs and Sutcliffe were time and again beaten and bruised. Hobbs had his cap knocked off; he gave a chance at slip when he could not get his bat away from a rasper that stood up at him off a good length; but he was too experienced to be rattled. At the other end Sutcliffe peered watchfully at every ball, taking fliers on his ribs without discomposure, his bat almost a second line of defence. When a ball could be hit they hit it; but more frequently they were employed in killing the spin or in leaving it contemptuously alone. Runs were not at present the chief consideration. Blackie, whom they feared for his great penetrative powers, bowled shorter than he should have; a'Beckett wasted priceless minutes and more on that lethal wicket by bowling innocuously outside the off stump, it is not clear why. Whether he thought to lure Hobbs or Sutcliffe into an injudicious dab is not on record; he might well have spared his pains. They rubbed themselves where they were hit and carried on.

Between lunch and tea they added 75, but the miracle was their survival, not their score. The sanguine old cricketers in the pavilion who had prophesied a total of 80 were disconcerted in their actuarial accuracy; they had not in Australia learned to reckon with this kind of opposition to natural upheavals. After tea, the pair continued as before, unhurried and philosophical, like a bomb-disposal squad. In the intervals of improvising safe strokes against unpredictable trajectories, Hobbs began to devise tactical plans. He signalled for a change of bat; and when the twelfth man came out with a selection, he methodically tried them all over with a professional eye and sent them back in again. The twelfth man went back with the bats and a message to the captain. Hobbs, becoming closely acquainted with the wicket and the bowlers, had conceived the idea that they would be less suited to the aggressive open freedom of the regular number three, Hammond, than to the close intellectual scrutiny of Douglas Jardine, and ventured in this way to put the proposition to Chapman for implementation should a wicket fall. Jardine was instantly commanded to put his pads on; and the absorbing struggle continued.

Against all predictable probability they put the hundred up; it was astonishing to find good bowlers so helpless to remove them. When Blackie finally ran one through too quickly for Hobbs, he had made a 49 altogether disproportionate in importance to its unambitious dimensions, and England had 105 on the board. True to strategy, Jardine entered in his place, and his long headed caution and impeccable technique saw away the last of the perilous day. There was still a long pull even when the wicket dried out, and England faltered more than once before completing it; but with Sutcliffe's massive and classic century to bind the later batsmen together, the victory came home at last; and graven on the hearts of every Englishman as the news came through that day were the twin inseparable names of Hobbs and Sutcliffe, who by this performance and their great hour at the Oval those few years before had qualified as the greatest bad-wicket batsmen in the whole history of this subtle and taxing game.

Hobbs and Sutcliffe relaxed happily against South Australia by collecting a hundred apiece, and they began the tense fourth Test, which we eventually won by 12 runs, by making 143 together in two and three-quarter hours. Hobbs made a classic 74, and in the vital closing stages swooped on a hard hit and threw Bradman out from cover as if he were twenty-five years younger. Unfortunately the great partnership had to be dissolved for the last Test, as Sutcliffe strained a shoulder and Hobbs was accompanied by Jardine. Hobbs did enough for both, scoring what proved to be his last Test century on the day when Leyland made his first, and following it up with an admirable 65 in the second innings; but a high-scoring match was lost. His last Australian tour revealed him as past his most magnificent greatness, but, as Melbourne very well understood, still the equal of any player then breathing. The majesty and power of Hammond, the lightning pertinacity and brilliance of Bradman, were both on view and vividly impressive; but in the severe crises of the higher reaches of the game, when man did battle not only with mortal flesh but with the elements as well, the great Shakespearian warning held—'tis better playing with a lion's whelp than with an old one dying.

Yet there were few signs of death or decay, whether his Test tempo gave signs of slowing up or not. He had in the intervening seasons met a New Zealand side that did not attain Test status, and he took off them at the Oval for Surrey a century so perfect in its artistry and mastery that these strong young men were nearly in tears with admiration. He played against the gay and volatile West Indians who came for their first Test series in 1928, and though he regretfully missed through injury the first Test match they ever played, he did not let them off without a beautiful 159 at the Oval, playing their virulent barrage of fast bowlers with the friendliest and most welcoming good-humour.

In 1929 and 1930 his background pattern fell into a shape which was now becoming familiar. He would begin by making an early series of high scores for Surrey—in 1930 he submitted Glamorgan in the first match of the season to the ambiguous honour of two centuries in the match—and would then find his years betray him by small sequences of minor strains and indispositions. He frequently found Test trial matches fatal to his muscles, and these infuriating games were often productive in this manner of more problems than they solved. Then the common run of representative matches, Gentlemen and Players and Tests alike, would very probably claim him when he was fit. The natural result was that Surrey had tantalisingly short leases of him. *Wisden* commented resignedly in 1930 that in the last 136 championship games that Surrey had played he had been missing from 53. In 1929 indeed he missed four of the five Tests against South Africa as well, owing to shoulder strain; in the only one in which he played he made 52, a little overshadowed by Sutcliffe and Hammond who made three centuries in the two innings between them. For the rest he scored with all his usual prolific grace; was still the leader of the familiar batting order at the Oval whenever blessed normality prevailed, still heard the shrill clamour of welcome from the schoolboys among the ginger-beer bottles as he came down the steps with Sandham. He still headed the Surrey averages, though the number of his season's innings would be 20 or 30 now and not 50; he was still the masterly artist of the great years, whenever his body forgot, as his soul never remembered, its rightful age.

CHAPTER III

THE SUNSET TOUCH

In the year 1930 he screwed himself at last to the melancholy and inevitable decision to make the unwanted break with Test cricket. He was as fit as he could normally expect himself to be, at forty-seven; and that season was less encumbered by minor strains than many of its recent predecessors had been. He still felt ready and competent to play Australia's present generation of fast bowlers with a broomstick if need be. Gregory had dropped out of cricket, with chronic cartilage trouble, and there were no immediate successors to his pace or quality in the ranks of his own compatriots; even if there had been, it would have caused little concern to one who in these very years dealt so consummately with Larwood, Constantine, Macdonald. "There could be no fast bowling," remarked Edmund Blunden of this batsman, "to that immense clarity." His defence was as sure and compact as it had ever been, his hooking and pulling as precise, his rare late cutting and square driving timed as perfectly as of old. Only his feet moved infinitesimally slower into position; he went for his runs less, knowing well that if he waited inside his crease they would come to him, and they still came quicker to him than to most, like homing pigeons knowing their place. He still cherished in his consciousness the knowledge that the first over of an innings was far likelier than the second, and the second than the third, to contain the gift of a loose ball. Bowlers did not take long to realize that a loose ball in the first over to Jack Hobbs was never neutralized by the batsman's nervous tension. A loose ball in the first over got belted smack against the fence as soon as look at it; and I have seen him despatch

three such in a row for four, to the general demoralisation of the
bowler and the encouragement of the principle of aggressive opening batsmanship. Yet in these days, taking stock of his apparently
inexhaustible skill, he must have reckoned up the cumulative strains
on his stamina and health and decided that he must not longer
aspire to the highest tensions. He never wanted to have to be
hidden in the field; he never had to be. For just as long as his body
could keep up with his still youthful spirit of adventurous expertise,
he would be proud and happy to be in his rightful place; but at the
first sign of deceleration, he would know it was time to step down
at least one stage.

The announcement that after the end of the Australian tour of
this country in 1930 he would no longer be available for Test cricket
came as less of a surprise than a regretful wrench. We had known
for years that he was older than we could wish; as long ago as 1926
Neville Cardus had written of the famous Oval Test as if it might
be his last; and the continual little strains and pains and indispositions and inexplicable absences hinted far more strongly than
plainly-worded bulletins could have done that the age of com-
promise was here to stay. He still looked trimly youthful, coming
out with Sandham or Sutcliffe, walking with the easy distinctive
light step with the latent spring in it, fiddling absently with his
shirt-collar, looking with screwed-up eyes past the long inquisitive
nose under the peak of the England cap. There were crows' feet
and seamed wrinkles in his brown weathered face, and the pouted
lips broke ever and again into the famous slow grin; he pushed his
cap further back on his head as the runs mounted and the work
got warmer, and on hot days he would take it off by the peak and
wipe the sweat from his forehead with his forearm, all in one
engaging movement. Then he would rest back at ease on his heels
as the bowler began to walk back and with elbows at his sides would
give his bat the distinctive twiddle as he looked once more round
the field, then down into the easy stance with the left toe cocked
and active ready for the lightning strategic move as he gauged the
length and positioned himself for the stroke—and whether this
was the feather-light leg glance that so often served him to open his
score, or the pile-driven hook that took his whole body round with
it and sounded like a great whip cracking, or the demure push to
within ten feet of cover with time in plenty for the batsmen to go

through for the impossible single, it was the neatest and most unobtrusive manoeuvre possible and it was no more the distinctive
Hobbs stroke than the next one was, for he had and used them all.
Hammond had the great cover-drive, Sandham the late cut, Sutcliffe the pull, Hendren the eyebrow-hook and the square cut—but
Hobbs had all these too without privilege of specialization, and all
the others round the clock as well. The completest batsman in all
cricket was going to his old age unwearying, with the variety of
his talents quite unimpaired.

Looking at him as we did then, say in 1930 which was the last
year of his Test career, we saw a great batsman whom we had not
known as anything other than the player whom we followed and
applauded so faithfully that day. He did not give us then the
impression of a great tradition coming to its end, the last few pages
as it were of a self-contained history. Had we had at that stage
and that age more historical sense, we would have marvelled not
only at the supreme batsman he clearly was but at the huge attainments he carried with him as he went. These we knew of, but, as
far as most of us were concerned, not thoroughly. We merely
accepted him, rightly or wrongly, as the greatest living batsman,
playing there on the Oval in front of us. When he stole a run we
did not stop to reckon that over 50,000 had already preceded it;
we merely waited impatiently for the next, and hoped they would
come four at a time; we never calculated that he had been doing
this, and doing it in this place, twenty-five years ago, before many
of us were born. He did not look like a survival; but among many
other things, that was what he was.

The faces of his companions were changing. His Surrey
colleagues remained hearteningly constant, though his old friend
Strudwick had retired a year or two back to the concentrated
assiduity of the score-box, and Bill Hitch had gone the way of
most fast bowlers too soon. Another year or two and Alan Peach
would go, and Mac Ducat; and soon Percy Fender's wonderful
term of captaincy would end and the unhappily short reign of
Douglas Jardine begin. Sandham remained a perpetual and reassuring bodyguard, as Sutcliffe did in the higher spheres, whence
only in this very season would the indestructible Rhodes depart,
bowling in his last match most enigmatically and bafflingly to

Bradman, who had all his work cut out to stay in against the retiring mage, much less score runs off him.

Hobbs for the moment journeyed on untroubled. He was no relic and he did not feel like one. There was a late afternoon at Lord's that season, May 31st, 1930, the precise date, when fortunate spectators to the number of about 15,000 were treated to a dual performance which chance rather surprisingly decreed should be in the historical annals of the game a somewhat conspicuous rarity—a long and fruitful partnership between Hobbs and Hammond, the old master and the new. (It may be a cosmic coincidence that at the precise moment of their prolific association their chief rival Bradman was completing his 1,000 runs in May at Southampton; only a Thomas Hardy-like Spirit of the Years could have been so situated as to observe all three in operation at one and the same time, but it is of curious interest to know that there was at least one hour or so of Time when all these immortals were at their wonderful best simultaneously.) The Lord's match was a Test Trial; the Rest on a slow wicket were hurried out in an undistinguished manner, and when the England eleven batted Sutcliffe for once lost his wicket almost immediately, and Hobbs and Hammond added 113 in an hour and three-quarters. In all their long association in England and representative teams at home and abroad I can discover virtually no instances of a long partnership between these great batsmen. Hobbs was often out before the younger man came in; and even when he wasn't, some obscure polarity of fortune expelled the one in no long time from the other's presence. It is a noteworthy fact that twenty years or so later that other pair of magnificent incompatibles, Hutton and Compton, had a similar failure in correlation. But on this occasion the malevolent genie forgot to strike. Hobbs and Hammond batted beautifully. Allom and Clark, Jack White and Stevens, Worthington and Wyatt, and other auxiliaries, were the bowlers. They bowled at Hobbs, and he scored a single; and they found they were facing the massive contempt of Hammond. They tried again, and the batsmen crossed once more; and the bowlers were up against the easy but commanding technique of the world's best batsman. That night their various masteries were deployed in full before those doubly-blessed spectators, who had once and for all, for an hour and three-quarters that they would remember all their lives, been privileged to be in the presence of the two greatest batsmen in modern English cricket at the height of their distinctive skills. It is not a famous match; I have rescued it myself from the obscurity in which *Wisden* enshrouds it; it is not talked of much, but to me it is a key moment, the fusion of the older powers and the newer, of the mobile genius with the massive, of the lightness and the strength of classical cricket; the rare but entirely happy combination of all that we think of when we say "Jack Hobbs" and all that we remember when we think of Walter Hammond.

From this time on we must not shirk the decline; it was mathematically, scientifically inevitable, though at the time we hoped and believed it possible to postpone it indefinitely. Its chief outward and visible sign was his announced intention of withdrawing from Test cricket; we were consoled meanwhile with the unspoken but implied assurance that he still wanted to play for Surrey; also that the present Test series against Australia would not go on without him. When the Australians arrived for it, compact of new promising players and well-grounded veterans of past series, we in England thought of Chapman's tour and happily anticipated a modest repetition of it.

Unfortunately for us we had not taken into account the inevitable cyclical changes that appear to govern the fortunes of Anglo-Australian cricket. In the short meantime the young Australians had developed and hardened; the older Englishmen had grown older and if anything softened. Our bowlers with all their available variety had not gained in accuracy; our admirable wicket-keeper Duckworth was prone to off-moments at crucial times; several of our more illustrious and time-honoured batsmen failed to retain their places in the side. The only new batting success was Duleepsinhji, the only established batsman to retain his reputation throughout was Sutcliffe. Hobbs began with two beautiful innings of over 70 each in the first Test which England won (and followed it up in the very next game, which was Surrey v. the Australians, with a not-out century which saved the match for his county) but could not in the matches which followed recapture the necessary knack. And in addition nobody was prepared for the comparative mediocrity of Hammond; and it is quite certain that nobody on earth in their wildest megalomaniac dreams could have dared to envisage the impossible performances of Bradman, who in five games altered Test cricket for ever. A single century, two double centuries, and a treble century compensated fairly enough for his three other Test innings of 8, 1 and 14 (the last of which represented a strangely uneasy half-hour against Peebles' baffling googly on a wet Manchester wicket; but he took it out of Peebles later, be sure of that). And with Bradman eclipsing Hammond's great record and average, and four other batsmen averaging over 50 in the Tests, coupled with great accuracy from Grimmett and close efficiency from his supporting colleagues, and who can wonder that England let the Ashes go, especially as they panicked before the last match at the Oval and dropped Chapman through the same trap-door as had swallowed Carr four years before?

After the victory at Nottingham and the deceptive euphoria that followed it, Hobbs' Test fortunes faltered. At Lord's, in that game which England began so prolifically but which was lost from the moment of Bradman's entry, he was deprived of Sutcliffe through injury and had Woolley as his partner. He was out very early in the first innings and made no great mark on the second; and in that third Test of Bradman's mammoth three hundred and plenty, Hobbs and Sutcliffe on Sutcliffe's home ground suffered the inexplicable humiliation of being rudely barracked for successfully appealing against the light. This ironic ignominy was crowned after the resumption by the unusual experience of their being separated by a run-out, the quicksilver Bradman, who never forgot a thing and never in any circumstances ended otherwise than one up, revenging his two-year-old run out by throwing Hobbs out marvellously from deep mid-off as he went for a sharp run. The game itself dribbled away into a draw, and so did the Manchester Test, curtained with drifting rain as usual and tantalisingly indecisive. The last Test at the Oval, Jack Hobbs' clearly stated farewell, was also to be the decider of the series.

The Fates who wrote Jack Hobbs' story for him were no compilers of schoolboy romance; they gave him over-brimming successes, but they ever denied him the high romantics of the Technicolor finish. So it was at the Oval in August 1930. The great timeless struggle, to which the whole ponderous campaign had been perceptibly moving as to a loadstone rock for its great consummation, failed in the act to be more than a ragged repetition of the fatal Lord's Test. England's first innings of over 400 would

in series gone by have been accounted an extravagance; in this one
it merely whetted the insatiable Bradman's appetite. The match
began under the ambiguous shadow of Chapman's replacement;
the excellent Wyatt was catapulted into the seat of honour without
warning, and required to exercise the same hoodoo as the similarly-
honoured Chapman had decisively manipulated in 1926. There
was no reason why this should work again and it did not, though
Wyatt himself was gratifyingly successful with the bat. Looking
back over thirty years I cannot honestly feel that it made any
difference. It would have needed two cricket teams of world status
to have contained Bradman that summer; and his ten colleagues
should not be under-rated either. England were properly crushed,
and it would be foolish to go about imagining alternative
possibilities.

Hobbs and Sutcliffe began in the old reassuring way, surviving
a nerve-racking moment in the first over when some mischance led
to a slip and a scamper, relieved by someone throwing wide. Apart
from this they consolidated without excitement; runs came steadily
though not freely, two from Hobbs to every one from Sutcliffe, an
easy competent seeing-off of the not very penetrative opening
attack. Wall and Fairfax, Grimmett and McCabe, none on the
clean hard surface presented much problem, the pace being easy
and the surface unresponsive. Ten minutes before lunch, with the
score in the sixties, Wall came back to bowl down wind from the
Vauxhall end and dropped one in his first over a shade shorter
than the rest. Hobbs held it in the line of his eyes and slammed it
to the square leg boundary as if he had hit it with a powered steam-
hammer; the stroke paralysed the fielders, nobody moved while
the ball was flung back to the wicket and the cheers echoed round
the Oval. Hobbs twiddled his bat and got down to it again as Wall
ran up, saw and relished the same ball repeated, laid his head
behind it again, gave it the full meat, and was gloriously caught
by Alan Kippax by the square-leg umpire as we looked to the
boundary for it. Hobbs turned smiling to the pavilion to meet the
cheers, 47 to his name out of 68. The ground buzzed and mur-
mured, excited but a little disappointed, having hoped like Hobbs
for a hundred.

How England slithered, rallied, fell, recovered again, and
ultimately through Sutcliffe and Wyatt reached 400; how Ponsford

made it soft for Bradman by punching the confidence out of Larwood and Tate; how days and nights went by and Bradman was still there, whether with Woodfull or Kippax or Jackson or McCabe no one could rightly tell but there he was—how till the verge of Wednesday night the vast Australian innings accumulated its runs, 400, 500, 600, until it stopped short of 700 by five and there rested, is a kaleidoscopic horror easier to experience in the memory than set down on paper.

Fate had set no easy stage for a final glory. England were drooping and exhausted, they were nearly 300 in arrear, such reward as might be burrowed out of disaster would not come without days of uphill struggle and conflict. It was the worst time of the day to go in to bat, a quarter to six; after a sunny day the evening clouds were gathering in over the gasworks, the light was none too bright. Hobbs must have walked in to his last Test innings under the double strain of a heightened nervous tension and two days' field fatigue. The crowd can have hardly embodied its hopes for him in anything but the vaguest form; but it cheered the two of them heartily enough as they appeared in the Australians' wake, and settled down to help tide them over the day's awkward end.

It was Woodfull who so generously and happily signed the occasion with the warrant it might otherwise have lacked. Quiet, charming, undemonstrative, this most friendly of opponents gave character to the day with his most moving gesture. He grouped his fieldsmen round the wicket as the batsmen approached, and as Hobbs arrived among them Woodfull called for three cheers. I believe this to have been the first time that this kind of tribute had ever been paid to a player by his opponents; it has since been imitated by other captains. Hendren and Woolley were both the centre of similar happy demonstrations, and long years later Bradman stood for his own tribute from his English friends where Hobbs stood on this day. Woodfull's frank and straightforward integrity had fashioned a precedent that instilled sweetness into the regret of many a later parting.

The crowd added to Woodfull's three another twenty thousand or so of its own and the scene broke up, the Australians to their places, Hobbs to master the emotions of the unexpected moment and, as best he could, to face Wall. He says the incident in no way affected his concentration; and indeed he played a few minutes afterwards a beauty of a forcing shot past mid-wicket off his toes, great batsman signed all over it, a compact and wristy delight. He flexed and limbered his shoulders and bent to the batting again; the heightened emotional hum died down among the crowd. Normality returned.

And there, I am afraid, is the end. There are no heroics to chronicle, merely a depressing and insignificant anti-climax. A few overs later he attempted a forcing shot outside the off-stump off Fairfax, it moved in to him a shade quickly, and he played on off the inside edge. You could hear the cavernous gasp as the bails fell, the sigh breathed out of all those well-wishing throats as for just that second longer than usual Hobbs stood motionless, looking at the broken wicket. If it had been 0 now, as Bradman's last Test innings was, there had been some perverse distinction in the failure; but 9 was neither here nor there. The foundations were kicked away from the excitement, the evening dusk gathered above the players, and nobody protested when ten minutes later someone appealed against the light and play ended for the day. The crowd sloped home in sadness, feeling for their hero, England's looming defeat a minor thing beside his disappointment. Yet Jack Hobbs, savouring the ill-fortune no less bitterly than they, consoled himself then and for ever after with the warmth and good-fellowship of Woodfull's graceful gesture, which he has never forgotten and never will.

Next day the clouds broke in rain and when after a blank Thursday England took up the struggle, it was on a soft pudding of turf on which the lanky Hornibrook exercised even more tortuous wiles than Grimmett. Sutcliffe, Duleepsinhji, Hammond, all opposed such arts of defiance and aggression as became their natures, but there could be only one end. In the last stages Hobbs, of course, took no part; after that melancholy moment on the Wednesday evening he had sunk without any trace but his past imperishable greatness, which unhappily could not affect the present game. He went out of Test cricket with his customary lack of fuss, with 5,410 runs as his total showing in his sixty-one appearances for England. He had made the Australians over a period of 23 years or so field out to a dozen separate hundreds from his bat; and he would no doubt have been willing enough to sacrifice any number of these in exchange for one just like them in his last Test at the

Oval. Not for the first nor the last time Jack Hobbs found the element of drama and occasion denied to his otherwise enviable gifts.

He finished the 1930 season with over 2,000 runs and an average in the fifties; and in 1931 he was to do even better with an aggregate of 2,418 that in the illimitable length of his prolific career he only exceeded eight times—this at forty-eight, an acknowledged has-been. He got to the thousand before anyone else in the country, he made ten centuries, seven of them for Surrey, and showed no falling off in inventive and executive skill. He and Sutcliffe put on a masterly dual performance at Scarborough when in successive matches they achieved stands of 227 and 243 at the respective expense of the Gentlemen and the touring New Zealanders, who never came on a tour these days without being simultaneously drubbed and delighted by the batsman they honour to this day as the greatest. Surrey had an indifferent year both in 1930 and 1931; the older men were falling away, the newer generation was slow in establishing itself; changes were in the wind. At the beginning of the 1932 season the mysterious dictates of circumstances removed Fender from the captaincy and set Jardine in his place, Fender in the most co-operative way continuing to play as valiantly and valuably as ever. The reliability of Hobbs and Sandham remained constant through these vicissitudes; they were for the time proof against the winds of chance. But old ties were being severed one by one; the huge Scarborough successes of 1931 proved to be his last appearances on a ground that had always attracted him and on which he had always been a favourite. It was an excellent thing that it should so turn out that he and his great Yorkshire partner should at that same time bring their wonderful tally of century partnerships to such a resounding close.

In the winter of 1930-31 he had accepted an invitation from the Maharaj Kumar of Vizianagram (the same who later captained an Indian side on its tour through this country) to take part in a privately-arranged tour through India and Ceylon. This he was delighted to do, especially as his wife was invited along with him and Herbert Sutcliffe was to be of the party (having for some reason, which at this distance of time is worse than obscure, been left out of the M.C.C. team to tour South Africa). He travelled to India and enjoyed the experience as well as the cricket; but was the innocent cause of an outbreak of unrequired publicity on his stating politely but firmly that he objected to playing cricket on Sunday. It says much for his prestige that the tour was rearranged accordingly; it says even more for his simple moral courage that he proclaimed his convictions and stood by them. Even among cricketers and cricket-lovers who were by no means Sabbatarians, his firmness won him additional respect. It also, on the debit side, was inclined to pep up his stock in revivalist and Wayside Pulpit contexts, a concern to which he no doubt paid little attention. "Good old Jack!" announced to my knowledge one over-familiar cleric, fist on the pulpit and head portentously wagging at the congregation, "He never played a straighter bat than that!"

Good old Jack entered his fiftieth year apparently untouched by Time. He scored as regularly and prolifically for Jardine as he had for Fender, opening with Sandham almost from memory or in his sleep, creating over again the illusion that time, which had overseen them in their partnership's inception in 1919, could stand still for ever over an institution that it cherished. At Taunton, that haven of hallowed memories, the two put on 264 together, a devastating business; at the Oval against that other symbol of revengeful satisfaction, Essex, Hobbs for the sixth time in his life made two centuries in a match. His second innings, when with Gregory he piled on 232 runs in two and a half hours to win a tense and memorable game by nine wickets, was a masterpiece out of his great matured period, a prime and expert beauty that enchanted all who watched it. This was the innings that caused Jardine, partly one supposes in a lightly joking mood but partly out of a deeply rooted and deeply-felt admiration, to apply to him the epithet, "The Master," a name which curiously stuck to him and gave him an unusual sanction and honour for the rest of his career.

We must look in 1932 for the great innings that caused him the most satisfaction and distinguishes itself beyond all others as a late landmark with now not many successors, not to Surrey matches but to the last time he took bat in hand for the Players against the Gentlemen at Lord's. Over the past quarter of a century he had engraved his name deeply on this great fixture, had made it as much part of his own tradition as of England's, had delighted to play in it and felt deprived when occasionally he did not, had made in the course of his honourable association with it a record number of centuries, by this time fifteen. The 1932 match was, perhaps partly by luck and partly by judgment, a wonderfully constituted balance of sides; Jardine led a gifted and aggressive band of amateurs that compassed it seemed the whole attractive scale of amateur cricket of a dozen fruitful years, Wyatt and Duleep, Chapman and the Nawab, Allen and Brown and Peebles, all names of a richness and rarity to haunt the mind. Only Robins of the vintage amateurs of that time was missing from the list, a team of the most adventurous and various talent. Facing it under Hobbs' own leadership was the greatest Players' side of the post-1914 generation; it is difficult to see how it could be easily strengthened. The roll-call began with Hobbs and Sutcliffe, proceeded through Woolley to Hammond and topped off the batting with Hendren and Paynter; Larwood and Tate opened the attack and Voce and Freeman were there to support them, with Duckworth behind the wicket. (If one substituted Ames for Duckworth and Leyland for Paynter, you would have an England team to take on any comer you could name, let alone a Players' side.) With beautiful appropriateness this noble galaxy surrounded Jack Hobbs for his last appearance in the series; he could not have wished for a happier farewell. He took no thought of farewells at the time, of course; but it seems in the light of history an almost instinctive mobilization of the great names for a leave-taking, names whose echoes are still most powerfully evocative—

> *"Not hear? The noise was everywhere: it toll'd*
> *Increasing like a bell. Names in his ears*
> *Of all the lost adventurers his peers"—*

—the roll-call was almost ceremonial in its richness and authority. The Master among his fellow-masters, enjoying with the cooperation of their skills one last exercise of his supremacy.

And at last Fate let him work what his spirit willed. He went unknowing out of the series on a note of triumph—not complete, for the match was drawn, but his personal satisfaction must have been great. The game began in a faulty light, and neither he nor the greater part of his renowned compeers could make much headway against a nagging attack and a green lifting wicket. Sutcliffe, Woolley and Hendren were pegged down and overcome; Hobbs himself cut out a cheerful little pattern for an innings before Allen clipped his bails for 24; the famous names were coming and going, and the Lord's wicket was performing its regular incalculable tricks. The valiant cross-batted Paynter set himself sturdily to resist, while at the other end Hammond honoured the occasion with a free and forcing hundred, a determined and aggressive answer to determined and aggressive bowling. The Players topped the 300 that night, and got rid of Wyatt in the few overs that could be bowled before the grey day turned black and sent them all in early.

The Gentlemen gave Hobbs good measure on the next day; their three finest batsmen saluted him with rare appropriateness by flogging his illustrious bowlers all over Lord's. Jardine made a classic 64 in a hundred minutes; but the great feature of the day was a beautiful partnership by the two young Indians, Duleep and the Nawab, whose centuries of brilliant and enterprising resource are still a gay and memorable part of the history of the series. We can see these innings now in an ironic perspective, although at the time they were merely two in a row—for Duleep's hundred was his last ever; he had barely a month to go before illness removed him from first-class cricket for good at the age of twenty-seven; and death has come to both these captivating players, and to their captain Jardine, tragically early. They decorated Hobbs' last Gentlemen and Players game with a delicate joint artistry that nobody ever saw again.

The Players, with a day to fight through, were 130 behind; and again the leading lights shone rather more dimly than they might. Sutcliffe, Woolley, Hammond, Hendren, all the lost adventurers his peers, played and promised and faltered and were gone before the leeway was made up. Only Hobbs at this last ditch gathered to himself the authority and power of the whole team and used the amateurs' bowling as he had used it in his greatest days. He stayed in all day and he carried his bat, each modest partner helped him and the side to take the total further from defeat, but his was the burden and the glory. When Duckworth and Freeman departed at the close of the innings to successive balls, Hobbs was left high and dry with 161 not out made in five hours, an innings ripe with patience and experience and skill. Jardine, who had taken the full brunt of it, congratulated him at the end on a great personal triumph; and though the Players had perhaps slightly the worse of the draw, the honour of the game lay indisputably in Hobbs' hands. The great innings linked up over twenty-one years with that classic 154 not out with which he had rescued a similar eleven of giants from shame if not from defeat. One other note should be made against this honourable and still-remembered occasion. When he walked out on that last morning to take his second innings, it was the very last time that Hobbs and Sutcliffe came in to bat together in a first-class match. Behind them were nine years of wonderful attainment, twenty-six opening partnerships of a hundred or more, a legendary technique and a repute unequalled by any other pair; the lean, active, quizzical Hobbs and the neat wiry imperturbable Sutcliffe, who set a standard that can serve as a guide but defies all attempts at emulation.

In the winter of 1932 Jack Hobbs took a busman's holiday and reported the Tests in Australia for the *Star*. This was the "bodyline" tour of unfragrant memory; he committed himself on that contentious subject as little as he might, for he was too close to the main participants for objective comment. He had given personal indication in the previous summer of what his views might have been, when he allowed his disapproval of Bill Bowes' action in repeatedly bowling short to him at the Oval to take the form of a public and unmistakable protest on the spot. But whatever his views on the bodyline controversy they set no curb on the violence and unfortunate distemperature of that unhappy series, and nothing of what he may have said or thought affected either the bitterness at the time or the reconciliation which eventually prevailed. He came back to England fifty years old and as ready to take up the old routine as ever; but, aware more than before of the advisability of husbanding his stamina, he arranged with Surrey that he could not be expected to be available regularly. This was, in effect, no innovation; strains and fatigues had been operative upon him for years; and Surrey were content to have him at all, on whatever terms he liked to propound. In the event he did not begin his season until the last match in May 1933, when the fiery West Indians came to the Oval to play Surrey and Hobbs proceeded to bat for six and a half hours while making 221. Sandham was injured and did not bat; but Hobbs was not baulked of his century opening partnership, Gregory being the very worthy

other half of it. He has recorded that this outstanding performance
made him abominably stiff; and who can wonder at it?

It was a fine dry season that year, and the sun shone on his back
encouragingly enough to tempt him into ten Championship
matches. He pleased himself very much by getting a hundred at
Blackheath—that age-old ghost took a deal of laying—and he
dealt out another pleasurable century against the academics from
his old home University. Somerset, too, had the benefit of yet
another, not unaccompanied by closely-cherished memories; and
he was overjoyed to achieve another on Bank Holiday against
Notts at the Oval. As he went back to the pavilion after this one,
the crowd of 15,000 rose in a body to cheer him home; as if they
knew by instinct what they could only have guessed, that this was
the last hundred he would make at the Oval. There seemed no
relaxation in the standard of his play; his eyesight was keen, his
stamina equal to the demands his intelligent and economical plans
made upon it. He played less often than before, but he played
every bit as well. He made eleven hundred runs that season, with
the tidy little average of 61. In the field, in the distance, he looked
a trim thirty-five. We knew that some day he must retire, but as
yet there seemed no sign of it.

CHAPTER IV

THIS IS THE WAY THE WORLD ENDS

HE spent part of the winter of 1933-34 reporting for the *Star* once more. This time it was India's turn to receive a touring team, and again Jardine was entrusted with the command—M.C.C.'s gesture of confidence after the frictions of the bodyline season. Once again Hobbs enjoyed the sensation of accompanying a touring side while escaping the stresses and strains of the accustomed responsibilities. Once again he looked forward to a new English season with confidence. While in India, he had been immeasurably delighted to receive a cable from the Surrey Club asking if he agreed to an appeal being made to members to subscribe to a new main entrance at the Oval, to incorporate a set of gates to bear his name. The compliment, the unusual honour, moved him very much; that the gates of his beloved home ground should be set up under the name of the Hobbs gates was a thought that overwhelmed him whenever it recurred. It is a rare honour; Lord's accorded it to W. G. Grace, but only after his death, and Sussex have since done the same for the services and memory of Maurice Tate. Jack Hobbs, acceding to the suggestion with deep gratitude, has never ceased to count this gesture of his Club's as the most moving and satisfying compliment that any cricketer could be privileged to receive. The gates were duly installed and in 1934 they were formally opened, handsome and unostentatious like the batsman whose name they bear. If Jack Hobbs' cricket needed any memorial, their design could not have expressed better in its wrought iron grace the elegance and strength that were at the heart of his achievement.

Parallel with this happy commemoration may be recorded
another, that had been carried out and completed three or four
years before. At the time of Hobbs' second benefit a proposal was
put forward to honour his oldest associations by building a pavilion
on Parker's Piece. He eagerly agreed to this, remembering over the
years the discomforts of dressing in a tent; and after some while a
sufficient number of subscriptions had been received to make the
proposal a reality. He and his wife went down for the opening
ceremony in April 1930; and in September of that year he took to
Cambridge a team of all the talents to play on Parker's Piece a
charity match for the benefit of the local hospital. The Hobbs
Pavilion on Parker's Piece; the Hobbs Gates at the Oval; he seemed
to be raising wherever he went monuments more lasting than
bronze.

The presence of the Hobbs Gates made him anticipate the season
of 1934 even more readily than usual; and there was already in his
mind, and it must have been hovering there for more than a season
or two, the possibility of the achievement of the crowning performance of his career—his 200th century. In the previous season
he had only played eighteen innings, and he had made a hundred
every third time he went in. What was more, his last hundred, that
against Notts on Bank Holiday, was number 196 in the canon.
Given a reasonable season, the quarry should be in the bag without
undue difficulty in about mid-season. It is interesting, and perhaps
a little surprising, to realize how much stock this great batsman
set by this and other somewhat arbitrary records. There is no
doubt whatever that he cherished the anticipatory pleasure; probably, at this stage of his career, it was his sole remaining ambition.
One thing he harboured at his heart; he sorely yearned to reach it,
if it could be reached at all, at the Oval. The Oval had been deprived
of his hundredth hundred, of his 126th and 127th and 150th; he
had disappointed the loyal Oval crowd in his last Test. There was
a powerful emotional *rapprochement* between Jack Hobbs and
the Oval crowd whom he had delighted for so many years; and
his keen hopes were compounded partly of a desire to hear their
admiring applause (and nobody in their reasonable senses is going
to blame him for that), but partly of a strong sense of obligation
towards a public who had encouraged him all his life and to whom
he would like to make a really special presentation before he retired.

Surrey began their season under a new captain. Jardine, to everyone's regret, had found it necessary for one reason and another to resign. Surrey had been somewhat rudderless during the previous year, when injuries and business commitments had kept him away oftener than was good for the side. The long stabilization under Fender was receiving unexpected and distracting jolts. Jardine's successor was Errol Holmes, a cheerful and optimistic cricketer without the chess-player's subtlety of Fender or the autocratic intellect of Jardine. At school he had been an outstanding batsman, and at Oxford he had imparted to University cricket a style and a punch that were commoner then than they are now but which even in his day arrested the eye of the spectator attracted by quality. His county record had been uneven and his appearances few; in fact he had barely played six first-class matches since 1927. Yet here was a free and stylish batsman of character and grace; in three or four years from 1934 he enjoyed days of immense success; he played for England at home and abroad, he captained a minor tour to New Zealand, and he was invited to make the major tour to Australia later but had to decline it. He played cricket with a captivating buoyancy and enthusiasm, and his professionals ate out of his generous hand. Jack Hobbs' last county captain brought a long and distinguished line to a cheerful and friendly end; he admired Jack Hobbs, and always admired him, several degrees on the other side of idolatry; he played his own beneficent part, witting or unwitting, in the close of a great career.

Jack Hobbs did not know, when he began to play in 1934, that this would be his last season in first-class cricket. It seems that he had no present intention of putting a date to his retirement; he would be content to clock up the 200 centuries first, and then perhaps look about him. Holmes respected the senior man's freedom of choice, as Jardine and his substitutes had done. He never picked him specifically for any match; he asked him if he would be willing to play, and was delighted when he said yes. For the first few matches in May everything seemed to go well. Hobbs began the season by making 50 at Lord's against the M.C.C. who were comprehensively beaten; he made it in an hour and a half and *Wisden* refers once more to his masterly style. It was early May and we can picture him as nearly all who saw him that season remember him, a little thicker than of old, his hair silvering at the ears under his England cap, a white scarf round his neck, more often in a bulky sweater than not, yet his eyes as keen and his nose as inquisitive as ever as he looked down the wicket. That game in May was in fact his last at Lord's; Surrey moved over to the Oval and were unexpectedly put through the hoop by Glamorgan who found in Hobbs, who made a careful 62, the only formidable opponent to Clay's biting off-spinners. Hobbs by this time could play off-spinners in his sleep and did so, but nobody else stayed and Glamorgan did not have to bat again. He fared indifferently with 7 and 37 against Warwick, and inexplicably ran himself out for 19 against Gloucester. Even this early in the season he had begun to notice that runs were not coming so readily as they had the year before. He had little trouble with his stamina, but was more disturbed by the failure of his timing, for so many years a precision instrument of wonderful accuracy. He thought he was hitting the ball just as hard, but it made no pace off the bat. He says too that while he continued to enjoy plenty of time to play the fast bowling, the spinners for the first time began to fox him. Clearly his co-ordination was ever so slightly out of true; his spontaneous re-actions were perceptibly slowing down. After the Gloucester match Surrey had a week's rest, and he did not travel to their next game, which was the Whitsun match with Notts. He held himself ready for the Lancashire match at Old Trafford on 26th May; it was the benefit match of his old friend George Duckworth, who had made a special point of asking him to play.

The Old Trafford crowd, whom he had often obliged in the past, were glad to see him and gave him a cheer of his own when he took the field with Surrey on the Saturday. Lancashire were all out, late in the afternoon, and Hobbs and Sandham had a couple of hours to play through at the end. When they appeared at the gate the whole crowd rose as a man and cheered their old friend to the wicket as he had hardly ever been cheered before. Undisturbed by this, he and Sandham batted out the evening. It has to be confessed that the Lancashire attack that season was a shadow of its illustrious greatness of the 'twenties, honesty and accuracy taking the place of devil and guile; but it does not detract from the performance of Hobbs and Sandham in scoring 184 together, some that night but most on the Monday morning, before the first wicket fell. (It is beginning to sound monotonous; but it was their last century partnership.) Before Sibbles finally got him, Hobbs had reached his longed-for hundred. He took four hours over it, a lengthiness unthinkable against such an attack in the days of his prime; but he had got it, and he was one step closer to the visionary goal he had set himself to reach. As he turned from the wicket the crowd rose at him in applause again; they bayed their admiration and gratitude from their North-country lungs, they proclaimed with dizzying communal noise their appreciation and perhaps their farewell. As he arrived at the pavilion gate some unidentifiable genius broke into the opening bars of "Auld Lang Syne", and before he had his foot on the steps the members in the pavilion had taken it up. Neville Cardus, in a most admiring notice of this sure and masterful innings, criticized the tribute as lacking resonance in the tenors, though he pronounced himself satisfied with the bass quality; he characterized the whole performance as one of the most moving pieces of sportsmanship he had ever known. It was nearly too much for Hobbs; it was all he could do not to break down. He cherishes that moment in his memory along with Woodfull's impulsive gesture at the Oval four years before; he can never forget it. Had the Manchester crowd known that they were singing him home after the very last of all his centuries, they could hardly have celebrated him more warmly or touched his gratitude more closely.

He had another ovation at the end of that same drawn game, which left him not out for 51 in the second innings. As the players trooped in together the crowd surged to its feet again and the friendly warmth came near to melting him once more as he hurried in. George Duckworth, coming in close by him, thinks he was in tears. It was this match, and the moments it brought him, that reconciles him in retrospect to a season which otherwise is a tale of frustration and disappointment. The goal he had set himself seemed to recede rather than approach now that last year's touch was missing. The hundred at Old Trafford had emphasized rather than lightened the difficulty.

He played next day at the Oval against the Australian tourists, in an inconclusive match of fabulous scores. Sandham made 219 and Gregory 116 in a Surrey innings of 475 for six; the Australians overtopped this with ease and made 629. Hobbs' modest 24 was a drop in the bucket; and in the curious match at Brentwood that followed, when Essex, fresh from being defeated by Kent by an innings and 192 runs, promptly defeated Surrey by (believe it or not) an innings and 192 runs, Hobbs was the first victim of a tear-away destroyer named H. D. Read and only made 5 and 28 as his share of a general martyrdom.

Ten days later he turned out against Sussex at Horsham. He showed himself perfectly capable of playing Tate still, and his second innings nearly brought him one nearer his ambition, for when Surrey went in hundreds of runs in arrear he batted for four solid hours for an uncharacteristically defensive 79 which postponed but did not avoid defeat. So near he was to the hundred and yet through his own error it eluded him, for he ran himself out for the second time that season. Was his frustration at last beginning to disturb the coolness of his native judgment?

Once more a melancholy landmark has to be chronicled. In his next match against his favourite old opponents, Somerset, with who knows what conjectures in his thoughts, he batted, I do not know why, at number four, and was out for 15. He walked off the Oval not knowing that he would not bat on it in a first-class match again; and indeed, though this was but the middle of June, he had only one more innings for Surrey. Even then he was reluctant to turn out, as he was short of practice; he had by this time been out of the game for weeks and weeks, and it was the end of August and Surrey's last match; not at the Oval, but at Cardiff, against Glamorgan. The wicket was soaking and play was much curtailed; Fender took 8 for 79 in dismissing the home side for 173, and Hobbs and Sandham walked out to bat in the murk and wet, an unfitting end to their rousing times together. A few balls in Clay's first rasping over, and Hobbs was out, l.b.w. for 0, clean as a whistle. The game was swamped in a flurry of showers and there was not time for Surrey to have a second innings; and that was Jack Hobbs' very last game for Surrey. It leaves the chronicler blank and distracted, as if over a bottomless pit.

From Cardiff he journeyed to Folkestone, where two Festival matches saw the season out. The first promised better than it performed, as rain cut it to the bone; for an England XI bristling with notabilities faced a solid Test team of Australians. Every single member of the England side bar one played at some time or other for England; and it is difficult to see what right the remaining member of the side had, apart from his charm as a man and his ability as a cricketer, to be in such a side at all, as he was the gifted Indian all-rounder Jahangir Khan. The sadly truncated match saw an admirable opening stand by Hobbs and C. F. Walters, that lovely stylist who like Donald Knight before him was not out of context in such a partnership. McCabe caught Hobbs off Fleetwood-Smith for 38 after Walters was out and Woolley and Hobbs together had sketched a recollection of thirty years of batsmanship; and when Hobbs got out Hammond came in and made 54. At the ruined game's end the irrepressible Bradman made 149 in an hour and three-quarters; the spectators who paid money for that match got it back in bags of pure gold.

The next game lacked the *cachet* of such eminence, though there was a generous sprinkling of Test players. This time it was an unofficial Gentlemen v. Players match; Hobbs went in first this time with the attractive and aggressive Charlie Barnett, and Woolley and Hammond waited with their pads on. The destroying Read of Essex, who had had a remarkably successful season for one so inexperienced, once more made the ball fly and spit; the great batsmen faced him gingerly. Hobbs was proof against him in the first innings; Allom bowled him for 24. The Players were well behind on the first innings and once more made a poor start. Barnett and Woolley went early and Read induced Hobbs, by bowling a bumper at his face, to give a catch to Garland-Wells when he had made 18. George Geary made 100 and the Players perked up; but next day the Gentlemen won by three wickets after a happy holiday game. The winning hit brought Lionel Tennyson's fifty and was made off Freeman, and Jack Hobbs walked off the field with Hammond and Ames and Woolley and Tate and Geary, the old friends along with the new; and so, unheralded and indeed unremarked, the greatest first-class cricket career of modern times came to its end. His last score has a delicate appropriateness; it was 18, the same score that he had achieved in his first innings on that remote cold April morning at the Oval when he came in to bat with Hayward. In his end was his beginning.

He made an end there, but he did not make it then. It must have cost him much thought during the winter; for it was not until February that he wrote to the Surrey Club announcing his intention to retire. The two-hundredth century had faded sadly from his ambition; there must have come a time in that last frustrating season when he faced himself honestly with the realization that he would never do it now. The ifs and the ands pile up to the consciousness as they piled up to his—if the 1914-18 war had not come; if he had accepted the invitation to tour South Africa; if he had not missed most of 1921, that hard batsman's season; if he had been able to play for Surrey two or three years earlier; if he had distributed his prodigal runs a little differently; if this, if that, and if the other. But he had not, and the number of his hundreds stood, and stands, at 197.* It is a virtually unchaseable record, Hendren coming next with 170; but he would dearly have liked the extra honour that those other three would have brought him. It is quite clear even to-day that the strange little disappointment went deep. At the end of a career which took him to the wicket 1,315 times for a record aggregate of 61,237 runs and an average of 50.65, it is strange to encounter a regret, but a regret exists. Looking back one can read the nervous tension and distress into a final season which may have been a rather less than happy one. It was not that he went on too long; it was that he was not quite able to go on long enough.

He wrote his letter of retirement in the February of 1935. In March he heard from the Surrey Committee of the regret that this had caused. The only gesture they could make was to confer upon him the highest honour that they were empowered to give, and they made it. The letter informed him that he was now a Life Member of the Club. This handsome recognition of the admiration and gratitude that they felt for the greatest cricketer who had ever served them, together with the already-existing tribute of the Hobbs Gates, did a little to compensate him, not only for his private disappointment over the centuries, but for the loss in future of his matchless art and craft and his incomparable practice of it.

It is a loss we do not often pause to measure, being too much taken up with our own deprivation. If ours is sore enough, we have substitutes to solace the void with; Sandham and Sutcliffe, Hammond and Hendren and Bradman and Woolley, journeyed on

---

*A year or two ago, some enterprising statistician sought to elevate into first-class status certain centuries he made during the Vizianagram tour of India in 1930-31 and so credit him with 200 and more at last. The attempt failed, and I doubt if he supported it.

their public way for our delight long after Hobbs gave up. But what of him? He has no valid substitute for his art, which is still active in his will and his brain and his instincts; only his muscles fail him, only they betray the darting imperishable *esprit* that used to control them but finds that they no longer answer. For this there can be no consolation but the satisfaction of the achievement permitted to him before the inevitable decline; and in that achievement is his life.

The life of a cricketer is his public life on the field, and when he retires he is little concern of ours. Jack Hobbs' life before he came to the first-class game was of interest to us because it showed the birth and development of a kind of genius, the quality of whose maturity was determined by his early adventures and experiments. Jack Hobbs' life away from the cricket field, whether during his active career or after it, must of necessity be his private affair in the way that the life of another kind of artist, a writer or a composer perhaps, could not be. A man whose art resides solely in a game finds it affected less by personal circumstances than a man whose art is in the expression in words or music or paint of an imaginative response to life. That is why I have concerned myself little, although he concerned himself much, with his wife and family, his home and his friends, the full and happy existence which he led away from cricket grounds. The shop he opened is a famous shop, but I have not thought it my province to chronicle its history. One day perhaps a multiple store will take it over; but no multiple organization whatever could ever have taken over Jack Hobbs. Apart from his cricket he never asked to be celebrated, never pretended to an unusual greatness. A man of far from usual character, perhaps; but a man of specialized genius can never be quite the same as his fellows, even in regions which his genius does not touch. Jack Hobbs went down into retirement in 1935 to the lasting impoverishment of hundreds of thousands of people for whom the close of his career was the close of a phase in their own lives. He is still almost as active as he was then; but the Hobbs who set his greatness as a common ideal and a common possession of cricketers ceased to exist in 1935 as anything but a remembered inheritance.

He did not cut himself off at once from active cricket, as some have been known to do. He was happy to play from time to time for scratch sides, in occasional Surrey Colts or Club and Ground fixtures, for charity elevens. Many young players of that time cherish the delighted memory that his appearance in their game gave them. For many years he had taken his own side to play Wimbledon and District on the Merton C.C. ground in late September; this he continued to do until the war came, augmenting the annual income of the local hospitals by a very satisfactory amount every year. He made a happy practice of travelling each week to Kimbolton School in Huntingdonshire, whose headmaster was a friend of his, and helping in the coaching and once in a while playing in a game against the school. This he went on doing throughout the war as far as he was able, and to the best of his recollection it was against this school that he played his last innings in a cricket match. Appropriately it topped the hundred; even more appropriately, for his endings had always been unawares, he did not think of it at the time as his last match.

The first-class cricket game did not forget him, and never will. He had built up a prestige unprecedented for a professional, for he was the first of these to attract so intensely to himself the public idolatry that from time to time attaches to a national sporting hero. Characteristically, he had done little to court this; it was the manner and quality of his performance rather than any publicizing trick of personality that fascinated his followers, and at a distance of a quarter of a century or more fascinates them still. He was honoured for it during his career, and honoured for years afterwards wherever cricket was known and loved. Soon after the war the M.C.C. made the excellent and popular gesture of awarding honorary membership to twenty-five eminent professionals renowned for conspicuous service in the past. There is no need to specify whose name led the list. Later he was elected to the committee of his own county, on which he still actively and usefully serves. And the culmination of official honours arrived in 1953 when, nearly twenty years after the game had seen the last of him as a participant, he was called to Buckingham Palace to receive a knighthood.

Most sportsmen honoured in this or kindred ways have received their acknowledgments while their names and their exploits have been fresh in the public memory. This, with a common sportsman, implies barely a season's lapse between present popularity and official honour, memory and popularity being the unreliabilities they are. There have of course been older cricketers, Warner and Leveson-Gower in particular, whose honours have rewarded administration as much as personal performance and whose cricketing excellence has been less in question. Those honoured for their batting—and it has been wryly remarked that the last man knighted for bowling was Sir Francis Drake—have generally received it at the end of their last season, or thereabouts. Not so Sir Jack; it came to him when he was seventy. It meant that somewhere in the public consciousness was living, warmly and excitingly, the memory of his greatest days. The accolade itself was a welcome honour, of course; in bestowing it the Sovereign gave effect to the previously unsymbolized wishes of her people. But it was merely a late acknowledgment of a public accord of which years and years before he must have been well aware.

Jack Hobbs got his knighting from Queen Elizabeth in 1953; but he had had the substance of it long ago. He got his knighting from the Oval crowds who milled and chattered and roared their approbation at so many of his matchless innings. These crowds whom he believed himself to have disappointed gave him all the honour that was in their power to give; their admiration and their encouragement and their personal hopes, their respect and their gratitude and their love. After that, the official endorsement from on high could only be in the nature of a rubber stamp.

The Oval is an ungentle ground, with no exterior graces. Gaunt patched buildings old and new surround it, the bulbous and overpowering manifestations of the most famous gasworks in the world overlay it, the air about it is assailed with all the attendant noises of motorization and industry from Lambrettas to ship's sirens, and the atmosphere is oppressive with a gamut of odours ranging from brewer's waste through Marmite and paint-spray to Military Pickle. Lord's, retired demurely behind the quivering plane-trees, preserves its remote control and avoids contamination; the Oval is down among the sounds and smells of the people, arid and headachy and uncushioned, offering no enticements. Yet Jack Hobbs, loving it as his own home and infusing into it the wonderful adornment of his own genius, made generations of spectators forget all this. When Oval-time meant Hobbs, the Oval was a place of rapture and enchantment. For thirty years he was the tutelary genius of the place, and it suffered a sea-change into something rich and strange. He is now, even to the present generation that can never have had the chance of seeing him, the first among all the great names associated with this great ground, where he played first in 1905 and last in 1934 and scored as many as ninety of his immense tale of centuries. The Oval made him, and to his own generation and those who followed it, he made the Oval. Henceforth they are indissoluble.

And in the countless succession of schoolboys who poured excitedly through its turnstiles, Jack Hobbs has his liveliest and most receptive posterity. If his active cricket ceased in 1934 it lives most enduringly still in the memories and imaginations of those who were fired by his art when they were at their most responsive. The schoolboys of the period before the First War are now unhappily a greatly lessened band; they met destruction head-on as they stepped out of school, and their memories of that early time are seen through a strangely distorted curtain; yet there are still enough of them to recall and record the rise of his adventurous genius. Nevertheless their successors of the nineteen twenties must constitute by far the most powerful army who will defend his immortality against oblivion. In rain or shine they flocked in with their sandwiches and their autograph books and their bottles of pop, and for almost a decade took the full glory of that magnificent Indian summer, were for years the enviable beneficiaries of a notable bestowing. In their hands and in their memories the immortality of Jack Hobbs is safe, so long as they retain within their middle-aged frames the receptive and responsive essence of boyhood, which knows and acclaims genius with a ready generosity less often found among the adult tribes. It is for the schoolboys of the 'twenties, inheritors through the luck of their birth of one of the rarest individual possessions in the recent history of English life, to keep the quality of this man's cricket as a living influence on the spirit and the continuity of this great game, in their own minds and in the minds of their own successors. A man cannot achieve this kind of immortality unless he can bequeath to his admirers the urgent conviction that this quality must not lapse or be forgotten, must be re-created and passed on. I am one of the schoolboys of the 'twenties, conscious of my inheritance; I have written this book to help preserve that immortality.

Sir Jack Hobbs himself, hale and friendly, in his late seventies, a retiring unobtrusive figure looking back on his life, has borne the test of time with the easy resilience which anyone watching him in his prime would naturally have expected. He is lean, brown, active and light as always, looking upwards of a dozen years younger than his true age. He still spends more than half of his retirement at his Fleet Street shop; back home at Hove, he and his wife are once again on their own after more than fifty years of marriage, their grown-up family scattered about in satisfying stages of prosperity as happy families should be. He tries out his eye and skill as regularly as he can on the golf course, accompanied as often as not by his old friend Strudwick, curbing no doubt an in-bred tendency to follow up a short putt by going for a short run. He reviews his great career with an expected modesty, but with an altogether disarming certainty that it was a great one. He is very properly and quite unblushingly proud of it. There is no question of throwing it deprecatingly aside; he still enjoys it. He is still pleased at having made a hundred both home and away against every first-class county; he is still proud of his good fortune at never having bagged a pair. He is still touchingly disappointed at his failure to make 200 centuries. He cherishes very much the fan-mail which still arrives for him, welcomes with delight the chance visitor to his shop who remembers seeing an innings of his, it may be forty or fifty years ago, it may be in Australia or South Africa. He is pleased at the honours and recognition, great or small, that may still come to him; pleased when the Press remembers him; pleased when some officious upstart writes a book about him. He goes to Lord's and the Oval when he can, he drops in for an hour or two at Hove, he watches present-day cricket and does not know what answer he would have to the inswingers and the leg-side field that are sealing up the enterprising batsmen to-day. He is dined and wined on his birthday by a collection of his friends and admirers calling themselves the Master's Club; Strudwick will be there and Sandham, Hendren, George Geary and G. T. S. Stevens, and out of his far past, J. N. Crawford. Crawford is now the only traceable survivor of that first cold game at the Oval in April 1905, except Hobbs himself; that first game, when W.G. played—the continuity runs strong, for while W.G. played in Jack Hobbs' first match, Jack Hobbs played in W.G.'s last, and when he came to his own

last appearance he was playing with Hammond; the strand of
great batsmanship spanning not much less than a hundred years.
His memories must be so multifarious as to confuse and hypnotize
him as he voyages among them picking on his great moments, and
which are his greatest it is almost as difficult for himself to say as
for someone else—whether one of the supreme key innings of his
career, like the hundred in the fifth Test in 1926, or the stand
with Sutcliffe on the death-trap at Melbourne two years later, or
the memorable partnerships with Wilfred Rhodes when Warner's
team brought back the Ashes; or does he sometimes think more
evenly and pleasurably of some of his long routine stands with the
calm and reassuring Sandham, the 428 perhaps or the heightened
glories of the undefeated partnership at Taunton which brought
Surrey victory and Hobbs his 127th century? Or the day before,
when all England came to watch him equal the record? Or of the
rough thorny spaces of distress through which he struggled to his
hundredth hundred? Or of the day when he batted through the
blazing Bank Holiday afternoon with never a thought of war? Or
of the taming of Gregory and Macdonald at Old Buckenham Hall
before his thigh muscle gave out? Or of throwing Bardsley out
from cover, or of making 154 not out against the Gentlemen at
Lord's when they had asked him to stand down, or of breaking
the clock at Bradford, or of the Manchester crowd singing "Auld
Lang Syne", or the Sydney crowd applauding him round the
ground, or Woodfull's Australians giving him three cheers? It is
a rich mélange of gratifying days and hours, and there is
bounty beyond belief to choose from; but we may be sure that
most often of all his thoughts rove back, after tender reminiscences
of Parker's Piece, to the Oval which he made into a home and
a palace and a shrine; the Oval on to which he first walked into
first-class cricket by the side of his hero Tom Hayward, long ago,
to begin a career for which there was no precedent and no rival as
a contribution of variety and enrichment to the game of cricket;
an enrichment, moreover, of the lives and the memories of thousands of people whom he himself could not ever know, of the
schoolboys particularly, and the last word should be with the
schoolboys, who date their full appreciation of this great and lovely
game from the days when Summer-time meant Oval-time, and
Oval-time meant Hobbs.

INDEX

(*N.B. I have not thought it necessary to point specific references to Jack Hobbs himself. Those interested in him may care to read through the preceding pages, beginning at the beginning, and going on until they come to the end.*)

a'Beckett, E. L., 176
Abel, R., 29, 34, 35, 37, 42, 47
Abel, W. J., 118
Ainley, Henry, 127
Alcibiades, 72
Alcock, C. W., 27
Allen, G. O., 191, 192
Allom, M. J. C., 183, 201
Altham, H. S., 39
Ames, L. E. G., 191, 201
Andrews, T. J. E., 172
Armstrong, W. W., 43, 60, 61, 69, 70, 85, 86, 88, 90, 94, 96, 119, 125-129, 132, 167

Bailey, Sir A., 95
Baker, A., 37, 41, 45, 49
Bannerman, A. C., 15
Bardsley, W., 68, 69, 86, 89, 94, 98, 126, 150, 167, 168, 208
Barnes, S. F., 58, 61, 62, 66, 77, 78, 83-93, 96-98, 102, 103, 147
Barnett, C. J., 201
Bedser, A. V., 93
Beldam, G. W., 39, 40
Belloc, Hilaire, 54
Bernhardt, Sarah, 3
Best, Edna, 127
Bird, M. C., 72, 102
Birtles, T., 106
Blackie, D. J., 176, 177
Blake, William, 22n.
Blunden, Edmund, 180
Blythe, C., 45, 51, 58, 60, 69, 70, 107, 109, 116, 121
Booth, M. W., 102, 116
Booth, General W. (Salvation Army), 102
Bosanquet, B. J. T., 52
Bowes, W. E., 193
Bowley, E. H., 149
Boyle, H. F., 15

Bradman, D. G., 10, 93, 142, 167, 175, 177, 178, 183-188, 201, 202
Braund, L. C., 53, 58
Brearley, W., 39, 40, 48, 56, 57, 65, 66, 71
Bridges, J. J., 159
Brockwell, W., 34, 37
Brooke, Rupert, 104
Brown, F. R., 191
Brown, G., 67, 169
Brown, J. T., 35
Buckenham, C., 41, 77, 78
Bunyan, M. J., 28
Burrows, R. D., 49

Cardus, Neville, 171, 181, 199
Carr, A. W., 166, 168, 169, 185
Carr, D. W., 107, 108
Carter, H., 60, 61, 63, 86, 89, 92, 96
Catterall, R. H., 141, 142
Chapman, A. P. F., 13, 148, 151, 153, 167, 169, 170, 173, 177, 184-186, 191
Churchill, Sir Winston, 107
Clark, E. W., 183
Clay, J. C., 198, 200
Collins, H. L., 93, 125, 126, 150, 170, 172
Commaille, J. M. M., 141
Compton, D. C. S., 4, 7, 29, 36, 67, 76, 183
Constantine, L. N., 180
Coriolanus, 72
Cotter, A., 43, 60, 61, 69, 70, 85-89, 96, 116
"Country Vicar" (Rev. R. L. Hodgson), 31-32
Craig, Albert, 41, 42
Crawford, J. N., 27, 35, 49, 50, 54, 56, 57, 60-62, 66, 71, 84, 85, 117, 119, 120, 121, 207
Crawford, V. F. S., 39
Cricketer, The, 31

209

Jackson, A., 187
Jackson, Hon. F. S., 16, 48
Jahangir Khan, 201
Jardine, D. R., 10, 132, 133, 140, 159, 174, 177, 182, 189, 190, 191, 192, 195, 197
Jeacocke, A., 132, 133
Jeeves (P. G. Wodehouse), 148
Jephson, D. L. A., 34, 35
Jessop, G. L., 33, 48, 53, 69, 98, 102
Joel, Mr. Solly, 144
Johnson, I. W., 167
Jones, A. O., 16, 57-60, 69, 71, 116
Joyce, James, 84n
Jupp, V. W. C., 129, 130

Keats, John, 116
Kelleway, C. E., 86, 88, 93, 126, 150
Kennington Oval, passim
Key, K. J., 34
Kilner, R., 10, 143, 152, 153
King, J. B., 66
Kinneir, S. P., 83-86
Kippax, A. F., 186, 187
Knight, D. J., 9, 79, 105, 108, 118, 121, 122, 129, 130, 132, 133, 158, 201
Knox, N. A., 27, 40, 45, 48, 49, 54, 119
Kotze, J. J., 52, 53

Laker, J. C., 167
Larwood, H., 173, 174, 180, 187, 191
Laver, F., 43
Leavis, F. R., 13
Le Couteur, P. R., 77
Lee, H. W., 8
Lees, W., 35, 41, 42, 45, 48, 49, 78
Leveson-Gower, H. D. G., 66, 68, 71, 72, 76, 205
Leyland, M., 191
Lilley, A. A., 57
Lockwood, W. H., 34, 35, 134
Lohmann, G. A., 34, 35, 134
Lyons, J. J., 16

McAlister, P. A., 63
Macartney, C. G., 60, 61, 62, 68, 69, 70, 94, 96, 126, 167, 168, 169, 171
MacBryan, J. C. W., 149, 159
McCabe, S. J., 186, 187
Macdonald, E. A., 90, 119, 120, 129, 130, 131, 170, 180, 208
MacLaren, A. C., 10, 48, 57, 68, 69, 70, 129
McLeod, C. E., 43
Mailey, A. A., 126, 127, 130, 150-152, 169-171, 173, 176

Makepeace, H., 125
Marsh, J. F., 30
Marshal, A., 66, 72, 79
Matthews, Stanley, 4
May, P. B. H., 13
Mayne, E. R., 85
Mead, C. P., 10, 27, 47, 67, 83, 85, 89, 101, 103, 132, 174
Milton, John, 13
Minnett, R. B., 85, 86, 88, 90, 94
Mitchell, F., 52
Moynihan, Sir B. (later Lord Moynihan), 57, 131
Mozart, W. A., 3
Murdoch, W. L., 15

Newman, J., 166
Newstead, J. T., 66
Noble, M. A., 43, 60, 61, 63, 69
Nourse, A. D. (Snr.), 96, 141

O'Connor, J. A., 62, 70
Oldfield, W. A., 126, 153, 154, 169n
Ovid, 6

Palairet, L. C. H., 48
Palmer, G., 15
Parker's Piece, 18, 19, 21, 24, 26, 55, 56, 196, 208
Parkin, C. H., 126
Pataudi, Nawab of (Snr.), 30, 191, 192
Paynter, E., 191, 192
Payton, W., 71
Peach, H. A., 8, 133, 134, 182
Peebles, I. A. R., 185, 191
Pellew, C. E., 126
Peter Pan, 127
Podder, Mr. (All Muggleton v. Dingley Dell), 74
Ponsford, W. H., 150, 186
Prinzip, Gavrilo, 107

Quaife, W. G., 123
Quiller-Couch, Sir A., 13

Ranjitsinhji, K. S., 10, 11, 16, 18, 19, 48, 116
Ransford, V. S., 68, 69, 86, 90, 94, 96
Raphael, J. E., 37, 44
Ratcliffe, A., 30
Read, H. D., 200, 201
Read, W. W., 34
Reay, G. M., 123
Reeves, W., 24, 41
Relf, A. E., 102, 103
Rembrandt, 3

All books from the Pavilion Cricket Library are available from your local bookshop, price £12.95 hardback, £6.95 paperback new titles, £5.95 backlist, or they can be ordered direct from Pavilion Books Limited.

New Titles

Farewell to Cricket
Don Bradman

Jack Hobbs
Ronald Mason

Backlist

In Celebration of Cricket
Kenneth Gregory

The Best Loved Game
Geoffrey Moorhouse

Bowler's Turn
Ian Peebles

Lord's 1787–1945
Sir Pelham Warner

Lord's 1946–1970
Diana Rait Kerr and Ian Peebles

P.G.H. Fender
Richard Streeton

Through the Caribbean
Alan Ross

Hirst and Rhodes
A.A. Thomson

Two Summers at the Tests
John Arlott

End of an Innings
Denis Compton

Ranji
Alan Ross

Batter's Castle
Ian Peebles

The Ashes Crown the Year
Jack Fingleton

Life Worth Living
C.B. Fry

Cricket Crisis
Jack Fingleton

Brightly Fades The Don
Jack Fingleton

Cricket Country
Edmund Blunden

Odd Men In
A.A. Thomson

Crusoe on Cricket
R.C. Robertson-Glasgow

Benny Green's Cricket Archive

Please enclose cheque or postal order for the cover price, plus postage:

UK: 65p for first book; 30p for each additional book to a maximum of £2.00. Overseas: £1.20 for first book; 45p for each additional book to a maximum of £3.00

Pavilion Books reserve the right to show new retail prices on covers which may differ from those previously advertised in the text or elsewhere and to increase postal rates in accordance with the Post Office's charges.